TRADE STRATEGY FOR RICH AND POOR NATIONS

B

Edited by Harry G. Johnson

NEW TRADE STRATEGY FOR THE WORLD ECONOMY

by Harry G. Johnson, Gerard and
Victoria Curzon, Lionel Gelber,
Maxwell Stamp and Harry Cowie,
David Robertson

Second impression

Edited by Hugh Corbet

TRADE STRATEGY AND THE ASIAN-PACIFIC REGION

by Hugh Corbet, G. C. Allen,
Sir Robert Scott, Leonard Beaton

Trade Strategy
for Rich
and Poor Nations

EDITED BY

HARRY G. JOHNSON

UNIVERSITY OF TORONTO PRESS

FIRST PUBLISHED IN 1971

First published in Canada and the United States by University of
Toronto Press, Toronto and Buffalo

MICROFICHE ISBN 0-8020-0046-0

© George Allen and Unwin Ltd, 1971

ISBN 0-8020-1761-4

PRINTED IN GREAT BRITAIN
in 10 on 12 point Baskerville type
BY THE DITCHLING PRESS LTD
DITCHLING

THE ATLANTIC TRADE STUDY PROGRAMME

The Atlantic Trade Study, registered as an educational trust, was formed in December, 1966, by a private group in London to sponsor a programme of policy research on the implications for Britain of participating in a broadly based free trade association as possibly the next phase in the liberalisation of international trade.

It is under the chairmanship of Sir Michael Wright, formerly Permanent Head of the British Delegation to the Geneva Disarmament Conference, while the Director of Studies is Professor Harry G. Johnson, of the London School of Economics and Political Science and the University of Chicago. The programme is now being administered by the recently established Trade Policy Research Centre, the Director of which is Mr. Hugh Corbet, previously of *The Times*. Set out below is the committee responsible for the programme:

As a basis on which to proceed with research, the proposed free trade association was defined as initially embracing the United States, Canada, Britain and other member countries of the European Free Trade Association; open to the European Communities and to Japan, Australia and New Zealand, as well as other industrially advanced nations; and affording less developed countries greater access to their markets.

Several proposals along these lines had already been receiving serious attention at academic, business and official levels in North America. The ATS was in fact a British response to a new trade strategy proposed in May, 1966, by the Canadian-American Committee, a non-official group sponsored by the Private Planning Association of Canada and the National Planning Association in the United States.

With the expiry on June 30, 1967, of President Johnson's authority under the Trade Expansion Act of 1962 to negotiate trade agreements with other countries, and the completion of the so-called Kennedy Round of multilateral tariff negotiations, made possible by the Act and conducted under the auspices of the General Agreement on Tariffs and Trade, the United

States Administration and Congress was expected to embark upon a thorough reappraisal of trade policies and practices with a view to formulating a fresh negotiating authority. The proposal for a multilateral free trade association initiated by North Atlantic countries has been one of the policy options to have subsequently come under consideration.

Meanwhile, the British Government had made a second application for United Kingdom membership of the European Communities. But whether Britain gained admission or not, the concept of a potentially world-wide free trade association was deemed, in either eventuality, as likely to prove of large significance. For in the event of membership being negotiated it was considered that the United Kingdom would then require an informed policy for the development of closer commercial and political relations between Western Europe and North America. If on the other hand the European Communities rejected Britain again, even if only temporarily, it would be important to have examined beforehand whether there exists a viable alternative.

CONTENTS

Part I

BROAD TRADE STRATEGY
FOR THE SEVENTIES

by

HARRY G. JOHNSON

Professor of Economics, London School of Economics and Political Science and the University of Chicago; formerly Professor of Economic Theory, University of Manchester; author of The World Economy at the Crossroads (*1965*), Economic Policies Toward Less Developed Countries (*1967*) *and* Essays in Monetary Economics (*1967*).

Part II

OPPORTUNITIES FOR
DEVELOPING COUNTRIES

by

DAVID WALL

Lecturer in Economics, University of Sussex; economic consultant to Overseas Development Administration, London; author of The Commonwealth Preference System (*1970*).

Part III

HARMONISATION ISSUES
UNDER FREE TRADE

by

HANS LIESNER

Fellow of Emmanuel College and Lecturer in Economics, University of Cambridge; Deputy Director (Economics), British Treasury, on secondment since October, 1970; co-author of Case Studies in European Economic Union (*1962*).

Part IV

AMERICAN CAPITAL
AND FREE TRADE

by

M. D. STEUER

Reader in Economics, London School of Economics and Political Science; economic consultant to Department of Trade and Industry, London.

PREFACE

This volume examines certain specific aspects of the proposal for a free trade treaty among developed countries as the next phase in the liberalisation of world commerce. That proposal has been the subject of a programme of studies in Britain which has been concerned with exploring the economic, political and strategic implications of such a multilateral free trade association. The three papers which appear here, in the pages following my introductory part, were carried out as part of the project, known as the Atlantic Trade Study Programme, and have been revised since they were first published in 1968 and 1969 as individual monographs.

Other papers under the programme have appeared in two earlier volumes. The first one, entitled *New Trade Strategy for the World Economy*, which I edited, dealt with the politico-strategic and general economic aspects of a free trade treaty initiative. It was published in 1969. The second volume, *Trade Strategy and the Asian-Pacific Region*, was published a year later. It was edited by Hugh Corbet and dealt with the Asian-Pacific interest in a multilateral free trade agreement.

When the free trade treaty proposal is raised, three broad issues are commonly among those that come to mind. Where would an arrangement among developed countries leave the developing countries? Since tariffs are becoming less significant, it is asserted that non-tariff distortions to trade are what matter now. Could a free trade treaty cope with them? And then there are the misgivings that are aroused in lesser industrial countries by the prospect of a closer economic association with the United States. Would not British industry be taken over by American giants? The papers in this volume examine these issues of popular concern and attempt to put them in perspective.

The paper by Mr. David Wall, of the University of Sussex, first appeared as a pamphlet under the title, *The Third World Challenge*. It links the question of tariff preferences for developing countries to the formulation of a broad strategy for maintaining the momentum of trade liberalisation in the world as a whole. The idea has since been taken up by the International Chamber of Commerce and has become a common feature of other writings in the area of trade policy. The paper by Mr. Hans Liesner, of the University of Cambridge, published in 1968 as *Atlantic Harmonisation*, examines the implications of a multilateral free trade treaty for the national economic policies of the participating countries, in the course of which he deals with the non-tariff distortion problem. Mr. Liesner has taken a special interest in policy harmonisation questions. His paper incidentally serves to throw some light on the progress made in this area by the European Community and the European Free Trade Association. It also gives some indication of the consequences for British economic policies and institutions were the United Kingdom to join the European Community. But the paper does not try to provide a systematic comparison of the harmonisation implications of the alternative commercial policies open to Britain. The paper does not deal either with two key problems, the reserve role of sterling and temperate-zone agriculture, which have been the subject of other studies under the Atlantic Trade Study Programme, namely Sir Roy Harrod's monograph, *Dollar-Sterling Collaboration*, and the one by Mr. Brian Fernon, *Issues in World Farm Trade*, published in 1968 and 1970 respectively. The paper by Mr. M. D. Steuer, of the London School of Economics, first appeared in 1969 under the title used here and draws to some extent on the research project which the author has been directing at the British Board of Trade on foreign investment in Britain.

While the Atlantic Trade Study Programme has provided the opportunity, and the encouragement for their work, the contributors to this volume have been solely responsible for the views expressed in their respective papers.

HARRY G. JOHNSON

London
Autumn, 1970

Part I

BROAD TRADE STRATEGY FOR THE SEVENTIES

by

Harry G. Johnson

country by the multinational corporation and the influence of trade and other policies on such investment and on its economic consequences. All three studies should therefore prove interesting and useful to readers concerned with international trade policy, regardless of whether or not they are attracted by the free trade association proposal itself, for they deal with the issues that are of prime concern to the less developed countries and those that are of prime concern to the more developed countries and which, moreover, will need to be taken into account in any broad trade strategy directed towards the achievement of an open world economy.

Retreat towards Protectionism

Any research programme, and particularly a research programme concerned with economic policy, has to be formulated in a temporal context that suggests what the important problems are and how they should be approached. But as time passes, events occur, new policy decisions are made, and the elusive "climate" of public opinion changes; some aspects of the research problem wax, and others wane, in importance. So it has transpired with the Atlantic Trade Study Programme.

To be specific, when the programme was started, the Kennedy Round of negotiations for tariff reductions was approaching its eventually successful conclusion, and it seemed both logical and prudent to consider what the next step towards freer trade should be. The programme therefore called for a discussion of the relative merits of the alternatives that at that time appeared plausible, namely: (1) a temporary standstill while the Kennedy Round tariff reductions were being digested, (2) another Kennedy Round, (3) sector-by-sector negotiations in industrial products of both export and import interest to the advanced countries and (4) a free trade treaty among like-minded industrial countries.[2] The possibility of Britain's admission to the EEC still left open the question of a global strategy for further liberalisation of world trade.

In the intervening years, however, the situation on the trade liberalisation front has deteriorated far beyond what many had initially expected. (One must, in policy matters, distinguish between what is logically possible or conceivable, and what one

[2]See Curzon and Curzon, "Options After the Kennedy Round", in Harry G. Johnson (ed.), *New Trade Strategy for the World Economy* (Allen & Unwin, London, 1969; and University of Toronto Press, Toronto, 1969).

4

1 CONTEMPORARY SITUATION

When the Atlantic Trade Study Programme was first devised, in the autumn of 1966, its instigators were concerned with exploring the potentialities and possible problems of the formation of a free trade association among the advanced countries of the Atlantic area. The concept emerged naturally from the post-war history of trade negotiations among these countries. It was envisaged as a way of maintaining the momentum towards the liberalisation of international trade and payments that had characterised the period and that had obviously contributed greatly to world prosperity and economic growth. To that end, the task of the Atlantic Trade Study Programme was to examine not merely the general concept and its potential economic advantages to the United Kingdom, but also the "nuts and bolts" of a feasible arrangement together with the problems that might arise in various other areas of concern to British public opinion.

The present volume presents three major studies in the latter *genre*, which extend well beyond the confines of a plan for a free trade association into basic issues of the consequences of trade and the problems of economic policy formation in an open economy. Mr. David Wall's contribution (Part II) deals with the general issue of trade policy as a means of promoting the economic development of the poor countries of the world—a subject which, as will be elaborated on below, has increased considerably in importance since he wrote his study. Mr. Hans Liesner (Part III) deals with the question of how far freedom of trade requires harmonisation of national economic policies—a subject of importance not only in connection with the negotiations for Britain's entry into the European Communities (EEC), but also in connection with the growing post-Kennedy Round concern about non-tariff barriers to international trade.[1] Mr. M. D. Steuer's study (Part IV) deals with an issue that promises to be a matter of major concern in the next decade, the benefits and costs of direct investment in a

[1] For a discussion of non-tariff distortions to trade see Gerard and Victoria Curzon, *Hidden Barriers to International Trade* (Trade Policy Research Centre, London, 1970).

3

is in very grave danger of back-sliding into protectionism as the consequence of the accumulation of petty self-interests, each looking to protectionism and trade restriction as either a source of immediate profit or a temporary cure for an immediate and concrete problem. What is lacking, and what is urgently needed, is a bold conception of the global benefits of much enhanced freedom of trade, and a global strategy for working towards trade liberalisation on a planned and programmed basis capable of securing the benefits while avoiding any incidental problems that might arise. Such a strategy must be capable of absorbing into itself, and resolving, the problems that are currently pushing the legislators and the public opinion of the advanced countries in the direction of protectionism.

The Free Trade Treaty Option

Of the various possible strategies that have been examined under the Atlantic Trade Study Programme, the free trade treaty proposal appears in my judgment to be the most promising under contemporary circumstances. The main reason is that the traditional approach to the negotiation of reciprocal tariff reductions, through the instrumentality of the General Agreement on Tariffs and Trade (GATT), has demonstrated definite weaknesses in the face of contemporary concerns about trade policy.

In the first place, as the 1964-67 Kennedy Round of tariff-cutting negotiations showed, it is extremely difficult to deal with the problems of agricultural trade in the context of the GATT. Agricultural protectionism is a social policy of redistributing income towards farmers, the protective side-effects of which, while serious enough for other countries, are incidental to the main purpose. Consequently it is difficult to subject agricultural protectionism to hard bargaining on a commercial interest basis, especially as, in terms of their agricultural sectors alone, countries tend to be either exporters or importers without much possibility of exchanging import concessions for export concessions. If the problems of agricultural trade are to be resolved, or at least mitigated, they will have to be tackled as part of a much broader negotiation, and in terms of rationalisation and regularisation of existing policies aimed at the achievement of greater economic efficiency for the participating countries. This will require a commitment of the participating countries to the objective of would not be surprised to see happen; one tries to hedge one's arguments against the logically possible, while continuing mentally to rule out certain conceivable developments as too unlikely or too potentially disastrous to be taken seriously.) In mid-1970, rather than being prepared for further steps towards trade liberalisation, the major nations seem bent on a reversal of the post-war trend towards freer trade, and on a retreat into the protectionism that so disastrously crippled the world economy in the inter-war period.

The retreat into protectionism is evident on both sides of the Atlantic. On the European side, it is evident both in the series of agreements by which various peripheral European countries have been progressively tied into the discriminatory trading arrangements of the EEC, and in the firmness with which the Common Market countries have insisted that Britain and the other applicants for membership must accept the Communities' arrangements as they stand. On the American side, it is evident both in the growing emphasis on the importance of "reciprocity" in trade negotiations (and the growing scepticism about whether past trade negotiations have achieved "genuine" reciprocity), and in the growing enthusiasm of the United States Congress for quotas designed to guarantee American industries a minimum share of their domestic market. The most ominous development of all, in the USA, is the fact that the American labour movement has abandoned its long-standing commitment to the principle of free trade. This leaves American support for freer trade to the advocacy of two minority groups: the farm lobby, whose interests are unlikely on their own to find an effective focus in future trade negotiations, given the strength of agricultural protectionism in Europe; and the giant multinational corporations, which are chronically suspect in the mythology of American democracy and which have increasingly become a focus of suspicion for the American labour movement, on the grounds that they "export jobs" and "weaken the collective bargaining process" through their power to choose to locate production abroad.

In this situation the prospects for rational and informed discussion of alternative strategies for further trade liberalisation are bleak to say the least. On the other hand the need for such discussion is far more urgent than it appeared to be when the Atlantic Trade Study Programme was inaugurated in 1966. The world economy

C

increasing efficiency in general through the liberalisation of international trade, rather than to a narrower effort to obtain specific advantages in the form of tariff and other concessions on particular types of trade, at the "expense" of reciprocal concessions on other types of trade. A proposal for a free trade association, aimed at moving all the way to free trade, could provide a context of negotiation within which a start could be made on the dismantlement of existing agricultural protectionism and the inauguration of a more rational system for dealing with the social and economic problems of agriculture in a world in which efficiency requires an acceleration of the movement of labour off the land into the industrial and service sectors of the economy.

In the second place, the Kennedy Round negotiations called attention to the importance of non-tariff barriers to trade, barriers whose significance increases as the formal barriers to freedom of trade posed by tariffs and other "general" governmental interventions such as exchange controls and quantitative restrictions are reduced. It has become increasingly clear, during and since the Kennedy Round negotiations, that non-tariff barriers pose some very complex problems, which must be negotiated on a case-by-case basis. They do not lend themselves easily to the legal process of establishment and codification of principles and rules which has been the general GATT procedure. Instead they must be approached on a basis of mutual goodwill and a readiness to discuss and modify procedures in the light of economic reality and a concept of the common interest. Again, negotiations for a free trade treaty could provide the opportunity to bring non-tariff barriers to trade into the bargaining process, and to establish both the basis of agreed principle and shared goodwill and the machinery of discussion and review required to permit the reduction of such barriers in an orderly and amicable fashion.

Thirdly, the GATT framework has proved extremely cumbersome and relatively ineffective in dealing with the main problem that has emerged in post-war international trading experience, that of market disruption associated with the unexpectedly rapid growth of imports of manufactured goods from relatively low-wage sources of supply. This problem has constituted an important part of the demand for quota protection of domestic production against imports in the USA. It should be possible in the context of negotiation of a free trade treaty to work out principles and procedures to govern and contain such cases of market disruption in an equitable fashion consistent with the longer-run achievement of the benefits of free trade and international specialisation according to the principle of comparative advantage.

The problem of market disruption is largely but not exclusively one specific aspect of a much more general and more fundamental problem, that of promoting the economic development of the poor two-thirds of the world by integregating these nations into a liberal system of international trade, payments and investment. The importance of this objective has been recognised from the start by the proponents of what would initially be a North Atlantic free trade association[3] and also by the proponents of a Pacific free trade association.[4] The former have advocated unilateral extension of free market access to the developed countries, subject to safeguards against market disruption, while the latter have gone even further in advocating deliberate diversion of trade in agricultural products towards the developing countries. But the objective has become urgent with the emergence of the so-called "crisis of aid"—that is, the growing public disillusionment, particularly in the USA with the whole process of official aid-giving from developed to less developed country governments, and the consequent prospect of a serious decline in the volume of such aid. Further, it is quite clear from the failure of the Kennedy Round to accomplish anything significant in the way of opening new export opportunities specifically for less developed countries, and from the failure of the second (1968) United Nations Conference on Trade and Development (UNCTAD) to produce the hoped-for package of concrete new trade policies for development, that little can be hoped for from attempts to solve the problem within the existing framework of trade policy negotiations. Generosity in trade policy towards the less developed countries, if it is to be exercised at all, is only likely to be exercised in the context of a much broader negotiation aimed at establishing freedom or virtual freedom of international trade (in manufactures, with ancillary arrangements for agricultural trade), such

[3] *A New Trade Strategy for Canada and the United States* (Canadian-American Committee, Washington D.C. and Montreal, 1966). Also see David Wall, "Opportunities for Developing Countries", Part II of this volume.

[4] Kyoshi Kojima, "A Pacific Economic Community and Asian Developing Countries", *Hitotsubashi Journal of Economics*, Hitotsubashi University, Tokyo, June, 1966.

as would be constituted by negotiation of a multilateral free trade treaty.

This is the broad conclusion reached by Mr. Wall in Part II of this volume. But the study pre-dates some important developments —unfortunately of a highly discouraging kind— and hence reflects more optimism about the possibilities than seems justified in the contemporary situation of development policy. It has therefore seemed appropriate, in this introductory essay, to bring the picture on the development front up to date.[5]

[5]The following section is based on Johnson, "The North-South Problem in the World Economy, and the Implications of UNCTAD 1968", in Kojima (ed.) *Pacific Trade and Development*, Vol. II (Japan Economic Research Centre, Tokyo, 1969, pp. 3-14.

2 THE DEVELOPMENT PROBLEM

The development problem (sometimes referred to as "the North-South problem") derives from the wide gap between the average incomes of the developed industrialised nations and the poor nations anxious for development, and also between their normal rates of economic growth, especially of growth in *per capita* incomes. This latter gap is aggravating the existing disparities of living standards between the two groups of countries. The problem of development, as it concerns the developed countries, is to narrow the gaps by the adoption of appropriate policies designed to accelerate the development of the less developed and poorer nations. Recognition of, and concern about, this problem on the part of the developed nations has always been the outcome of a mixture of motivations: humanitarian concern about the relief of poverty; economic concern about the development of markets for exports and about securing favourable treatment of foreign investments by nationals; and, particularly at the outset, politico-military concern about the attraction and adhesion of allies in the cold war and the establishment of economic conditions conducive to political stability in the poorer nations. These motivations do not necessarily lead to the same kind of economic policies for promoting economic development. On the contrary, some of them have led to policies contrary to that end, at least in the judgment of some experts—for example the preservation of ruling oligarchies and the support of substantial military capabilities by lavish economic assistance. Confusion about the objectives of economic assistance of various kinds, generally lumped together as "development assistance", is in fact largely responsible for the current state of wide-spread disillusionment in the developed countries about the effectiveness and usefulness of development assistance. A contributory factor to this disillusionment was the initial illusion on the part of the USA that the development problem could be solved in the same way as the problem of European economic recovery, by modest pump-priming with American capital and technical assistance, over a short period of time, of economies that otherwise possessed the prerequisites of industrial competence. In fact, the poor countries were and are poor in all senses, not just that of shortage of capital to co-operate with the other factors of production, and much capital was wasted in the process of learning that development requires much more than an addition to the stock of capital equipment and will take a much longer and more sustained effort than the Marshall Plan.

In addition to the disillusionment with development assistance just mentioned, other more objective tendencies in the world economy have been operating to attentuate the concern of the developed countries with the poor countries and to reduce their willingness to prvide such assistance. Politically, the attainment of a *modus vivendi* between the USA and the Soviet Union, signalised notably by the outcome of the Cuban missile crisis of 1962, has greatly reduced the pressure to compete for political allies by generosity of assistance—a competition which in any case was proving itself to be self-defeating. Militarily, the development of new technologies of offence and defence has greatly reduced the dependence of the major powers on far-flung strategic bases, and therefore the need both to spend on the maintenance of these bases and to purchase political acceptance of them. On the economic side, two of the major aid donors, the USA and Britain, have been in chronic balance-of-payments deficit, and hence under mounting pressure to reduce their foreign aid contributions, while— as a consequence of the growing malaise of the international monetary system—surplus countries have been reluctant to increase their aid donations unilaterally for fear of the balance-of-payments consequences. Finally, on the side of humanitarian concern for the relief of poverty, that concern has in the USA been shifted by domestic disorders from the relief of foreign poverty to the relief of domestic poverty and the provision of greater opportunities for the minority to share in the general affluence. Other developed countries have in various ways been subject to mounting internal pressures and discontents, which can only be relieved by substantial increases in public expenditure. Hence these problems lower the political priority of assistance to the economic development of the poor countries.

In short, the motives for concern in the North about accelerating development in the South have been gradually whittled down by the general trend of international economic and political relations to the primarily humanitarian; and the humanitarian motive

11

has been increasingly preoccupied with pressing domestic problems of poverty amid affluence. In these circumstances there has been a need for a reaffirmation of the moral commitment of the developed countries to help promote the development of the poor countries. To provide such a reaffirmation was one of the major functions of the Commission on International Development (the Pearson Commission), appointed in 1968 by the President of the World Bank, the 1969 report of which will be discussed below.[6] There has also been a need to explore new policy techniques that might be employed by the developed countries to foster the growth of the poor nations, and the arguments for so employing them.

The prospective inadequacy of foreign aid to cover the net foreign exchange requirements of the development plans of the less developed countries became increasingly apparent towards the end of the 1950s, and naturally directed attention towards the alternative of expanding opportunities for earning foreign exchange by means of exports, and also towards ways of increasing the real contribution of existing aid flows. In addition to the foreign exchange motivation of interest in expanding export opportunities, the experience of some of the more industrialised developed countries with industrialisation based on protection in the domestic market ("inward-looking industrialisation") had convinced their experts that such industrialisation was highly inefficient and prone to be self-limiting if not self-defeating, and that what was required was access to larger, foreign markets, both in the advanced countries and among the other developing countries. Moreover, experience of attempting to develop exports of their manufactures had disclosed the existence of substantial barriers placed in their way by the trade policies of the developed countries. Finally, there were long-standing grievances over the prices and the price-instability of the primary products that formed the mainstay of their exports—characteristics of the trade in these products partly attributable to the agricultural protectionist policies of the advanced industrial countries.

Success of First UNCTAD: Geneva, 1964

This was the background of the first UNCTAD held in Geneva from March to June, 1964. In the background document for the

[6]*Partners in Development: Report of the Commission on International Development* (Praeger, New York, 1969).

conference,[7] its Secretary-General, Dr. Raúl Prebisch, presented a powerful argument for a new trade strategy for development, based on an appeal for equity and parity of treatment of producers in less developed countries in competition with those in developed countries. Specifically, he called (1) for international commodity agreements to give less developed producers of primary products the same sort of price-support and price-stabilisation assistance as were enjoyed by the farmers of the developed countries; (2) for preferential access for exports of manufactures and semi-manufactures from developing countries to the markets of the developed countries, to enable them to compete on equal terms with the manufacturers of those countries, their preferential advantage over other advanced-country manufacturers in that market compensating for the competitive disadvantages of under-development; and (3) for preferential arrangements among developing countries, falling short of the free internal trade arrangements which are the only exception allowed to the GATT rule of non-discrimination, to permit them to gain the advantages of specialisation in a large market.

As I argued in my study of the issues raised at the 1964 UNCTAD,[8] the developing countries had valid and weighty grounds for complaining that the trade policies of the developed countries, and the system of regulating international trade within the framework of the GATT, were biased against their exporting interests. These included: the *de facto* exemption from the GATT of domestic price support schemes for agricultural products, implemented by quotas, which both narrowed export markets and accentuated the instability of prices; the tariff bargaining procedure of the GATT, which until the Kennedy Round of multilateral tariff-cutting negotiations concentrated the reductions of tariffs to manufactures of prime interest to the large developed countries (and even in the Kennedy Round retained vestiges of such concentration through the exemptions lists); the typical escalation of tariff rates in national tariff structures by stage of production, which discriminated in favour of imports of raw materials and against imports of manufactures, and hence impeded the industrialisation of the developing countries; and the application within the GATT

[7] *Towards a New Trade Strategy for Development* (United Nations, New York, 1964).
[8] Johnson, *Economic Policies Toward Less Developed Countries* (Brookings Institution, Washington D.C., 1967; and Allen & Unwin, London, 1967).

of quota restrictions on the exports of cotton textiles from the less developed countries. A further point, to which I confess I gave inadequate attention at the time, was that the formation of the European Economic Community (EEC) and subsequently of the European Free Trade Association (EFTA) greatly extended the market area of protection of manufacturers in developed countries from their competitors in the developing countries, by giving members of these arrangements free entry to the markets of other members.[9]

While the developing countries had cogent grounds for complaint against the existing system of national and international economic policies, and for demanding sweeping changes in that system designed to improve its equity and promote their own economic development, the changes they demanded, or at least the two most important of them (commodity agreements and manufacturing preferences), were in my judgment poorly considered, for a variety of reasons. First, the ideal solution in principle would be to eliminate the discriminatory protectionist barriers to free international trade, and to seek to promote world economic development on a basis of dynamic comparative advantage.[10] The inversion of existing protectionism in favour of the producers of the developing countries is economically a second or third best solution to the problem. Second, the very political forces which generate and maintain protectionism in the advanced countries are likely either to resist strongly the resulting exposure of domestic producers to competition from the developing countries, or to accept it only in return for safeguards which might actually worsen the market opportunities of the developing countries in the longer run. Third, a great deal of pre-war and post-war experience with international commodity agreements has shown them to be extremely difficult to negotiate and operate. Moreover, the probable effect of preferences on the exports of the developing countries is an

[9]It is true that some developing countries—the associated overseas territories of the EEC—also obtained this preferential entry, without having to reciprocate. But the effect was to accentuate the discriminatory effect against other developing countries not among the associated overseas territories.

[10]By this is meant the gradual transfer of production from advanced to less developed countries in response to wage differentials and the gradual standardisation of new technologies of production. For a fuller statement of a dynamic theory of comparative advantage see my Wiksell Lectures: Johnson, *Comparative Cost and Commercial Policy Theory for a Developing World Economy* (Almqvist and Wiksell, Stockholm, 1968).

empirically unknown quantity, while theory indicates that the net real resources for development contributed by additional exports could only be a fraction of the increase in the quantum of exports itself. Thus there are strong reasons in both cases for doubting whether the contribution to foreign exchange earning and to development resources that would result would justify the complex changes in trade policies that would be required to bring them about.

Be that as it may, the 1964 UNCTAD was a substantial success in calling the manifold grievances of the developing countries in the field of international trade policy, and to a lesser extent aid policy, forcibly to the attention of the developed countries. Most notably, from the standpoint of the basic principles for the conduct of international trade and trade policy, the USA which at Geneva had stood firm on the principle of non-discrimination in opposition to the demands of the developing countries for trade preferences, reversed its stand in April, 1967, and subsequently co-operated with the other members of the Organisation for Economic Co-operation and Development (OECD) in preparing an agreed set of principles for a preference scheme in manufactures for presentation at the 1968 UNCTAD. Not long after the GATT agreed to the establishment of partial preference schemes among developing countries.

Failure of Second UNCTAD: Delhi, 1968

The second UNCTAD was originally projected to be held in 1966, but was delayed until March, 1968, by organisational difficulties, both in setting up and staffing the institution itself and in preparing for the conference. This delay was extremely unfortunate, from the point of view of the interests of the South, because during the interim occurred the events mentioned above as sapping the commitment of the developed countries to the assistance of the developing countries—the rapid worsening of the US balance of payments position, the deterioration of the British position culminating in the devaluation of 1967 (a particularly serious blow since in the 1964 conference Britain had exerted considerable moral leadership), an increasingly unstable international monetary situation, and increasing preoccupation of the developed countries with their internal affairs. As a result of these developments, and also of the emergence of conflicts of interest among the developing countries which had been successfully papered over at the 1964 conference, and the eclipsing of the conference by the international monetary disturbances of the autumn and winter of 1967-68, the second UNCTAD was a virtually unrelieved failure.

A significant contributory factor to this outcome was the so-called "group system" of arriving at decisions and resolutions at the conference. A great deal of the success of the 1964 UNCTAD as a forum for effective expression of the grievances of the developing countries about the trade and aid policies of the developed countries was due to the fact that the developing countries, under the leadership and inspiration of Dr. Prebisch, had welded themselves into a majority voting bloc, whereas the minority of developed countries arrived at the conference with diverse positions that reflected their different national situations and approaches to policy and also the divisions among them that had arisen during the preparatory stages of the Kennedy Round negotiations and, indeed, had their roots in the complex diplomacy of post-war European economic integration. The developed countries were therefore taken by surprise and the differences among them were exploited to the disadvantage of their public images. The developing countries ("the Group of 77") sought to repeat this political success— necessary to assert the maximum moral pressure on the developed countries to grant concessions that could not be extracted from them by majority voting alone—at the 1968 UNCTAD by drawing up an agreed set of demands (the "Charter of Algiers") at a preparatory meeting. But the natural response of the developed countries, after the experience of Geneva, was similarly to group themselves into a bloc ("Group B") and concert their positions in advance. Moreover, given the asymmetrical relationship between the "Group of 77" (by then enlarged to 86 countries) as demanders and "Group B" as suppliers of concessions, it was equally natural— though highly unconducive to successful negotiation—that the "Group of 77" should tend to achieve unanimity on the basis of the most extravagant demands of some members, and that "Group B" should correspondingly tend to achieve unanimity on the basis of the least generous concessions individual members were prepared to offer. This polarisation, and other organisational weaknesses inherent in large conferences, tended both to encumber or paralyse negotiations and to divert the proceedings from negotiations to declamations and confrontations.

The central objective of the 1968 UNCTAD, as a sequel to the 1964 UNCTAD, was to contribute to the formulation of a development policy for the second Development Decade "by approving a series of concrete measures to accelerate the rate of economic and social growth of developing countries and by inserting these measures into the basic framework of a broad strategy for development, as encouraged by the General Assembly".[11] The prime emphasis was on the production of an agreed strategy, which the UNCTAD Secretariat had prepared but which it withheld "before it became clear whether fundamental positive results would emerge; and they did not. A global strategy without concrete measures would have been another document of pious declarations without any practical consequences."[12]

The conference thus failed in its longer-range aim of producing a global development strategy because it failed in its proximate aim of producing concrete solutions to sufficient important problems of promoting development. For this the group system, and more specifically the insistence of the developing countries as expressed in the Charter of Algiers on the need for special measures for the least developed countries so that all the developing countries would derive comparable gains, was largely responsible—because the way in which the subjects for discussion were divided up ensured that equality of benefit would be impossible to attain. As had become clear from the 1964 UNCTAD, the individual developing countries have widely divergent interests. Most obviously, the more developed are interested in exports of manufactures, and the less developed in exports of primary products; in addition, they are divided among those in the Commonwealth preference system, those associated with the EEC, and those excluded from either preferential system. Thus while, as had been cynically remarked of them at the 1964 UNCTAD, it was easy enough for them to agree on the highest common denominator of demands on the developed countries, it was also—as had been predicted by some analysts of the first UNCTAD, and as proved the case at the second UNCTAD—very unlikely that they could find any common interest in practical proposals for trade policy change, and therefore agree to them without extensive wrangling, if at all.

[11]Raúl Prebisch, "The Significance of the Second Session of UNCTAD", UNCTAD, TD/96, May 7, 1968, p. 2.
[12]*Ibid.*, p. 8.

This probability was verified, most surprisingly to the Group B countries, with respect to the proposal for a preference scheme in manufactures and semi-manufactures for the exports of the developing countries. As recorded above, this was the most hotly contended proposal to emerge from the 1964 UNCTAD, and one with respect to which the USA reversed its original opposition and co-operated with the other OECD countries in the production of an agreed plan for a general preferences scheme for presentation to the conference. That plan was a collection of principles and elements rather than a concrete scheme, and it left unresolved the question of abolition of "reverse preferences" (preferences for developed countries in the markets of developing countries under Commonwealth preferences and EEC's association of overseas territories); but it did represent a major concession of principle, and the developed countries expected it to be warmly welcomed. The welcome was indeed warm, but in a quite contrary sense. Developing members of an existing preference area were worried lest they should lose more by sharing their existing preferences with other developing countries than they would gain from access to the markets of the developed members of the other preference area and the USA. More important, preferences in the manufactured items envisaged for inclusion in the scheme were of interest only to a minority of the developing countries, those with a manufacturing capability. To extend the range of beneficiaries in accordance with the principle of equitable sharing of benefits, the "Group of 77" insisted to the last possible minute that the general preferences scheme must include processed and semi-processed agricultural and other primary products from the beginning, in place of these products being dealt with as proposed on a case-by-case basis as the scheme evolved. In consequence, instead of positive adoption of the proposal, a special committee was set up to continue work on the details of the scheme, with the objective of having a definite scheme ready by late 1969. This objective was far too optimistic, given the deep division between the Americans and the Europeans over the issue of "reverse preferences" and over the issue of non-discrimination generally. Progress at a rather glacial pace has only been made possible by means of an agreement that each side can introduce its own preferred form of preference system. The fact that progress in the discussions is being made may perhaps be counted as some sort of achievement of the 1968 UNCTAD. But with the contemporary upswing of protectionism in the USA, there is a serious danger that any preference scheme proposed to Congress by the US Administration would be seized on as a means of imposing fresh barriers to the exports of the less developed countries to the USA. (This was, of course, one of the main practical objections made by American experts to the original preference proposals produced at the 1964 UNCTAD.)

With respect to other major areas of discussion, significant positive results failed to emerge for a variety of reasons, involving the unwieldiness of the group system, the balance of payments difficulties of the UK and the USA, and fundamental economic problems. The work on commodities schemes advanced little beyond the recommendation that existing efforts to negotiate such schemes on certain eligible commodities, and a variety of research programmes, should be continued. Nothing was accomplished with respect to improved access of developing countries exports of primary products to the markets of developed countries. The proposal prepared by the World Bank for a supplementary financing scheme to enable countries suffering shortfalls in export earnings below projected levels to continue their development plans was sent back for further study, because the countries that would have had to supply the required resources were unwilling to do so for balance of payments reasons.

The only potentially significant concession from the developed countries to the developing (the general preferences proposal apart) was in the field of finance, where it was agreed to change the denominator used in applying the "one per cent of national income" principle for financial resource transfers from the former to the latter from net national income at factor cost to gross national product at market prices. This would raise the required aid volume by about 25 per cent of existing levels. The value of this concession, however, remains problematical owing to the unwillingness of most developed countries to specify a target date by which the change would be implemented. Given the evolution of the international monetary system and the balance-of-payments and inflation problems of the UK and the USA since then, it appears extremely unlikely that the aid levels prevailing at the turn of the decade will be maintained, let alone the new targets be implemented.

The 1968 UNCTAD was therefore a virtually unqualified

failure. Of its two noteworthy positive accomplishments, the increase in targeted aid levels is a very wishful hope rather than a firm commitment, while the general preferences proposal remains to be worked out in detail and its outlines themselves are still nebulous—and, as already mentioned, its final form may well be trade-restricting rather than trade-creating.

Future of UNCTAD?

The failure of the 1968 UNCTAD raises two important questions. The first is whether UNCTAD in its present form has ceased to serve a useful purpose. The 1964 UNCTAD caught the developed countries by surprise and enabled the developing countries to dramatise their grievances sufficiently to change the thinking and approach of the developed countries, notably on the issue of trade preferences (including preferences among the developing countries). But the developed countries learned from the experience and at the 1968 UNCTAD they were able to let the divisions of interest among the developing countries themselves prevent much of importance from happening, and at the same time to shed some of the burden of responsibility for the ills of the developing countries that had been heaped upon them at the 1964 conference. It therefore seems that the process of confrontation of the two groups at time-consuming monster meetings has lost its moral shock power and that its expense, inefficiency and irrelevance to the solution of concrete issues are no longer justified by its possibilities of forcing progress. On the other hand, it is clear that understanding of the real issues has been furthered by the research that has been stimulated and carried out, both inside and outside the UNCTAD organisation, as a result of the 1964 confrontation. Perhaps UNCTAD would be well advised to eschew monster international rallies in future and to emphasise research and discussion by small expert groups in co-operation with other established international institutions.

Future of Development Promotion?

The second and more important question is how, if at all, efforts to promote the economic development of the developing countries by increases in development assistance can be intensified, given that the UNCTAD route has probably reached its limits, and has possibly passed them, in the sense that the failure of the 1968

UNCTAD may well have given the developed countries the feeling that they have done everything reasonable for the developing countries, and may henceforth leave them to stew in their own juice.

As mentioned earlier, there has been an obvious need for a renewal of the moral commitment of the developed countries to help the developing countries; and, as also mentioned, it was widely hoped that the report of the Pearson Commission would provide such a moral reaffirmation. Unfortunately, while the Pearson Report is in many respects an excellent document, inasmuch as it provides a useful review of past experience with development and with the promotion of development by official aid, points to problems for the future and makes many sensible suggestions for changes in aid provision and administration, it completely fails to provide the new motivation for aid-giving that had been hoped for. The reasons for this failure are readily understandable.[13] The only remaining argument for aid is the humanitarian or charitable argument. Charity is difficult to discuss in public at the best of times and a group representing both donors and recipients is very unlikely to be able to arrive at non-self-contradictory statements about it. Thus the Pearson Report proceeds from a brief and inconclusive discussion of the motives for aid to the establishment of targets for aid-giving, which targets appear as a practical compromise between the estimated needs of the developing nations and the hoped-for generosity of the developed countries, unsupported by motivating arguments for the latter. Hence the report can easily be interpreted as a tombstone rather than a milestone to international co-operation in the promotion of economic development.

This in fact seems to have been its consequence so far as one can judge at this early stage. The Pearson Report contained two major recommendations—a substantial increase in the amount of aid, especially official aid, and a substantial shift towards the provision of aid through multilateral institutions (primarily the World Bank) rather than as heretofore through bilateral government-to-government transactions. The subsequent Petersen Report, [14] which presumably reflects the trend of official American

[13]For a fuller commentary on the Pearson Report, see Johnson, *The Crisis of Aid and the Pearson Report* (Edinburgh University Press, Edinburgh, 1970).

[14]*US Foreign Assistance in the 1970s: A New Approach*, Report to the President of the United States from the Task Force of International Development (US Government Printing Office, Washington D.C., March 4, 1970).

thinking on the aid question, in broad terms endorses the objective of multilateralisation but refuses to commit the USA to an increase, or even a standstill, in the level of its development assistance. The Petersen Report thus lends itself ominously to the interpretation that the USA intends to extricate itself gradually from the aid business through a combination of a reduction of total aid and an abnegation of responsibility for the allocation and administration of the aid it continues to provide. This interpretation is only too consistent with the trend towards protectionism in trade policy mentioned above, and with the general impression noted by many observers that the USA is moving rapidly into a phase of economic and political isolationism.

The prospect of a decline in the volume of US development assistance in the 1970s, and even more important of an abandonment by the USA of its previous leadership responsibilities in this field, implies important changes in the nature of and approach to the development problem in the years ahead. Two major changes are particularly noteworthy. First, there is likely to be a growing emphasis on private foreign direct investment by the large multinational corporation as a substitute for official aid transfers between governments. Development by private foreign investment rather than by inter-governmental transfers raises a host of economic and political problems that are as yet largely unexplored.[15] Second, export opportunities, for both primary products and manufactured goods, will be of increasing importance to developing countries obliged to rely increasingly on their own capacity to earn foreign exchange to finance the requirements of their development programmes.

It is this prospect of heavily increased dependence of the development process on ready and assured access to large and expanding export markets that makes trade liberalisation in the 1970s a crucial factor in the further progress of the whole world economy. The developed countries by themselves are rich enough to absorb the inefficiencies that stem from protectionism, both industrial and agricultural; and there is little reason for them to fear that whatever new protectionist policies they introduce will jeopardise

[15]See Johnson, "The Multinational Corporation as a Development Agent", *Columbia Journal of World Business*, New York, May-June, 1970, pp. 25-30; and also Johnson, "Direct Foreign Investment: A Survey of the Issues", Paper prepared for the Third Pacific Conference on Trade and Development, Sydney, Australia, August, 1970.

their international interests and influence. But for the developing countries, the trade and aid policies chosen by the developed countries may prove of vital economic significance.

The best and most effective contribution that the developed countries could make to the promotion of economic development in the poor regions of the world, given the contemporary disillusionment with official aid, would consist of non-discriminatory reduction or elimination of barriers to exports of manufactures and semi-manufactures from developing to developed countries, including both tariffs and quota and other restrictions, coupled with an effort to regularise and liberalise trade in agricultural products. Thorough-going steps in this direction would require both procedures for dealing equitably with the problem of market disruption, and a substantial development of methods for providing adjustment assistance to industries (and farm enterprises) in the developed countries adversely affected by import competition. A far inferior second-best, and one that might even prove counter-productive in its effects, would be a preference scheme on the lines that seem to be emerging from UNCTAD discussions.

Even here, however, there are better and worse schemes available. Preferences might be given on a basis non-discriminatory among developing countries, or they might be given by particular developed countries to particular client groups of developing countries. The latter has the political attraction to the developed country concerned of creating a definite obligation on the part of the clients, as well as permitting discrimination in favour of the client countries at the expense of other rivals; but for the same reason it involves political dangers both for the clients and for the world polity. US policy has thus far favoured the non-discriminatory alternative; the European countries, by contrast, lean towards the client relationship and the European Communities have in recent trade agreements been making special arrangements for particular developing countries. This trend would be accentuated if Britain were successful in gaining membership in the EEC. The adverse consequences of this on the trade of the Latin American countries with Western Europe might well lead the USA to reverse its present stand, and espouse a "hemisphere" arrangement involving preferences in the American market for Latin American countries only.

Such a development in the direction of regionalisation of world trade would be unfortunate in itself; and it might have serious international political consequences, because it would in effect assign Latin America to the USA, Africa and the Mediterranean to Europe, leaving the less developed countries of Asia out in the cold with only the Russians to turn to. (While Japan and Australia could, and in the course of time probably would, do substantially more for South-East Asian developing countries, they obviously lack the capacity to take on the problems of the Indian sub-continent.)

Part II

OPPORTUNITIES FOR
DEVELOPING COUNTRIES

by

David Wall

1 FACTORS AGAINST DEVELOPING COUNTRIES

This paper is concerned with the problems that might be created for less developed countries by the formation of what has been described as a free trade treaty initiated by Atlantic countries and, too, with the policies that might be adopted by participants to meet these problems.[1] The major change in the international environment of trade relationships which would result from a North Atlantic free trade area (NAFTA), as the arrangement would initially be, would have an important impact on the trade prospects of developing nations. In the years since World War II, less advanced countries have come to assume a bigger voice in world affairs. The group of nations that might comprise NAFTA would accordingly have to take account of their needs. It has in fact become increasingly accepted in recent years that any changes in the set-up of international trade should accommodate Third World interests. It is urged in some quarters that satisfying such interests should be the prime purpose for reforming the world trade environment.

The motivation of the free trade treaty idea is the desire to move further towards world free trade. The establishment of NAFTA by itself, however, would involve some conflict with this objective, inasmuch as it would result in increased discrimination against poor nations. To avoid this effect, which would be contrary to the obligations the developed countries have assumed to help the development of backward economies, the NAFTA arrangement would have to devote special attention to the trading requirements of less developed countries.

---

[1] If implemented, the free trade treaty idea would probably embrace Pacific and Atlantic countries in a multilateral free trade association, but it has been assumed that the proposal would need to be initiated by North Atlantic countries and hence the use in this paper of the shorthand expression, NAFTA. The writer is aware, though, of the semantic problems posed by this pnemonic word.

The phrases "less developed countries", "developing countries", "poor nations", "the Third World", "the South" and "under-developed countries" are used interchangeably in this study, as are "developed", "advanced", "industrial" and "rich".

More than a hundred countries fall into the less developed category. The term "less developed" covers a wide range of situations, from peasant societies more or less totally involved in subsistence activities to diverse economies with large industrial sectors which are only classified as less developed because of their low *per capita* incomes. All less developed countries are committed to accelerating their economic development. Development is a complex process. The form it takes necessarily differs from country to country. A common element, however, is a stress on modernisation, through accelerated industrialisation of the various sectors of the economy. Less developed countries depend upon trade with the developed world to assist their attempts to grow and develop through industrialisation. Trade, by making imports available, and by providing export markets, helps industrialisation in several important ways. On the import side, it affords a country access to sources of essential commodities which would otherwise be unobtainable (or which could only be produced domestically at prohibitive cost); and it provides competition from the products of established industries abroad as a spur to efficiency. On the other side, exports earn the foreign exchange required to finance the imports of essential commodities. Production of export commodities often provides employment for factors of production, especially labour, which would otherwise be unemployed or barely earning a subsistence level of income. Finally, the optimum size of many modern industries is often larger than the domestic markets which poor countries can sustain, and the availability of export markets enables these countries to reap economies of scale.

The modernisation of a less developed economy requires inputs of industrial goods the economy is unable to produce. In the case of the urban manufacturing sector the need for machinery is obvious. It is also true, however, that if agriculture is to be modernised, mechanical implements and industrial products such as fertilisers and pesticides are required. Although the availability of such products does not in itself ensure development it does facilitate the process. It was largely the belief that the inability to import adequate quantities of industrial products was frustrating the attempts of poor countries to achieve an adequate rate of growth that led, in 1964, to the establishment of the United Nations Conference on Trade and Development (UNCTAD).

A second argument for development policies that are trade-orientated is that competition from foreign suppliers encourages efficiency on the part of the domestic producer. This is valid whether the market in question is the domestic market or the export market. But the argument carries greater force in the latter case. If a producer is to establish an export market he must be able to sell at world prices. Trade also encourages efficiency by stimulating the interchange of ideas, knowledge and skills. Thirdly, the less developed world depends on commodity exports to earn the foreign exchange needed to provide the capacity to import the materials required in the industrialisation process. Aid, though important in extending the import capacity of the less developed countries, is responsible for just a minor proportion of their import finance, constituting only about 15 per cent of the total import bill.

Most under-developed countries are small. Only five[2] have populations greater than 40m; 72 have less than 15m. Even these figures over-estimate the size of the markets as a great proportion of the population in these countries is either outside the money economy or has miniscule purchasing power. Yet modern industry, typically based on high capital investment, requires large markets in order to operate efficiently. This problem leads to the fourth argument underlining the importance of trade as a means of benefiting from economies of scale. If a country wishes to develop on the basis of industrialisation, then unless endowed with a large home market, access must be had to markets abroad. This is the other side of the coin to the argument that if industries are to be able to compete on world markets they must be efficient. To be able, though, to operate efficiently industries must have export markets available to them. The circularity of this problem has led to many proposals for commercial policy measures which would effectively subsidise export industries in less developed countries during the early stages of their development.

Finally, an important aspect of the trade and development issue is that many factors of production in several poor countries are specialised in the production of one export commodity. Examples are coffee land in Colombia, textile workers in India and capital equipment in the Malaysian tin industry. Loss of export markets in cases such as these would mean much hardship for the factors employed. At best alternative employment for the factors would be much less remunerative; at worst they would be unemployed.

[2]Nigeria, India, Pakistan, Indonesia and Brazil.

Almost all less developed countries depend on a few[3] export commodities. They consequently rely heavily on the maintainance of markets for their exports for the employment of their factors of production.

Trade, then, has an important role to play in the industrialisation process on which the under-developed countries are depending to support their economic development. An expansion of trade opportunities is essential to help them support their rapidly expanding populations and to realise current ambitions to increase their rate of growth. Although the successful realisation of these ambitions will largely depend on self-help, there is little they can do to expand trade flows. According to the rules of the General Agreement on Tariffs and Trade (GATT) a country may protect, with tariffs, an "infant industry" which is producing for the home market. But it cannot give equivalent support to export industries in the form of subsidies. Some countries have devised measures equivalent to subsidies, like tax policies favouring exporters. The scope for such devices, however, is limited and are in any case at the implementing country's own expense. Less developed nations are, to a large extent, dependent on rich countries for providing widened opportunities for trade expansion. The need for widened opportunities has been intensified in recent years by the decline in the real value of aid flows. Capital aid from the developed to the less developed countries has been on a plateau since the beginning of the 1960s. Its real value has been falling due to a worsening of the terms on which it is extended and because increasing amounts of new aid are absorbed by interest and amortisation payments on old loans. Furthermore, the failure of aid to increase at a time when the incomes of advanced countries have been rising rapidly, means that it represents a falling share of those incomes.

Worsening Position

The rich countries have been moving away from, instead of towards, their Development Decade commitment to give 1 per cent of their incomes as aid to less developed countries.

In spite of the increased needs of developing countries for a widening of their trade opportunities, in the years since World War II their

[3]In 1965, 72 countries derived more than 25 per cent of their export earnings from one commodity. In 39 cases the percentage was 50 or over.

relative position has worsened and they have been unable to maintain their share of total world trade. The fall in the poor nations' share of world trade has been fairly constant. Whereas the rate of growth of the imports and exports of the industrial areas over the period 1960–67 attained an annual average 13.3 per cent and 13.9 per cent respectively, those for less developed countries averaged only 5.8 per cent and 5.1 per cent.[4] Although the total exports of the less developed countries rose some 90.0 per cent over the period 1953–67, their share of total world trade declined from 25.5 per cent to 18.8 per cent. Over the same period total exports from the industrial areas increased 178.6 per cent and their share of total world trade rose from 64.2 per cent to 69.7 per cent. The change in the relative shares reflects the fact that the trade of the industrial nations is being increasingly carried on among themselves and is mainly in manufactured goods. The share of the total trade of industrial areas which is accounted for by trade among themselves rose from 63 per cent in 1953 to 75 per cent in 1967. Over the same period the share of manufactured products in world trade rose from 45 per cent to 61 per cent.

Various explanations have been advanced for the relative worsening of the trade position of less developed countries. These fall into two categories. One is concerned with the contemporary economic environment, the other with development in international and domestic commercial policy.

From the point of view of the developed countries the economic factors which have been stressed[5] are: (1) the internationalisation of tastes developed by modern communications and stimulated further by the growing preponderance of companies (especially American) operating internationally and marketing their own products; (2) international advertising of mass-produced goods manufactured in the increasingly large quantities made possible by international specialisation and the growth of demand; and (3) the marked lowering, on a discriminatory basis favouring industrial economies, of unit transport costs.

From the point of view of poor countries, though, the decline in their share of world exports (on the average, because the experience

[4]Inclusive of petroleum exporting countries. If these countries are excluded the export figure is somewhat reduced.

[5]See John Pincus, *Trade, Aid and Development* (Council on Foreign Relations, McGraw-Hill, New York, 1967).

of individual countries has varied widely) can be attributed to several features of the natural economic environment stressed by spokesmen for less developed countries at the 1964 UNCTAD. The principal ones were: one, a slow growth of demand for food in the developed countries, a consequence of the falling share of income which consumers there need to spend on food; two, the development of synthetic substitutes for natural raw materials; three, increases in productivity in developed manufacturing industry requiring smaller amounts of inputs of raw materials per unit of output; and, four, insensitivity of demand to changes in prices of food and raw materials. A further factor, in connection with some commodities (coffee, cocoa, sugar and bananas, for examples), is increased competition among developing nations reducing the price received and thus total export earnings.

Commercial Policies of Industrial Nations

Although these economic factors have had an effect on the Third World's trade position, much of the explanation for its worsening is to be found in the post-war development of commercial policy among industrial countries, resulting in greater discrimination against the exports of either all less developed countries or certain groups of them. The heavier discrimination has stemmed from four sources: first, increased protection of domestic agriculture in almost all developed countries; secondly, the development of discriminatory trading systems; thirdly, the extension of quantitative restrictions imposed on imports of semi-manufacturers and manufactures from developing countries; and, finally, increased effective protection against the labour intensive exports of special interest to less developed nations, particularly low cost manufactured consumer goods and processed raw materials.

Protection of Agriculture

Almost all developed countries afford substantial protection to their agricultural sectors, using a wide range of devices such as tariffs, quotas, price supports, subsidies and income deficiency payments. At the instigation of the United States a waiver clause was included in GATT to allow such protection of domestic agriculture. This protection militates against the interests of poor countries, many being heavily dependent on exports of agricultural products which are competitive with the agricultural sectors of developed economies.

The extent of protection is illustrated by calculations which have been made[6] of the percentage excess of value of output of the agricultural sectors of developed countries measured by the prices received by farmers in the developed countries over the value of that output measured at import prices. For the years 1961–62 this excess value was 43 per cent for Norway, 41 per cent for Sweden, 39 per cent for West Germany, 29 per cent for the United Kingdom, 25 per cent for Italy, 17 per cent for France, and 16 per cent for the USA. Agricultural protectionism has been increasing in almost all developed countries since the last world war.

The protection afforded agriculture in industrial countries restricts exports from the developing countries in two ways: increased prices reduce total consumption and domestic consumption is substituted for imports. It is difficult to assess the value of expanded export income which would accrue to developing countries if protection of agriculture in the developed countries was to be removed. One observer[7], however, has put the figure at $2,000m, equivalent to an increase of about 15 per cent of earnings from agricultural exports. Professor Harry Johnson[8], of the London School of Economics, has estimated that free trade in sugar alone would result in a minimum increase of $897m in the value of sugar imports into the industrial countries and in addition would have released some $482m worth of resources which could be used for development purposes.[9]

The commodities which suffer most from the protective policies of advanced countries are cereals (including rice), meat, vegetable oils and oil-seeds, textile fibres, and sugar. In addition to agricultural products developed countries also extend substantial protection to their extractive industries, for examples, the coal industry of the UK and the oil industry of the USA.

One consequence of the developed countries subsidising agriculture has been large-scale surplus production, especially in the USA. Much of this surplus has been sent to food deficit countries as aid. The best-known example is the Public Law 480 "Food for Freedom" programme of the USA. Such programmes have a certain detrimental effect. They interfere with the food price mechanisms of the

[6]D. Gale Johnson, "Agriculture and Foreign Economic Policy", *Journal of Farm Economics*, December, 1964, pp. 922 and 923.
[7] *Ibid.*
[8]Also Professor of Economics at the University of Chicago.
[9]Harry G. Johnson, *Economic Policies Toward Less Developed Countries* (The Brookings Institution, Washington D.C., 1967), p. 257.

recipient countries, lowering the prices received by producers of similar or competitive farm products, thus discouraging efficient development of agriculture in the developing world.

Discriminatory Trading Policies

In the aftermath of World War II, developed countries tended to merge into self-interest groups. Initially, in Europe, this tendency was all-inclusive and was embodied in the Organisation for European Economic Co-operation (OEEC). Later, however, a clash of outward-looking philosophies led to the separate establishment of the European Free Trade Area (EFTA) and the European Economic Community (EEC) and at the same time Canada was moving closer to the USA. The establishment of discriminatory trading systems is the second policy development which has adversely affected less developed countries. It has done this in two ways. On the one hand the lowering of trade barriers on a mutual basis among the members of the groups has created large preferential trading areas resulting in a diversion of trade from cheaper foreign sources. Although it is difficult to estimate the quantitative size of the effect such data as is available indicates that that diversion is indeed taking place. For example, over 1961–67 the value of trade among EEC members increased by about 106 per cent while imports of the EEC countries from all other developed countries increased by only 42 per cent and from less developed countries by 50 per cent. Comparable figures for EFTA are 84 per cent for intra-EFTA trade, 46 per cent for imports from other developed countries, and 22 per cent for imports from developing countries. The exports of less advanced economies which have been most affected by the diversion of trade are agricultural products (for instance, sugar and oil seeds), processed agricultural products (vegetable oils, cocoa products), and some manufacturers (especially textiles).

In the cases of France and the UK the extension of preferences to the products of their partners in the EEC and EFTA has reduced the value of the preferences that they extend to colonies in the franc zone and the Commonwealth. Over the last few years Britain has been expanding imports of cotton textiles from her EFTA partner, Portugal, at the same time as she has been reducing imports of these products from India.

On the other hand, the formation of these groups may have altered consumer preferences. The mutual reduction of tariffs among the member countries of the EEC and EFTA has altered the relative prices of goods available to the consumer in the member countries. The availability of cheaper manufactured goods may have shifted consumer demand away from the products of less developed countries. These two effects are not, of course, restricted to the products of less developed countries. They can affect the trade of member countries with all non-members.

There has in recent times been a proliferation of discriminatory preferential trade arrangements between some industrial nations and selected less developed ones. The Commonwealth preference system is the best known. But since the war the USA has extended preferential treatment to imports from the Philippines (mainly sugar, which is currently being phased out), Canada (automobiles), Puerto Rico (currently under discussion) and Cuba (abolished after the Castro Revolution). The system under which the USA imports sugar is also a form of preferential trading. Import quotas are granted to selected countries, the criteria on which the distribution of these quotas are based being political in nature. Since 1963 the discriminatory preferences that EEC countries gave to their colonies and ex-colonies have been generalised and extended into an EEC preference system in which the associated overseas states and territories of the members have preferential access (on a reciprocal basis, as in the Commonwealth system) to the markets of all EEC countries for their exports.

Quantitative Restrictions

To be effective the price equivalent of tariff preferences, offered to countries whose exports are priced higher than world market prices, must be greater than that price disadvantage. If the preferred country already has a prior price advantage, preferences are not required to divert trade. They do, however, allow the preferred supplier to obtain higher prices than would be possible in the absence of the preferences. If the effective tariff preference is less than the price disadvantage of the preferred supplier then quantitative restrictions in some form (usually quotas) will be required to substantiate the preference. There are many examples where such quantitative restrictions apply: imports of bananas into the UK, France and Italy; sugar into the USA, the UK and France.

In addition to discriminatory quantitative restrictions, global quotas have been imposed by most industrial countries on imports of a vast range of products. Besides the justification of agricultural protection, the more common reasons advanced are: (1) balance of payments difficulties; (2) protection of established manufacturing industries; (3) protection of infant industries; and (4) military and political strategy. Most commonly they have been imposed on low cost, labour intensive products exported by poor countries. A recent development has been the imposition of "voluntary restrictions" by less developed nations on their exports of cheap cotton textiles to the developed world. The "voluntary" element is voluntary only in the sense that failure to keep within the export restrictions would result in import restrictions being put on by the developed countries. There is almost no export, apart from a few non-ferrous minerals, of any less developed country which is not subject to quantitative restrictions in some developed countries.

Effective Protection

While the above limitations on the trade of less developed countries affect those products in which they have a comparative advantage, the industrial countries also maintain substantial barriers to the expansion of developing countries' exports of processed and manufactured products. The substantial dismantling of barriers to trade since 1945 has chiefly affected raw materials and capital intensive exports of developed countries. In the latter case this discriminates against the labour-intensive products of less developed nations; in the former case, against exports of processed forms of the raw materials. This is because the effective protection afforded by a tariff is not determined by the nominal value of the tariff itself but by the ratio of the tariff to the value added in processing. For instance, if we assume that imports of a refined ore bear a tariff of 10 per cent and that the cost of the ore itself (imports of which do not carry duty) represents 50 per cent of the costs of production then the effective protection afforded by the 10 per cent tariff is 20 per cent. That is, the 10 per cent tariff is effectively applied to that half of the total costs which is represented by processing costs or, value added. Thus the effective protection of the production of a commodity increases as tariffs are withdrawn from imports of inputs used to produce that commodity. One result, then, of the freeing of imports of raw materials from tariffs has been the discouragement of the development of processing industries in less developed countries.

A further policy development which has adversely affected the trade prospects of less developed countries has resulted from the operation of GATT. The prime purpose of GATT is to provide a forum in which the reduction of all barriers to trade may be negotiated. The rules and regulations of the agreement, however, are biased in such a way as to ensure that the successive rounds of tariff negotiations held since the last world war, the most recent of which was the Kennedy Round, concentrated on the liberalisation of trade in products of export interest to developed countries.

This introduction has argued that developing countries need greater trade opportunities to assist their attempts to develop. It has also argued that economic factors and policy developments have prevented such expansion taking place on an adequate scale over the last two decades. This study is concerned to show how a NAFTA arrangement might prevent further deterioration and, through a widening of trade opportunities, boost the development efforts of the poor countries. Attention is first directed to the possibility of achieving such an objective within the existing international institutional framework. Chapter 2 discusses the position of the less developed countries in GATT and their prospects under that agreement. Secondly, in Chapter 3, the feasibility and usefulness of the various proposals made in UNCTAD for improving the trade opportunities of less developed countries are discussed and assessed. Finally, in Chapter 4, a proposal for a NAFTA preference system designed to encourage exports from less developed countries is outlined and discussed.

GATT is an agreement by contracting parties (signatory countries) to regulate trade among themselves according to mutually accepted rules and regulations. It is viewed by developing nations as being so organised as to be, in effect, run by the industrialised members in their own interests.

The dissatisfaction of less developed countries is perhaps best illustrated by the following quotation from a report to the Economic and Social Council of the United Nations General Assembly preparatory to the 1964 trade conference:

> "By the very nature of its philosophy, which is based on liberalism, GATT inevitably shows a marked lack of understanding of the interests of the under-developed and developing countries. This is primarily due to the inequality between the industrialised and developing countries in the matter of bargaining power. Article I of the General Agreement is based on the fiction that there is complete equality among the contracting parties. There is, however, no equality of treatment except among equals.
>
> "The contracting parties to GATT have from the outset taken an essentially negative view of the special problems of the under-developed countries, less perhaps because of ignorance of the problems of economic development than because the needs of these countries seem to conflict with the long-term objectives of the General Agreement, which are:
>
> (a) The general elimination of customs tariffs and other barriers to trade;
>
> (b) Non-discrimination with respect to customs tariffs and the commercial relations of each country with all other countries.
>
> "The under-developed countries have persistently urged, though with little success, that GATT should recognise the special ties which exist between economic development and world trade. The industrialised countries have always adopted a

very liberal attitude towards trade among themselves, while maintaining restrictive measures towards under-developed countries."[10]

It is such arguments which have led under-developed countries to label GATT as a "rich man's club".

International Trade Organisation

GATT came into being at a conference convened in 1947 to establish an International Trade Organisation (ITO). The ITO was one of four important institutions envisaged after World War II to normalise the world economy. The other three were successfully established. They are the International Monetary Fund (IMF), the International Bank for Reconstruction and Development (World Bank) and the Food and Agriculture Organisation of the United Nations. The provisions for establishing the ITO were negotiated in Cuba from November 21, 1947, to March 24, 1948, and were embodied in a document known as the Havana Charter for International Trade Co-operation. Fifty-six countries took part in the discussions and managed to reconcile divergent positions and opinions—represented by the 800 amendments proposed to the draft charter—sufficiently to agree upon a charter embodying the first code of rules and regulations ever adopted for the conduct of international trade. The charter contained nine chapters and 106 articles which, apart from establishing the ITO and its regulations, embodied provisions on commercial policy and other aspects of international economic relations based on the principle that all impediments to the free and normal flow of trade should be abolished. Thus it called for the reciprocal reduction of tariffs and the elimination of preferential trading systems. It also required that fiscal duties or taxes and internal regulations on consumption should be applied only on a non-discriminatory basis. Subsidies of all types were to require prior international consultation and export subsidies were to be allowed only in exceptional circumstances. Stressed also was the need for international commodity agreements to be confined to short-term protective measures. "Unavoidable" export restrictions or fixed prices, it was stated, should be of limited duration. Finally, provision was made for the participation of the

[10] *The Proceedings of the United Nations Conference on Trade and Development* (United Nations, New York, 1964), Vol. V, p. 409.

consuming and producing countries in the formulation and implementation of commodity agreements on an equal footing.

The Creation of GATT

But the ITO was stillborn. From the outset the world's two major trading nations—the USA and the UK—made it clear that they would not ratify the charter. In 1947, though, during the preparatory sessions for the Havana Conference on Trade and Employment, a group of 23 countries agreed to negotiate the proposed tariff concessions. They also decided to guarantee the stability of negotiated concessions by the advance (provisional) application of certain commercial policy regulations proposed in the draft charter. These agreements were formalised into the GATT which came into force on January 1, 1948.

GATT is not an organisation in the accepted sense of the word. It is simply a contractual framework which incorporates a set of mutually agreed rules governing trade relations. It also constitutes a forum for the negotiation of trade issues among members—such as the successive rounds of discussions on tariff reductions. There are 78 countries that have acceded to GATT as full contracting parties; one other country has provisionally acceded (Tunisia has special arrangements) and 12 newly independent countries participate in GATT on a *de facto* basis. These 91 countries account for more than four-fifths of total world trade. An important feature of the membership is that under-developed countries account for more than two-thirds of the voting strength. A two-thirds majority vote is sufficient to relieve a contracting party of its obligations under GATT.

The rules and regulations of GATT are derived from four basic principles, namely:

"Member countries should grant one another at least as favourable treatment as they grant any other country (the 'most-favoured-nation' principle), subject to the right, provided certain conditions are met, to form free trade areas or customs unions;

"Protection should be afforded to domestic industries exclusively through the customs tariff and not through other commercial measures (such as quantitative restrictions), and the general level of tariff protection should be progressively reduced through successive tariff negotiations;

"Contracting parties should use the procedure of consultation, directly with other contracting parties or with the contracting parties collectively, in cases of dispute and to avoid damage to one another's trading interests;

"Contracting parties should take such joint action . . . as is necessary to further the objectives of the agreement."[11]

From these basic principles are derived the rules and regulations which define the functions of GATT, the behaviour of members and how trade should be conducted by them. The principles of non-discrimination and of protection through tariffs only establish the guidelines for the commercial policy of member countries. The principles calling for progressive reduction of tariffs, for consultation within GATT in cases of dispute and for joint action to further the agreement's objectives determine the mode of operation of GATT and the behaviour of members within it.

These basic, general rules are reflected in specific rules. For example, the non-discrimination principle is discernible in the important rule prohibiting new preferential arrangements. Also important are the rules prohibiting quantitative restrictions save to cope with a chronic balance of payments problem, to help establish infant industry in less advanced economies, to prevent market disruption or to help overcome serious agricultural surpluses.

But the most important of GATT's institutional functions is to provide the forum for multilateral negotiations for reducing tariffs and other trade restrictions. These are conducted according to the central principle of reciprocity: the exchange of trade concessions of equal value by negotiating countries.

Bias Against Developing Countries

When it has suited them, the rules and regulations of GATT have been interpreted, implemented, amended or ignored by industrial countries in such ways as to effectively discriminate against less developed countries. One significant weakness of the agreement in this connection is, however, built into its assumptions. This follows from the conjunction of the principle of non-discrimination—or most-favoured-nation (MFN) principle—and the principle of

[11]"The Role of GATT in Relation to Trade and Development" (General Agreement on Tariffs and Trade, Geneva, March, 1964), p. 6. Quoted in Harry Johnson, *op. cit.*, p. 12.

reciprocity, which ensures that negotiations will be dominated by industrial nations. For the rules assume that negotiations will be conducted among equals. They in fact accord the major bargaining strength, though, to those countries which have most to offer and most to gain in negotiations, namely, industrial countries with their large markets and highly developed agricultural and manufacturing industries. The superior bargaining strength of the developed world has meant that negotiations have been restricted mostly to manufactured products of interest to them, thus discrmiinating indirectly against third parties, largely the emerging nations.

A second weakness of the bargaining system is that the reciprocity principle is biased against those countries least able to make significant concessions. The typical experience of development has included heavy dependence on tariffs as a major source of government revenue and, too, on both tariff and import restrictions to facilitate the establishment and running of domestic industry. What might thus seem to a developed country to be a balance of advantage, against a concession, to a developing country would in fact call for a sacrifice from the less developed nation of a magnitude greater than the advantages it would receive or the sacrifice made by the developed country. Dissatisfaction on this score was implicitly recognised by the contracting parties in 1964 when they adopted a new chapter, Chapter IV, to the agreement which no longer required less developed countries to concede reciprocal concessions in GATT negotiations. At the present time, however, it seems unlikely that industrial countries will make any significant concessions under this reform.[12]

There are several ways in which the strong members of GATT have exercised their bargaining position to discriminate against the trading interests of less developed members:

(a) While the developed countries have been negotiating a mutually beneficial liberalisation of trade in industrial products they have used every conceivable kind of protectionist device, from quantitative restrictions to variable import levies, to shield domestic agricultural sectors from foreign competition. This protection explicitly discriminates against the less developed countries because agricultural products predominate in their exports. Typical, well-known examples are the protection afforded by industrial nations

[12]Witness, for example, the unsatisfactory experience of the developing countries in the Kennedy Round negotiations, as discussed below.

to domestic producers of sugar, wheat, vegetable oils and oil seed.

(b) Although GATT is the only institution concerned with the regulation of world trade there is no provision for encouraging or administering commodity agreements. The Havana Charter did contain measures along these lines. But they were not adopted in GATT. The developed signatories have since consistently refused to bring commodity agreements within GATT's framework.

(c) GATT, while tolerating the old colonial-based preference systems based on reciprocity from less developed participants, proscribes new preferential arrangements unless they are in the form of fully-fledged customs unions or free trade areas. Although such arrangements may be suitable to developed countries with well-established industries and economies well able to adjust to the rigours of competition, developing countries with whole sectors, if not whole economies, in an "infant industry" state may be quite unable to conform to GATT rules on customs unions and free trade areas without suffering serious setbacks to their development programmes. This is especially true of the most under-developed members of existing arrangements. At the same time developing nations are prevented from considering partial free trade areas or customs unions, being under a threat of retaliation. For partial arrangements are defined in GATT rules and regulations as departures from the principle of non-discrimination.

It has, however, been possible for the EEC members of GATT to establish a new and illegal preferential trading system with their 18 associated overseas states under the Yaounde Convention. Despite the fact that this convention is a direct contravention of the GATT by six developed member countries there has been no retaliation in any form against them.

(d) Finally, the success of some less developed countries in establishing competitive manufacturing industries has been accompanied by the emergence of a doctrine of "market disruption". This doctrine has been deployed as a protective device by developed GATT countries who have advanced allegations of "market disruption" as an excuse to erect restrictionary controls on import of competitive manufactured products from less advanced economies. The "voluntary" export restrictions forced upon developing countries which have established competitive textile industries is a conspicuous manifestation of this restrictionist attitude. It is difficult to avoid the conclusion that the industrial nations have only implemented GATT rules and regulations when they have seen themselves likely to benefit. When these countries, though, have seen themselves likely to bear a loss or incur a sacrifice under the agreement, they have consistently sought to amend or simply ignore the rules and regulations. This "implementation by convenience" usually militates directly against the interests of the less advanced. "Implementation by convenience" is exemplified by the contrast between two recent GATT exercises, namely the Kennedy Round, and the 1963 Programme of Action.

Tariff-cutting Negotiations

It has been consistently argued by developed countries that less developed countries benefit from tariff reductions negotiated, in the main, by the industrialised nations. Such benefits to developing countries could take various forms. They could benefit (i) from increased import demand in industrial markets due to growth of production in them stimulated by tariff reductions; (ii) by exporting goods on which tariffs had been reduced; and (iii) by introducing into negotiations commodities in which they have a special interest. In GATT's Programme of Action meetings of 1963, and at UNCTAD in 1964, delegates of the industrial world took the line that many of the demands of less developed countries would be met in the Kennedy Round and that further action was unnecessary.

The Kennedy Round began in 1963 with the novel US proposal for a 50 per cent linear (across-the-board) cut in tariffs. Four years of hard bargaining followed. The negotiations often seemed doomed to failure. But the interests of the industrial countries involved were such that a relatively successful conclusion was reached in the summer of 1967.

In the Kennedy Round's early stages spokesmen for the industrial governments frequently said less developed countries stood to gain, especially since it was explicitly accepted that reciprocity would not be required from them. The actual outcome was far less satisfactory to the Third World than had earlier been promised. *The Times*, in commenting on the result, concluded that "while Britain and the other industrial countries are, on the whole, well pleased with the outcome of their labours, the developing countries are not."[13] It went on to say that the poorer countries were perturbed

"because it is possible to hold a four-year-long series of tariff

[13] *The Times*, London, July 26, 1967, p. 21.

44

and trade negotiations without anything very positive emerging in connection with the products in which they are most interested. None of the major recommendations made at the first UNCTAD conference in Geneva in 1964 have come much nearer to implementation. The poorer countries are still waiting. What, in fact, have the developing countries to give thanks for from the marathon trade discussions at Geneva? One item, on the aid rather than trade front. . . .".

This "one item" was an agreement among industrial nations to raise the minimum price of their wheat exports by 12.5 per cent and to give 4.5m tons of their surpluses to the developing countries under the American sponsored food aid programme. To offset this, however, there is a three-year extension of the protectionist Long Term Cotton Textiles Arrangement.

The conclusion of *The Times* was perhaps too pessimistic. Sir Eric Wyndham White, then Director-General of GATT, said: "From the data we have at hand it is clear that the less-developed countries will derive substantial advantages from the Kennedy Round, and equally clear that all their legitimate desires and aspirations are not fully achieved." In comparison to the benefits received by developed countries Sir Eric concluded that "the results of the Kennedy Round [from the point of view of the developing countries] are less impressive".[14] On the basis of the data available it is not possible to identify the "substantial advantages". Very few significant tariff concessions were made in the important fields of tropical products, processed foodstuffs and textiles. With tropical products it was impossible to reconcile significant concessions with existing preferential trading systems so that the obstruction of negotiations was attributable in large part to the vested interests of some less developed countries in existing preferences. In the cases of processed foodstuffs and textiles however, the chief obstacle was clearly the protected interests in developed countries.

Taking all agricultural products (excluding cereals, meat and dairy products) of export interest to less developed countries the proportion of commodities entering developed countries free of duty has risen from 11 to 19 per cent, at tariffs of 0-15 per cent from 40 to

[14]Eric Wyndham White, "GATT Trade negotiations", *GATT Press Release* 993, Statement to GATT Trade Negotiations Committee, Geneva, June 30, 1967.

43 per cent and at tariff rates of over 15 per cent the proportion has fallen from 49 to 38 per cent. With manufactured goods of current or potential export interest to less advanced economies the proportion of duty free items has risen from 5 to 7 per cent, in the 0-15 per cent tariff range from 60 to 79 per cent and has fallen in the range over 15 per cent from 35 to 14 per cent. Much more detailed information is required before an adequate picture can be drawn of the benefits which will accrue to developing countries following the Kennedy Round. Developing countries will, of course, derive some benefit from the application of the principle of non-discrimination. But as yet we do not know what the relative benefits will be or how much exports from these countries are likely to expand.

In assessing the Kennedy Round's outcome from the point of view of the Third World it should be remembered that tariff cuts tell only part of the story. The four major policy obstacles to the exports of less developed countries—quantitative restrictions. agricultural support policies, effective protection of processing and discriminatory preferential systems—remained more or less unchanged. Effective protection of processing increased, in fact, to the extent that tariffs were reduced or removed on imports into the developed countries of the raw materials required by processing industries. In addition, the reaction of industry in the USA—the world's largest market—to the Kennedy Round cuts would suggest that quantitative restrictions might be increased on imports into the USA of several products of export interest to the less developed countries. In Washington in recent years several industries have been pressing Congress hard either to place quotas on imports or, where these already exist, to make them even more restrictive. The pressure of lobbies has been strongest in the case of commodities exported by less developed countries, particularly textiles, non-ferrous metals, footwear and meat.

GATT Programme of Action

The product groups receiving the deepest tariff cuts in the Kennedy Round were those characterised by advanced technology or capital intensity. These products are primarily exported by developed countries and include such categories as chemicals, machinery and transport equipment, non-metallic mineral products and professional and scientific equipment. The tariff cuts in these and similar commodity groups were fairly general and substantial, averaging 40 to 50 per cent.[15]

But as already stated, the relative success (from the rich nations' viewpoint) of the Kennedy Round contrasted greatly with the experience of GATT's 1963 Programme of Action. This programme, endorsed (with reservations) by the signatory countries, contained the following eight points:

"*Standstill provision*: No new tariff or non-tariff barriers should be erected by industrialised countries against the export trade of any less developed country in the products identified as of particular interest to the less developed countries. In this connection the less developed countries would particularly mention barriers of a discriminatory nature.

Elimination of quantitative restrictions: Quantitative restrictions on imports from less developed countries which are inconsistent with the provisions of the GATT shall be eliminated within a period of one year. Where, on consultation between the industrialised and the less developed countries concerned, it is established that there are special problems which prevent action being taken within this period, the restriction on such items would be progressively reduced and eliminated by December 31, 1965.

Duty-free entry for tropical products: Duty-free entry into the industrialised countries shall be granted to tropical products by December 31, 1963.

Elimination of tariffs on primary products: Industrialised countries shall agree to the elimination of customs tariffs on the primary products important in the trade of less developed countries.

Reduction and elimination of tariff barriers to exports of semi-processed products from less developed countries: Industrialised countries should also prepare urgently a schedule for the reduction and elimination of tariff barriers to exports of semi-processed and processed products from less developed countries, providing for a reduction of at least 50 per cent of the present duties over the next three years.

Progressive reduction of internal fiscal changes and revenue duties: Industrial countries shall progressively reduce internal changes

[15]The above summary of the outcome of the Kennedy Round from the point of view of less developed countries is based on *GATT Press Releases* 992, 993 and 995, Geneva, June–August, 1967, and on UNCTAD document number TD/6, United Nations, Geneva, September 4, 1967.

and revenue duties on products wholly or mainly produced in less developed countries with a view to their elimination by December 31, 1965.

Reporting procedures: Industrialised countries maintaining the above mentioned barriers shall report to the GATT secretariat in July of each year on the steps taken by them during the preceding year to implement these decisions and on the measures which they propose to take over the next twelve months to provide larger access for the products of less developed countries.

Other measures: Contracting parties should also give urgent consideration to the adoption of other appropriate measures which would facilitate the efforts of less developed countries to diversify their economies, strengthen their export capacity and increase their earnings from overseas sales."[16]

None of the contracting parties either abstained from voting on or voted against the Programme of Action. The EEC countries, in their reservation, said they considered the first seven points to be a *minimal* programme only. Nothing, though, of any significance has resulted from the Programme of Action.

This dualism in the attitude of industrial countries towards GATT, one of support when it is in their interests and one of disregard when it is not, has led to a debate among less developed countries over whether GATT provides an adequate body of law for the regulation of world trade. They have little doubt that GATT, as it stands, is not in their interests.

Prospects

There is no doubt that if GATT was implemented as originally intended a major improvement in the export opportunities of less developed countries would be effected. A significant improvement would result from the implementation of the rule barring new barriers to trade being erected and by ensuring that arrangements for cotton textiles operated in such a way as to ensure a steady expansion of exports from under-developed countries. In addition, new export opportunities could be opened up if trade barriers on products in which developing countries have an existing or potential comparative advantage were to be lowered *pari passu* with the

[16]"The Role of GATT in Relation to Trade and Development", *op. cit.*, p. 6. Reproduced in *The Proceedings of the United Nations Conference on Trade and Development, op. cit.*, Vol. V, p. 482.

reduction (in GATT) of trade barriers on products of export interest to developed countries. The implication of such an operation of GATT is that developed countries would be prepared to accept the adjustments to their industrial structures necessary to absorb greatly increased imports without appreciably disturbing their domestic economies.

Developed countries have urged, as earlier observed, that less developed ones benefit from GATT through the MFN clause in the successive rounds of tariff-cutting negotiations. But the machinery of the agreement is so constructed as to ensure that the "spillover" benefits accruing in this way have been minimal. The bargaining principle, the principle of reciprocity, and the principle of non-discrimination combine to ensure that the implementation of GATT is dependent on the trade policies and interests of the powerful trading nations. The strong bargaining position of the major trading nations and the weak bargaining position of the less advanced nations have combined to make the two decades of GATT's operation a period marked by increased protectionism in the developed countries against an important group of products of export interest to developing countries and by continuous liberalisation of trade in industrial products in which the developed countries have a comparative advantage. The outcome of the Kennedy Round exemplifies this pattern.

The UNCTAD secretariat raised, in a report on "The Developing Countries in GATT", the following question in their conclusion:

> "There is no dispute about the need for a rule of law in world trade. The question is: What should be the character of that law? Should it be a law based on the presumption that the world is essentially homogeneous, being composed of countries of equal strength and comparable levels of economic development, a law founded, therefore, on the principles of reciprocity and non-discrimination? Or should it be a law that recognises diversity of levels of economic development and differences in economic and social systems?"[17]

No doubt was left that the UNCTAD Secretariat consider the "law of world trade", as currently laid down in GATT, to be of the first type and as such is totally unsatisfactory from the point of view of less developed countries. They concluded that new institutional

[17]"The Developing Countries in GATT", reproduced in *The Proceedings of the United Nations Conference on Trade and Development, op. cit.*, p. 468.

arrangements are required to supervise world trade, either within the GATT framework or in the form of a completely new organisation. Whatever machinery is employed, though, they argued that it should be made responsive to the need for:

"(a) A full recognition of the significance of the problem of economic development for world trade;

(b) Differentiation between countries of various levels of economic development and of different economic and social systems;

(c) Positive and deliberate action to promote exports of developing countries, overcoming the obstacles of agricultural protectionism and industrial discrimination, and providing for preferential treatment and other special measures for aid and encouragement".[18]

It was this sense of dissatisfaction with the current order of international trade which led to the convening of UNCTAD in 1964. The hopes and aspirations with which the less developed countries arrived at the conference are aptly indicated by the title of the introductory report submitted to the delegates by Dr. Raul Prebisch, then Secretary-General of UNCTAD: *Towards a New Trade Policy for Development*.[19] This report, much of which was eventually embodied in the Final Act of the conference, effectively rejected the non-interventionist, non-discriminatory principles of GATT and proposed a positive, interventionist role for trade policy. It argued that "the international community must combine its efforts to ensure that all countries—regardless of size, wealth or economic and social system—enjoy the benefits of international trade for their economic development and social progress". From the standpoint of less developed countries this was to be achieved, broadly, through action along two lines: ensuring a more rapid rate of growth of earnings from traditional exports of primary products; and encouraging exports of manufactured and semi-manufactured goods by the developing countries. These two objectives were to be achieved, in the first case, by the extended use of international commodity agreements and the establishment of a commodity compensation fund and, in the second case, through the introduction of a new preferential trading system in which all industrial countries

[18]*Ibid.*, p. 469.
[19]*Towards a New Trade Policy for Development* (United Nations, New York, 1964).

would accord preferential access to their markets to semi-manu-factured and manufactured exports from less developed countries. These two proposals, as well as other aspects of the UNCTAD programme, are discussed in the next chapter.

3   FIVE UNCTAD PROPOSALS

UNCTAD I, held in Geneva from March 23 to June 16, 1964, was a remarkable event. The most remarkable feature was the common front presented by politically and economically divergent developing countries. Dr. Prebisch, in his introductory report[20] to the conference, was able to set forth a description of development, and its frustration due to the trade policies of developed countries, which all the 77 less developed countries present could subscribe to.

Dr. Prebisch's picture of development was based on his experience of Latin American countries, it being argued that all developing nations will eventually encounter, if they have not already done so, the problems faced by these more developed of the less developed economies. There are, it was argued, two basic problems of development. First there was the external imbalance which stems from the conjunction of a rapid growth in the import requirements of the development process—food, raw materials and machinery—and the slow growth in the traditional exports of poor countries. The increasing import needs of development arise as opportunities run out for development based solely on domestic factors of production or for feasible import substitution with low import content. The explanation offered for the slow growth of export income was in two parts. On the one hand there are "structural" reasons: a fall in the share of income in the developed countries which is spent on food and beverages; the fall in the primary product content of manufactured goods, partly due to a rise in the use of synthetics and partly to increased productivity; and finally the rapid expansion of agricultural output in the developed countries. The second part of the explanation is the aggravation of these structural factors by policy measures in the developed countries, such as: restriction of market access in various ways; domestic price supports and subsidies, especially of agricultural produce; export subsidies, again especially for agricultural surpluses; and heavy taxation of competing imports, applied to increase the domestic prices of these products and to maintain the incomes of domestic producers.

[20]*Ibid.*

52

The second basic problem was held by UNCTAD to be the difficulty of establishing the efficient manufacturing industry required to stimulate and support the development process. This was seen to derive partly from domestic shortcomings and partly from the fact that modern industry demands markets greater than can be provided by individual less developed countries if maximum efficiency is to be achieved.

At the conference the less developed countries—known as the Group of 77—called upon the developed ones to take a political decision accepting a responsibility to assist poor nations. The acceptance of this responsibility was to be in part a compensation for the damage inflicted on less advanced economies by the commercial policies of developed countries and in part, too, a moral commitment to aid the poor countries, much as the rich nations have come to accept an obligation to assist the poorer sections of their own communities. The conference debated a wide range of measures designed to achieve these purposes. In the Final Act of the conference there were proposals affecting almost every aspect of the international economy.

Proposals made at the conference[21] divide into two groups: those concerned with trade in primary products and those concerned with trade in manufactures. The important proposals in the first group called for a broadened access for developing countries to industrial markets and for more "price-raising" international commodity agreements. The aim of broadened market access is to reduce the protectionism of the developed countries and the aim of commodity agreements is to have that protectionism extended in favour of all less developed countries. Proposals concerned in the second group called for the establishment of regional groupings of backward nations and for the preferential treatment by developed countries of imports of manufactures from poor countries. These were aimed at (a) earning or saving foreign exchange and (b) getting access to the larger markets necessary for industrial efficiency. The various proposals are examined more closely below.

In its first six years of existence, and despite hectic activity, UNCTAD had brought about no notable changes in the international economy. But projecting the trade and aid problems of less developed countries to the forefront of world political discussion has

[21]For a more complete discussion of the 1964 UNCTAD and the proposals made there, see Harry Johnson, *op. cit.*

been a major achievement. There is certainly a greater awareness today in the developed countries of the problems and needs of the poorer countries. This greater awareness has not, however, resulted in any significant increase in the willingness of the developed countries to increase their assistance to the poorer parts of the world.

Rich countries in UNCTAD have, more often than not, accepted the validity of the Third World's grievances. They have consistently argued, however, that UNCTAD is not the right institution through which to make amends. Two general reactions have become familiar when industrial countries are faced in UNCTAD committees with proposals for action. On the one hand they assert that the appropriate forums in which decisions should be taken to modify international institutions are such organisations as OECD, the IMF, the GATT and the World Bank. On the other hand they argue that the methods which less developed countries and the UNCTAD Secretariat have suggested for increasing the flows of foreign exchange to the less developed countries may be less efficient than additional foreign aid. Developing countries reply they are not satisfied with what has so far been accomplished in other forums where developed nations exercise control. And the second argument is said to be beside the point because donor countries have been becoming less, not more, generous in providing aid.

Trade in Primary Products

The first of the UNCTAD proposals for trade in primary products required a widening of market opportunities in the developed countries for the exports of less developed countries. This was to be achieved by removing the extensive and complex structure of restrictions currently placed on such trade by developed countries. As shown in Table 1, opposite, a third of all rich countries' imports of primary commodities are subject to tariff barriers, a quarter are limited by quantitative restrictions and two-fifths bear fiscal charges. It can be seen in Table 2 that the commodities subject to the greatest restriction are basic foodstuffs and fuels. Of developing countries' exports of these commodities, 87 per cent are subject to some form of limitation. This reflects the high degree of protection accorded to agriculture in the developed countries in the first case and the prevalence of excise duties on petroleum and petroleum products in the second. At the other extreme less than a quarter of

Table 1

PRIMARY COMMODITIES: IMPORTS OF MAJOR INDUSTRIAL COUNTRIES SUBJECT TO VARIOUS TYPES OF POLICY IMPEDIMENTS, 1962*

Type of Impediment	Value of Imports† US $m	Percentage of Total
TARIFF		
Total:+	6,270	34
Protective Duties:‡	1,698	
Revenue Duties:§	4,572	
QUANTITATIVE CONTROL⁰		
Total:	4,804	26
Also Subject to Duty:	3,174	
Entering Duty Free:	1,630	9
FISCAL CHARGES**		
Total:	7,927	43
Subject to Duty or Quantitative Control:	4,648	
Free of Other Impediments:	3,272	18
WITHOUT RESTRAINT		
Total:	7,052	39
All Primary Commodity Imports:	18,231	100

Source: The Proceedings of the United Nations Conference on Trade and Development, op. cit. Vol. III, p. 17.

  * Belgium, West Germany, France, Italy, Japan, Luxembourg, Holland, and USA.

  † Measured c.i.f. except in the case of the USA.

  + This total includes an indeterminate—but probably small—amount of trade subject to zero duty.

  ‡ Levied on commodities produced in significant quantities in the importing countries; excluding duties on petroleum in West Germany and on petroleum products in the UK (These have been classed as fiscal charges).

  § Levied on commodities not produced in significant quantities in the importing countries; including all duties associated with quantitative controls; excluding duties on tobacco in the UK.

  ⁰ Including a number of controls operated in the interests of preferred partner countries.

 ** Taxes levied specifically on the commodity, whether in crude or processed form, by the central government of the importing countries; including duties on petroleum imports into West Germany and on tobacco and petroleum imports into the UK.

developed countries' imports of such commodities as metals, crude minerals other than fuels and basic agricultural raw materials (like fibres, hides and skins and rubber) are subject to import restraints. These commodities are manufacturing inputs and there is accordingly a strong tendency to avoid cost-raising obstacles to their trade, except where the commodity is also produced under protection in the developed countries, as, for example, is the case with raw cotton imports into the USA.

The effect of these barriers to trade is the disintegration of the world market. One manifestation of this is the existence of national prices, behind the barriers, which are totally unrelated to prices prevailing in world markets. National prices are often so artificially high that surplus production is encouraged and the excess supplies are then dumped on the world market, thus disrupting normal trade. Increased local production stimulated by high prices lowers the proportion of total world production entering international trade. The commodities for which the ratio of trade to production tends to be lowest are generally those for which the barriers to trade are greatest and the spread of prices widest. This lowering of the ratio of trade to output of primary products results in the limitation of exports from and reduction of prices received by primary producing countries— mainly developing ones. One observer has estimated that the protected production of primary commodities—especially agricultural products—in the developed countries results in an annual loss of some $2,000m in export receipts to less developed countries.[22]

There is considerable scope for increasing the export opportunities of poor nations based on reducing protection afforded to agriculture and other primary commodity production in rich countries. While the restrictions problem is mainly in the agricultural field, it also applies to certain "low wage" manufactures, notably cotton textiles. Much effort was made at UNCTAD I to draw attention to this situation and to recommend ways in which the desired changes could be implemented. Scope for improvement undoubtedly exists. But these trade barriers are deeply rooted in the politics and policies of developed countries. The industrial countries in GATT have refused to move away from agricultural protectionism. If they take this attitude in GATT, which they strongly support, there is little hope of their being persuaded in UNCTAD, which they regard as little more than a talking shop. Moreover, the Kennedy Round

[22]Gale Johnson, *op. cit.*

56

Table 2

PRIMARY COMMODITIES: STRUCTURE OF IMPORTS SUBJECT TO
COMMERCIAL POLICY MEASURES IN THE MAJOR INDUSTRIAL
COUNTRIES*

Commodity Group	Value of Imports in 1962†		
	Total: US $m	Subject to Barriers+	
		Amount: US $m	Percentage
Fuels	6,066	6,054	100
Basic Primary Foods‡	1,697	1,475	87
Organic Oils§	313	243	78
Other Agricultural Raw Materials⁰	645	423	66
Fruit and Vegetables	795	512	64
Oil Seeds and Foods	884	361	41
Beverages, Spices and Tobacco	2,805	1,100	38
Crude Non-fuel Minerals	276	61	22
Metals	2,468	1,511	21
Fibres, Hides and Rubber	2,222	210	10
All Primary Commodities	18,231**	11,179	39

Source: The Proceedings of the United Nations Conference on Trade and Development, op.
          cit. Vol. III, based on Table 1–6, p. 17.
      *   and † as for Table 1.
      +   Tariff, fiscal charge or quantitative control, including control in the
          interests of preferred partner countries.
      ‡   Chiefly cereals, meat, sugar and dairy products.
      §   Vegetable, animal, and marine.
      ⁰   Including wood.
     **   This figure, as in Table 1, includes imports from developed primary
          producers, notably Australia, South Africa and New Zealand.

agreement to continue the restrictive arrangements for cotton textiles affords little prospect of progress in the area of "low wage" goods.

Narrowing the range of possibility to a range of political feasibility greatly reduces the hopes of developing countries to achieve export expansion through trade liberalisation. To examine the political feasibility of liberalising trade in primary products it is useful to divide these commodities exported by less developed countries into three groups: (1) those *competing directly* with commodities produced in developed countries, notably temperate agricultural products and some metals; (2) those *competing indirectly* with commodities produced in developed countries, namely substitutes and synthetics; and (3) those *not competing* with commodities produced in developed countries, mainly beverages and tropical fruits. Only in the last category are there likely to be any short-term concessions from developed countries.[23] (For example, the EEC countries and the UK recently suspended tariffs on tropical hardwoods and tea.) As Dr. John Pincus, of the Rand Corporation, has put it: "The North is perfectly willing to endorse the demands of less developed countries for access with words by resolution after resolution in GATT, UNCTAD and other UN economic forums, but it is not disposed to move on any significant scale from words to actions that hurt domestic producers".[24]

An important aspect of the trade restriction problem derives from escalation of tariff rates according to stage of processing—a customary feature of developed countries' commercial policy. This militates against the establishment of processing industries in less developed countries. The combination of low tariffs on a raw material with a higher tariff on its processed form raises the level of protection for the processing industry above what is implied by the nominal tariff on the processed goods. This is because the protective effect of a tariff structure is measured not by the nominal tariff rate on a commodity but by the effective rate of value added in the processing stages. A tariff on an input into a processing industry is effectively a tax, whereas a tariff on its output is effectively a subsidy. Free or low-tariff entry of inputs thus reduces the tax element

[23]The likelihood of concessions being made by the EEC and the UK to developing countries in general for even these products is restricted due to the prevalence of discriminatory preferential arrangements which exist for these products.

[24]Pincus, *op. cit.*, p. 263.

and increases the subsidy element. As a result of such effective protection of processing in developed countries, the export earnings of primary producing countries are reduced below what they would be if they were to process their products themselves. In many cases this would be a move to a more rational international division of labour. With exports of primary products from developing to developed nations totalling about $32,000m in 1967, even the transfer to less developed countries of a relatively small percentage value added would make a significant contribution to their foreign exchange earnings and do much, too, to establish an industrial base.

The final act of UNCTAD I also carried a proposal calling for the abolition of discriminatory preferential trading systems, in effect those operated by the EEC in favour of associated overseas states and territories, by the UK in favour of other Commonwealth countries and by the USA in favour of several preferred suppliers, notably Puerto Rico and the Philippines. The abolition of these systems would certainly result in a shift in trade patterns, although to what extent is difficult to say. But the overall effect on the total export earnings of less developed countries as a group would be negligible, especially since the opening of the developed markets concerned would result in cut-throat price competition among suppliers of several products in excess world supply (for example, coffee, cocoa, bananas, sugar and oil seeds).

Commodity Agreements

This chapter has so far been concerned with proposals made at UNCTAD I for removing restrictions on imports of primary products from less developed countries, measures directed towards freer world trade. These proposals, if implemented (which is unlikely), could significantly boost the foreign exchange earnings of less developed countries, but they would still be insufficient to meet all their development needs. The developing nations and the UNCTAD Secretariat realised that the developed countries were unlikely to make any significant moves towards freer trade in these commodities. Consequently they put forward proposals designed to appeal to the protectionist philosophy of developed countries and extend it in favour of less developed countries. In the case of primary products the more widespread establishment of international commodity agreements was called for.

There were two basic motives behind this proposal. The first derived from the despair of less developed countries over the unlikelihood of developed countries making any significant concessions on market access for primary products. The second was based on the hope that commodity agreements could lift prices for existing exports of primary products.

In principle, commodity agreements could be used for either of two purposes. One is the stabilisation of export earnings, which has been stressed by less developed countries, whereas what they really have in mind is the second objective, that of raising prices. This second objective is really a disguised form of aid and should be treated as such. The first is based on the belief that fluctuations in receipts of foreign exchange are inimical to economic growth. Proposals for the use of commodity agreements as a means of increasing the flow of aid from developed to less developed countries result from frustration of Third World attempts to increase market access for their products and to increase direct capital transfers from rich countries to poor. Stabilisation is a secondary objective in so far as exporting countries would obviously prefer higher export earnings to stabilised earnings. In this context stabilisation has come to mean the establishment of minimum prices. The justification for commodity agreements as a means of attaining stabilisation of foreign exchange receipts has been questioned in recent years by several economists, who have proffered evidence suggesting there is little relationship between fluctuations in export income and variations in domestic economic variables.[25]

Stabilising commodity prices could, however, be useful to the *producers* of certain items, particularly metals and tree crops with long gestation periods and subject to substantial variations in demand. In these cases a sudden rise in demand causes sharp price increases, inducing the development of synthetic substitutes and greater investment, also, in expanded productive capacity which often does not lift supply until after demand has subsided consequently reducing prices and earnings. Even if demand does not subside, reduced prices and earnings might still result if several countries simultaneously expand productive capacity in response to sharp price increases. In this sense, however, efficient stabilisation

[25]See, for example, Alasdair MacBean, *Export Instability and Economic Development* (Allen and Unwin, London, 1967).

conflicts with the maintenance of commodity prices at the highest possible levels. The tendency is to regard high prices as normal prices.

We are left with the question of how effective can international commodity agreements be in stabilising or increasing the export earnings of less developed countries. This depends upon two factors: first, on the willingness of the countries involved—both producing and consuming ones—to negotiate and operate such agreements; secondly, on technical considerations.

The paucity of international commodity agreements, and the experiences of those in operation, reflects the inherent difficulties of such arrangements. Agreements involving, first, the possibility of increasing producer incomes are ruled out unless this aim is deliberately accepted by consuming countries against their own economic interests. Export restriction schemes, secondly, depend on the readiness of producing countries to co-operate in implementing them. This means that each producing country must believe the scheme to be to its advantage (a requirement almost impossible to achieve) and have the ability, also, to control production and/or store the commodity concerned. The latter may be difficult in a one-crop economy where the producers form a strong pressure group. Thirdly, agreements based on buffer stocks, or export restriction schemes requiring national stockbuilding, are only suitable for cheaply storable commodities. Easily perishable crops, such as bananas, are therefore excluded. Fourthly, buffer stock schemes necessitate an ability to forecast price trends successfully. An unexpected price rise may leave the manager without a buffer stock and thus powerless. A long-run price fall, at the other extreme, may exhaust his finances, again leaving him powerless. Fifthly, successful price support of a commodity may shift demand away to a natural or synthetic substitute. Finally, "important components of world trade in primary products are dominated by trade between producing and consuming developed countries, or between producing and consuming less developed countries, or between developed producing and less developed consuming countries, in all of which cases an international agreement may be less attractive than either bilateral negotiation or *laissez faire*".[26]

Despite continuous and fervent argument about the need for international commodity agreements, the inherent difficulties are such that only six have been established since 1945. Two, covering

[26]Harry Johnson, *op. cit.*, p. 140.

wheat and sugar, were specifically designed to protect producers in developed countries. One, for olive oil, is not concerned with trade. The tin agreement has been non-operational for most of its life, due to favourable market forces. The most recent agreement, that covering trade in tea, only came into force in 1969 and it is too soon, at the time of writing, to evaluate its impact on the market, although India quickly claimed that it was against her interests. Only one, the international coffee agreement, is both operational and effectively furthering the interests of less developed countries.

The coffee agreement has to some extent achieved its objective of supporting coffee prices. But it is questionable whether it could have done so without the active support of Brazil, the dominant supplier. The agreement operates through export quotas. Its problems derive from this arrangement. Several exporting countries produce quantities far exceeding their quotas and have had to build up vast stocks, leading to substantial smuggling of "cheap" coffee. Coffee, is, moreover, a non-homogeneous product. World demand is shifting towards African *robusta* type coffee used to make instant coffee. Producers in Africa have consequently become dissatisfied with their historically determined quotas. A similar dissatisfaction is found in countries which have only comparatively recently established an export trade in coffee. Steps have lately been taken to overcome these problems. But it is as yet too early to evaluate their effectiveness.

Compensation

Two major proposals were made at UNCTAD I for compensating developing nations for damage inflicted on them by the protectionist policies of rich countries. These were put forward as alternatives to the piecemeal and uncertain operation of commodity agreements. The first was a plan, put forward by France, for levies on imports by developed countries from less developed countries, to be refunded in whole or in part. The levies envisaged were of two types. (a) Where developed countries' domestic prices of products partly imported from less developed countries are above world market prices, the levy would be imposed at a variable rate to raise the prices of imports to the domestic level, the intention being to encourage exporting countries to raise their export prices sufficiently to make the levy unnecessary. (b) On primary products not produced in the developed countries (tropical products), the levy would be a tax on consumers and could be used in place of a commodity agreement to exploit the monopoly power of the less developed countries' products. The French plan, however, is subject to all the defects and weaknesses of orthodox commodity agreements.

The second proposal, submitted by Britain and Sweden, was for a Supplementary Finance Fund. It envisaged the fund providing compensation from developed to less developed countries in part payment for the effects on the latter's exports of adverse trends, whether arising from the natural working of market prices or from obstacles to competition imposed by policy. The IMF already operates a compensatory finance scheme. But it is limited to making short-term loans during balance of payments crises. The supplementary finance scheme would compensate developing countries for deteriorations in terms of trade because of falling prices of exports for which it was not possible to negotiate or operate a commodity agreement. When export earnings fall below the expected level, the developing country in question would receive from the fund a loan (in certain circumstances convertible into grants) in order to prevent the breakdown of its development plans. This proposal explicitly recognised that the various plans for new commodity arrangements contain an aid element. It sought to go beyond the proximate source of difficulty, the instability of export *prices*, to the real source of difficulty, the instability of export *earnings*, and to provide aid in a form not tied to commodity trade but to unexpected shortfalls in export earnings. Unfortunately there is little hope of a supplementary finance scheme being set up in the foreseeable future. At present, with aid flows dwindling in real terms and difficulties over replenishing the funds of existing international aid institutions, particularly the International Development Association, the climate of international opinion is not conducive to the acceptance of the proposals.

All forms of commodity arrangements are relatively inefficient means of transferring income from richer, consuming countries to provide resources for the development of poorer countries. Commodity agreements which raise prices involve a political decision by consuming countries to transfer incomes from consumers to producers. A major merit of the supplementary finance scheme is that it aims straight at the problem of shortages of foreign exchange for development financing. The basic mechanism of capital transfers to governments appeals to donor countries because it means they can maintain some control over the pattern of aid distribution. In a commodity agreement, though, the distribution of "aid" is automatic, depending only on the extent of each developing country's participation in the trade in the selected commodities. Another feature of the scheme that is attractive to developed countries is that whereas commodity agreements distort market mechanisms, in order to maintain the foreign exchange receipts of poor nations, the supplementary finance scheme would not interfere with market forces.

International commodity agreements are, in sum, beset with many problems and difficulties. Even if they can be successfully negotiated their implementation produces various inefficiencies—in both market mechanisms and distribution of "aid". Estimates of cash gains which might accrue to poor countries from the several possible commodity arrangements are all below $1,000m, some being substantially less. While $1,000m is not an insignificant sum, it would not go much more than a very small way towards meeting the foreign exchange requirements of developing countries. As Dr. Pincus has put it: "The dominant conclusion which emerges from investigating all these aspects of international commodity trends and policies is that the South must look primarily to Northern prosperity as a source of export growth, and not to the UNCTAD policies (for commodity trade arrangements). Should the effect of these policies be substantial, they are unlikely to be adopted; measures that are likely to be adopted are also likely to be unimportant as sources of increased capital or trade. Policies to increase or stabilise commodity earnings cannot proceed much faster than Northern willingness to act on the broader problem of developing-country growth."[27]

Trade in Manufactures

Despite their limited possibilities less developed countries will continue to press for international arrangements for primary products. For trade in these commodities is to them crucially important and (to them) is an obvious source of their difficulties. The idea of solving everything through the right arrangement over prices is, moreover, appealing in its simplicity.

One of the two proposals for trade in manufactured products made

[27]Pincus, op. cit., p. 294.

at the first UNCTAD suggested regional, preferential groupings of less developed countries. This proposal was based on the same kind of arguments (discussed below) for preferences in industrial markets for exports of manufactures from developing countries: "the need for a market larger than the protection of the national market could provide, in order to foster the development of infant industries and to permit the exploitation of economies of scale, and the inability of producers in the less developed countries to export in competition with producers in the developed countries". An additional supporting argument is that regional groups of less developed countries would allow members to economise on the use of currencies in short supply. Foreign exchange could be saved by substituting imports from each other for imports from developed countries.

In the short run, though, little benefit stands to be gained from this proposal, except in special circumstances. There are numerous reasons. Not the least important is that less developed countries are poor countries with limited markets unable, even in groups, to sustain the large-scale production necessary to compete with industrial giants. For all their differences, there is also a remarkable similarity among developing economies in agricultural production and the structure of infant industry. This makes for difficulties in reaching agreement on products to benefit from freer trade among themselves. Witness the difficulties met in the Latin American Free Trade Area (LAFTA). Even so, there are many advantages for small numbers of less developed countries agreeing among themselves on strategies for the complementary development of specific industries. But there is not much hope for groups of poor countries wanting to emulate the successes of the EEC. In the long run, with their vast populations and resources, they will undoubtedly come to be each other's most important trading partners. This is likely, though, to be a consequence rather than a cause of development.

The desire to industrialise is an accepted feature of all less developed countries' development programmes. The assumption underlying proposed preferential tariff schemes is that industrialisation calls for larger markets than can be provided by protected national economics. Preferential arrangements among groups of less developed countries are unlikely to open up significant export opportunities. Great emphasis has accordingly been placed in UNCTAD on the need for preferential access to developed country

65

markets for the exports of manufactures and semi-manufactures from the Third World.

The inclusion of manufactures in these demands has another origin, the belief that there is small real prospect for a major expansion of export earnings from primary products. In compensation developing countries want to share in the rapid growth of trade in manufactures. Over 1959-67 the value of world exports of commodities increased at the rate of only 4.9 per cent a year compared with 9.3 per cent for manufactures. Countries bent on rapid increases in export earnings are naturally attracted by the outlook for trade in manufactures. This attraction is reinforced by the experiences of the few less developed nations which export a significant volume of manufactures. Their receipts from such shipments rose at the annual rate of around 10 per cent over the same eight-year period.

Modern manufacturing industry requires larger markets than poor countries (even in groups) are able to provide. Successful establishment of such industry depends then on the availability of large markets in the developed world. The desire of less developed countries to participate in the fast expanding trade in manufactured goods and their desire to establish modern manufacturing industries thus complement and strengthen each other. Fulfilment of these desires is currently prevented by two over-riding obstacles:[28] the commercial policies of the developed countries, in the form of escalated tariff structures and quantitative restrictions; and various economic policies of the less developed countries themselves, in such forms as over-valued exchange rates and inappropriate fiscal systems.

It is perhaps useful to illustrate the problems of developing countries in this context by comparing the hypothetical experiences of two new firms producing plastic toys for the UK market; one firm is established in Liverpool, the other in a developing nation. In the first case, the Liverpool firm, being in a development area, will receive substantial (100 per cent) tax relief on the capital cost of its machinery. It will be able to employ labour which has been trained in the requisite skills at government expense. Its raw material will be locally produced and transport costs will be negligible. Various other subsidies will be reflected in the firm's costs. The

[28]There are of course many other obstacles, the analysis of which constititutes the subject matter of development economics. The two obstacles treated here are the most important in the context of the subject of this study.

wages bill, for instance, will reflect subsidised food, housing, health and education. On top of all these cost-reducing subsidies the firm will also benefit from a 25 per cent tariff on imports of plastic toys into the UK. By contrast the firm in the less developed country would probably receive little or no government grant; pay high interest rates on capital borrowed; have an unskilled labour force to train; and pay premiums on the foreign exchange required to finance imports of essential machinery and other inputs—in the forms, for example, of tariffs, higher transport costs and graft. It would have to face the cost-raising effects of breakdowns in the infrastructure (power failures, transport hold-ups and delays caused by an inefficient bureaucracy). Any exports it might achieve will in all probability be taxed and bear, also, the price-raising effect of an over-valued exchange rate. If, after all of this, and the transport cost, the firm managed to make large and rapid inroads on the UK toy market there would be the possibility of extra action being taken to restrict imports directly or indirectly.[29] The arrangements for cotton textiles best exemplify such action. In addition, the subsidy content of development area policies could be increased.

Preferences for Manufactures

The mechanism of a preference scheme is quite simple. It involves the discriminatory reduction of tariffs on imports from selected suppliers. This reduction of tariffs in the first place reduces the protection afforded to domestic producers. In the second place it gives the preferred suppliers a price advantage over competing non-preferred (developed country) suppliers. Less developed countries could in this way be helped in their early stage of cost disadvantage and, where they are already competitive, they could be compensated for the past policies of industrial nations.

The years since the first UNCTAD have witnessed much discussion on preferences in government, international and academic circles. Debate has principally concentrated on setting out the merits and demerits of a generalised system. Two basic arguments for, and one basic argument against, such a scheme have been put

[29]This hypothetical example may seem loaded to emphasise the problems of Third World exports. In fact, soon after the example was devised, the UK toy industry called upon the Board of Trade to impose quantitative restrictions on imports of plastic toys from less developed countries, particularly India and Hong Kong.

forward constantly. Supporters argue, on grounds of equity, that preferences would compensate developing countries, for the various forms of subsidies and protection afforded by developed countries to their domestic industries. They argue, secondly, that preferences would compensate poor nations for the current biases of the international rules and trends of trade policy against their interests and also go some way, on ethical grounds, towards helping less developed economies overcome economic weaknesses by enabling them to compete with the exporters of industrial states. In short, the case for preferences is based on the view that they would allow less developed countries to compete in an environment where they cannot at present.

Against preferences it is said they would disrupt the markets of developed countries. And the reply of the less developed countries? It is this. Many decades will pass before poor nations could possibly achieve a sufficient level of competitiveness on a sufficient number of products to constitute a major problem to the rich nations of the world. Secondly, it is answered that developed countries themselves would benefit from successful competition from developing countries, allowing factors of production to be moved out of inefficient, declining industries into productive activities where they enjoy a comparative advantage.

It is difficult to estimate[30] the cash benefits which would accrue to less developed countries from the implementation of a preference scheme. Much would depend on the range of products covered. Earlier in this chapter it was argued that free access for processed primary products would result in substantial and widespread benefits for less developed countries. Preferences for such products would significantly augment those benefits. At the other extreme, preferences solely for finished consumer goods would initially benefit only those countries currently exporting them. Several years would be required for other developing countries to establish the production processes and develop the manufacturing techniques. In any case, except for a few products with high (unskilled) labour content, finished consumer goods are the products in which industrial countries are likely to retain the comparative advantage.

The scheme, as proposed in UNCTAD, is in direct contravention

[30]Pincus, *op. cit.*, p. 231, estimates that such a scheme could increase the export receipts of developing countries by $1,300m per annum if processed products were included.

of the rules of GATT. For this reason it seemed in 1964 to be a political non-starter. The USA in particular was opposed. Since 1964, however, discussions in the OECD have brought the scheme, or some versions of it, into the realms of political feasibility. This development was initiated by a change in the US attitude reflected in a speech by President Johnson at the regional conference of Heads of State at Punta del Este, Uruguay, early in 1967 when he announced that his Administration was prepared to explore with private interests and other governments the possibility of establishing a generalised scheme. Indeed, the format of a generalised scheme was devised by Britain, France, West Germany and the USA which, after considerable discussion in the OECD, was presented to UNCTAD II in New Delhi. The scheme as proposed fell far short of the demands of the less developed countries, however, and all that was achieved in New Delhi was a unanimous commitment to implement some form of generalised preference system as soon as the details could be worked out and agreed upon.

It has not proved possible for the developed countries to agree on any single scheme and the danger has been that any compromise scheme would have its characteristics determined by the most protectionist minded of the developed countries. The basic problem has been that several developed countries have been apprehensive about the possible effects of a preference system, in terms of the potential increase of imports of products which they themselves produce in sensitive declining (and consequently heavily protected) industries. As it is largely these industries in which the less developed countries have a long-run comparative advantage, it makes economic sense for the preference system to be most liberal in precisely these products; such a preference system would, however, call for great concessions from developed countries in the form of structural reorganisation. If a preference scheme was, though, to be established concurrently with the establishment of a free trade association among developed countries, there would already exist the stimulus for the necessary reorganisation. A preference scheme would in this context assist industrial nations in achieving their own ambitions (as discussed in the next chapter) and consequently be that much more acceptable to them.

Table 3

	Value of Imports in 1965 from Developing Countries US $'ooo	Percentage Share of Total	Official Aid to Developing Countries in 1965 US $'ooo*	Percentage Share of Total	Private Investment in Developing Countries in 1965 US $'ooo*	Percentage Share of Total
USA	6,619	20	3,627	58	1,873	46
Canada	768	2	124	2	45	1
UK	3,929	12	481	8	517	13
Sub-Total	11,317	34	4,232	68	2,435	60
Rest of EFTA	1,262	4	118†	2	86†	2
Japan	2,712	8	244	4	242	6
Australia and New Zealand	507	2	122+	2	23+	1
All prospective NAFTA	15,798	48	4,716	76	2,786	69
EEC	8,782	26	1,498	24	1,289	32
Others	8,680	26	—	—	—	—
TOTALS**	33,260	100	6,213	100	4,075	100

Sources: Data on imports from *Direction of Trade Supplement, 1961–65* (IMF and World Bank, Washington D.C., 1966). Data on aid and private investment from *Development Assistance Efforts and Policies, 1967 Review* (OECD, Paris, 1967). Tables III:I and IV:I.

Notes: *The *total* figures for aid and private investment only covers flows from the countries of North America, EFTA (exclusive of Finland), the EEC, Japan and Australia.
†Excluding Finland.
+Australia only.
**Totals may differ from sums of columns due to rounding errors.

THE FREE TRADE TREATY OPTION
AND THE THIRD WORLD

In the initial stages an open-ended, Atlantic-based free trade area might include the USA, Canada, the UK and other EFTA countries and possibly Japan, Australia and New Zealand. As Table 3 opposite shows, these countries imported, in 1965, almost half of the total exports of developing countries. They were the source of more than three-quarters of the official aid and more than two-thirds of the private investment flows to the Third World from the developed Western world. Any major realignment, such as would be involved under NAFTA arrangement, could have immense effects on the interests of less developed countries. It is important therefore that the interests of less developed countries be taken into account in the drafting of a free trade area treaty. Positive policy measures should be incorporated for the purpose of furthering those interests.

It is assumed that NAFTA countries would want to assist less advanced nations, this being in line with their policies and official statements.[31] But why are they more likely to help in a NAFTA arrangement than they so far have in GATT, UNCTAD and other international organisations? In GATT and UNCTAD the developed countries have been called upon to make immediate concessions to less developed ones without any obvious short term benefits to themselves. The formation of NAFTA without arrangements to safeguard Third World interests would increase discrimination on products exported by developing nations which are also traded among NAFTA countries. Simply extending similar treatment to poor countries on such products would prevent increased discrimination and would not imply the creation of discriminatory treatment among NAFTA members—as would be the case in the UNCTAD scheme. The primary objective of NAFTA, however, is the establishment of trade arrangements of benefit to developed countries. The intentions are to increase trade, income, and economic welfare in member countries. In this context it would be much more feasible politically to incorporate in NAFTA provision for trade

---

[31]A fuller discussion of the motives of developed countries for assisting less developed ones is contained in Pincus, *op. cit.*

concessions or increased aid to less developed countries than it would be to offer similar concessions or assistance divorced from such arrangements.

An interesting parallel is provided by the less developed associated overseas states, territories and departments of the EEC. In the early stages of the Treaty of Rome negotiations France insisted that all EEC members should offer preferential treatment on imports from colonies and ex-colonies of member countries. The Six agreed, in addition, to establish a development fund to channel capital aid from EEC countries to the associated areas. At the GATT meetings in which the EEC sought to justify these new preferences, the Community's representatives argued strongly that the preferential arrangements would not harm the interests of third party less developed countries. The benefits it was said, of the customs union, namely increased income, would result in increased imports from all less developed suppliers. A similar argument—that NAFTA countries could accommodate assistance to less developed countries out of the increased incomes—could be put forward to support the inclusion of such a policy in any NAFTA treaty.

It is highly improbable, though, that a new institution, specific to NAFTA for channeling official aid, would be established. It is instead probable that NAFTA participants would take the view that the aid burden should be equitably shared among all developed countries and that existing aid forums, notably the OECD's Development Assistance Committee, are already adequate. Also militating against a NAFTA aid agency would be the possibility of undesirable competition with the EEC's Development Fund.

Assistance from Free Trade Countries

Assistance from NAFTA countries to poor nations could best take the form of liberalised trade in products of special export interest to the Third World combined with an extension of preferences for imports of semi-manufactures and manufactures from the South. NAFTA governments could additionally encourage the flows of private investment to developing countries which would be stimulated by the trade measures. The value of this assistance would depend on the structure and extent of the arrangement.

A possible model is the Commonwealth preference system. The UK has, in fact, already taken a lead in this respect. At the 1964 UNCTAD, Mr. Edward Heath, the then President of the Board of

Trade, stated that Britain would be ready to extend the operation of the Commonwealth system to all less developed countries if all other industrial nations were prepared to make similar concessions. If all the developed NAFTA countries were willing to adopt a modified Commonwealth preference scheme, extended to all participating less developed countries, it would be an important step towards establishing a NAFTA preferential system in favour of the Third World.

The Commonwealth preference system is based on the reciprocal extension by all members of tariff preferences on imports from all other members. With the UK, where the tariff preferences do not offer effective protection to Commonwealth suppliers, they are often buttressed with quantitative controls. Quotas are also used when competition from fellow members threatens to disrupt the home markets of a member country's domestic producers. The non-discriminatory preferential treatment means that in the case of commodities produced in both less developed and developed member countries the former have to compete on an equal footing with the latter in the markets of third members. It also means that some of the poorer members are obliged to extend preferences on imports from rich members.

Free Trade Treaty Preference System

The conversion of Commonwealth preferences into a NAFTA system, if it were to be of the utmost benefit to developing nations, would eventually involve modifying some characteristics of the Commonwealth system. The most important problem, as far as developing countries are concerned, would be the phasing out of preferences extended by developed Commonwealth countries to less developed ones. These preferences (particularly those extended by the UK) have often been sufficient to encourage the uncompetitive production of some commodities. These preferences would have to be faded out over an agreed period to allow protected producers to prepare for the rigours of competitive trade. They would be compensated to some extent for the loss of their preferential markets by a widening of the market for their exports to all NAFTA countries as the new preference system came into operation. In certain cases it would be necessary to extend financial assistance to those developing Commonwealth countries where the loss of

Commonwealth preferences would require a particularly difficult transformation of the economic base.

The NAFTA preference system, in terms of participation, could take any one of four general forms, similar to those which have been mooted in connection with the UNCTAD proposal. They are:

(a) a completely non-discriminatory form in which all NAFTA members extended preferences to all those less developed countries which chose to participate in the system;

(b) a discriminatory form in which NAFTA members would extend preferences to all participating less developed countries but the degree of preference given to each developing nation would vary according to its stage of development;

(c) either (a) or (b) with only those less developed countries which are prepared to allow non-discriminatory entry into their markets allowed to participate; and

(d) either (a) or (b) with only those less developed countries which are prepared to accord reciprocal preferential benefits to NAFTA members—from the outset or after a fixed period—allowed to participate.

Incorporating a preference system in the NAFTA treaty would combine the desire to provide assistance to the less developed countries with the desire to move towards freer world trade. For this reason NAFTA countries would probably prefer a completely non-discriminatory system as their ultimate objective. From the point of view of the free trade advocate interested in the efficient location of industry, there are two advantages in the completely non-discriminatory form. First, it would maximise the choice open to poor nations in deciding which export industries to establish and encourage. Secondly, from the standpoint of NAFTA members, it would widen the range of commodities which it may become possible to import more cheaply than to produce internally. The protectionist might argue that this form of arrangement would maximise the number of NAFTA industries which would be vulnerable to competition. The free trader could counter this, however, by pointing out that as far as NAFTA export industries are concerned, 50 per cent of all NAFTA members' imports come from other NAFTA countries and that the preference system would give less developed countries no advantage *vis-à-vis* this trade. Potential trade diversion would be limited to the imports of NAFTA from other industrial countries, which constitute less than a quarter of all NAFTA imports (on the assumption that NAFTA would include all developed countries except those of the EEC and the Soviet bloc). The NAFTA countries would simply shift their import trade from third party developed countries to less developed countries for those commodities which the developing nations were able to supply at competitive prices under the preference.

As far as the uncompetitive manufacturers producing for domestic consumption are concerned, the preference system would be relatively unimportant in the face of competition from efficient producers already established in other NAFTA countries. Replacing inefficient producers by efficient ones is the principal object of NAFTA. It would be possible to facilitate the decline and disappearance of inefficient producers, partly through ensuring that the elimination of trade barriers between NAFTA members is phased over a number of years. The phasing out of trade barriers would allow NAFTA members to extend an additional benefit to poor nations by instituting the preference scheme at once. This concession—giving imports from developing countries a tariff advantage in each NAFTA market *vis-à-vis* imports from other NAFTA countries—would disappear when the NAFTA arrangement was fully established. In fact, the nature of intra-NAFTA trade together with the condition of less developed countries, would prevent the Third World from taking full advantage of the concession. Trade between the prospective NAFTA participants is largely in increasingly sophisticated goods which less advanced economies would probably be unable to produce competitively with a preference diminishing in value over a period of, say, 15 years. This limitation would increase as the membership of NAFTA expanded[32] and the faster, too, that trade barriers were eliminated.

To point out to the protectionist that the impact of the preference system would only be marginal[33] is also, of course, to point out its limitations from the point of view of the less developed countries.[34]

[32]Conversely, the smaller the membership of NAFTA the less likely would the members be prepared to extend preferential trade concessions to less developed countries.

[33]To the extent that preferences resulted in the successful establishment of competitive manufacturing industries in less developed countries, the developed nations would lose their markets for the products of those industries in the Third World.

[34]The UNCTAD scheme would involve greater benefits for developing countries because they would not be watered down by the free trade area effects of NAFTA; it is, however, that much less likely to be adopted in a worthwhile form.

There is, however, little doubt that preferences could make a positive and significant contribution to the economic development of the Third World out of all proportion to the monetary costs to the countries extending them. (These benefits are discussed below after further discussion of the forms the preference system might take.)

The non-discriminatory[35] form can be supported on economic grounds in terms of efficient use of the world's resources, the inefficiency inherent in the diversion of trade from third party developed countries being justified in aid terms. The various modifications of the open system which have been suggested in UNCTAD derive either from protectionist lobbies in industrial capitals or from the economists of some less developed countries on principles of equity and are political in nature.

Some developing countries have argued that a preference scheme which treated all less advanced economies on an equal footing would in fact be discriminatory. They argue that in the stages of development there is a wide range. It would be the more developed countries which would benefit most from a non-discriminatory preference scheme. But the more backward countries are the ones in most need of assistance. For this reason it has been suggested that any preference scheme should adopt the second of the forms listed above; that is, preferences graded according to stage of development. Reaching agreement on the criteria for determining the stage of development of each country would be impossible. But the underlying argument is fallacious for two other reasons. First, equity would not be served by such a scheme. Underdevelopment measured in terms of a country's inability to produce manufactures at competitive prices is no measure of that country's poverty in terms of per capita income weighted by the distribution of that income. Leaving aside questions of nationalism, equity requires that those countries with the largest numbers of population living in poverty should receive the most assistance. On this criterion it is countries such as India, Pakistan and Brazil which are most in need of assistance. The combined populations of these three, amounting to almost half of the total population of the Third World, have an average per capita income of only $98 per year, almost a third less than the average of $141 for the population of all developing countries. In fact, in 1963

[35]"Non-discriminatory" is something of a misnomer. Any preferential system is by definition discriminatory. It is meant here, though, that any less developed country would be able to participate in the preference scheme and that all imports from all participating less developed countries would be treated on an equal footing.

these three countries accounted for almost a third of all exports of manufactures from all less developed nations.

And the second fallacy? The ability of a country to establish a competitive manufacturing industry is necessarily determined by its overall stage of development. Whether or not a less developed country can sustain competitive, export-orientated manufacturing is determined as much by government policy (on such questions as taxes, the exchange rate, foreign investment and public investment) as by economic factors.

If we stress the "aid" argument for preferences, a non-discriminatory scheme will not of itself ensure that the benefits of the scheme will accrue to the different less developed countries according to any criterion of needs. There are better ways, however, of compensating for the inherent biases of a non-discriminatory scheme than through grading preferences according to stage of development. The compensation can either be reflected in the overall aid programme of the donor countries or be incorporated in the preference scheme in a more efficient way than by making the preferences discriminatory on a country basis. (These possibilities, too, are discussed below.)

Finally, the last two forms that a preference system could take derive solely from political conditions. If NAFTA were to include all the countries mentioned at the beginning of the chapter then the only less developed ones which would be discriminated against would be those associated with the EEC. If the reciprocal preferences extended by those associates to the Community are at all effective, they involve losses to them in that they are forced to buy products from EEC suppliers at prices higher than those prevailing elsewhere. Even if the associated overseas states choose to sustain those losses, NAFTA countries would have no moral grounds for adding to them by denying these emerging nations access to the new preference system. Neither the free trade nor the aid arguments for preferences lend any support to the demand for reciprocal preferences contained in the fourth form of preferential system. These demands are political and protectionist in nature.[36] They have,

[36]Professor Harry Johnson has suggested that some less developed members of the Commonwealth preference system actually lose from the reciprocity to the UK demanded of them in that system. He calculates that Jamaica loses as much as £1.8m a year, with Singapore, Malaysia, Sierra Leone, Malta and British Honduras also losing significant amounts. See Harry Johnson, "The Commonwealth Preferences", *The Round Table*, London, October, 1966.

indeed, been dropped from the discussion on preferences within UNCTAD.

Commodity Coverage

The second structural aspect of the proposed NAFTA preference system to be considered is the problem of commodity coverage. Selectivity has been urged on protectionist grounds, too, and on the grounds that it would permit the desired discrimination among less developed countries according to their need for assistance.

To the extent, however, that those exports of developing countries which could effectively compete with producers in NAFTA countries were excluded, the potential benefits to the Third World would be reduced. If all competitive, or potentially competitive, products were excluded, there would be no point at all in establishing a preference system. The possibility of disrupting markets for individual domestic producers in NAFTA countries before the necessary adjustment processes can be implemented is a genuine problem. But more efficient methods of ensuring short term protection than product selection can be devised and these are discussed below. Selectivity would not of itself guarantee that the benefits accruing from the preference system would be distributed among the less developed countries according to needs. Once a preference had been established for a particular product, any less developed country could establish that industry and the richer one would obviously be better able to exploit the concession.

A related proposal which was made in the UNCTAD group on preferences suggested that "if some provision cannot be made for each developed country to exert a more or less equivalent effort as regards preferences, some developed countries might wish to grant preferences only on a restricted range of goods". Reflected here is the protectionist attitude of the developed countries in UNCTAD, embodying the belief that tariffs and other import barriers are beneficial to the countries imposing them. Rather ignored is the fact that import barriers mean a loss of consumer welfare and result in an inefficient allocation of resources. The same arguments which would be used to justify the creation of NAFTA, and which have already been used by developed countries to justify the establishment of the EEC and EFTA, should also be applied to trade relations between developed and less developed countries. Not to do so would be hypocritical. Thus the problem referred to in the above quotation is reduced to the problem, mentioned earlier, of devising some safeguards for the gradual running down of inefficient, protected industries in developed countries.

Given the entrenched agricultural protectionism in many of the prospective NAFTA countries, it would be naive to envisage agricultural products, particularly temperate-zone crops, being included from the outset in the preference system. Special arrangements would have to be devised for this group of commodities. The positions of the various groups of commodities in the trade arrangements between NAFTA and the less developed countries are later examined in more detail.

Short term protection for uneconomic industries in the NAFTA countries, designed to facilitate their gradual decline, can be incorporated into the preference system. But it is a residual problem. The only industries affected are those in which all NAFTA members' production is uneconomic *vis-à-vis* less developed producers. Creating NAFTA would imply that each member would be prepared, eventually, to adjust to full competition from other member countries. The threat of market disruption following preferential access for exporters from the South would therefore be less than would be the case under the UNCTAD scheme. This reduced threat could be allowed for in the decisions concerning the degree, timing and duration of the proposed NAFTA preferences.

Timing and Safeguards

The actual severity of competition from developing countries would depend on the effect on existing protection of the tariff cuts and, also, on the liberalisation of the quantitative restrictions, both in absolute terms and relative to the rate at which trade barriers are removed among NAFTA nations. In this context, the timing and duration of the preferences are important. Once barriers are eliminated on intra-NAFTA trade, the participating poor nations will lose their advantage in each NAFTA market *vis-à-vis* competitors from other NAFTA countries. What remained of the advantages of preferences would be confined to that portion of NAFTA's imports from third party developed countries on which the preference system gave the South a competitive edge. The optimum arrangements for the less developed countries would be for as rapid as possible a reduction and elimination of barriers on their exports to NAFTA countries, combined with a slow and gradual elimination of barriers among NAFTA countries and the maintenance of substantial barriers on imports of relevant products from non-NAFTA developed countries.

Under the UNCTAD preference scheme the threat of market disruption in individual industrial nations is much greater than under a NAFTA system. Discussion of the UNCTAD scheme has thus paid considerable attention to safeguard arrangements. Recent discussion has centred on two alternative safeguards: the application of "escape clauses" and the provision of uniform tariff quotas. Neither is satisfactory. Escape clauses would allow the application of the preferential treatment to be fully or partially suspended. Under tariff quotas each developed country would admit at the preferential rates only a certain pre-determined volume of imports corresponding to a fixed percentage of domestic consumption, production or total imports of the item concerned. The arbitrariness of both arrangements would mean that any developing country which successfully established an industry that with the help of the preference was able to compete with producers in NAFTA countries could face either a loss of markets or the imposition of an uneconomic ceiling on exports. No rational entrepreneur would undertake heavy investment in the face of such risks. Various modifications have accordingly been suggested, all intended to introduce flexibility. But the experience of the arrangements for cotton textiles suggests that devices of this kind tend to become rigidly protectionist.

If the prospective NAFTA countries are committed to the rationalisation of their economies, the optimum policy for bringing about the graceful retirement of uneconomic industries would be a "package" of subsidies to allow uncompetitive production to continue over the retirement period and of cash grants to finance the closing down of productive capacity. Facilities should be provided, in addition, for the retraining and movement of redundant labour.

Duration and Eligibility

How long the preference system should last requires close attention. The proposal for preferences is a variation of the infant-industry argument. It is based on the observation that in order to reach an efficient state and level of production modern industry must have access to a large competitive market. This condition is not fulfilled by the small protected markets of less developed countries. Hence the call for preferential access to the large, competitive markets of the industrialised world. In effect, this is a plea for income transfers from the consumers of developed countries to the producers in less developed ones, except to the extent that the maturation of the newly established industries has the effect of reducing world market prices. The advantages to poor nation exporters, conferred by the preference system, with respect to intra-NAFTA trade, would last as long as the period over which NAFTA members gradually removed barriers to trade among themselves, and, with respect to NAFTA imports from third party developed countries, as long as some developed countries remained outside NAFTA and the free trade area maintained barriers to imports from them. The duration of the preference scheme should be long enough to allow the successful establishment of some industries (in particular, processing industries), but not so long as to encourage the establishment of industries in which developing nations have no prospect of long term comparative advantage.

The final, organisational problem for which a solution would have to be found within the framework of the preference system itself is the question of the eligibility of less developed countries for participation in the scheme. In other words, a definition would have to be found for a "less developed country". The OECD preference scheme uses the principle of self-nomination; that is, any country can call itself developing. The implicit assumption is that nations would like to graduate from that status or can be forced to do so by the discretion allowed developed countries under the scheme.

By recalling that the preference system can be regarded as an aid programme, the problem becomes one of deciding some reference criterion for determining the *needs* of a country. If, for example, a country which managed to set up a wide range of competitive export industries also had a large population with very low per capita incomes, then that country would remain eligible for inclusion within the system. This assumes that the preference system involves a disguised form of aid and that an equivalent amount of assistance could not be extended in a more efficient manner. It should be noted that even if a developing country manages to establish an industry which could price its output below world market levels, preferences allow it to charge higher prices than would be possible without them.

In sum, the proposed NAFTA preference system should be open to all less developed countries in need of assistance, cover all their exports and be continued for as long as possible. It should be free of protectionist safeguard devices, although assistance should be given to declining NAFTA industries in the forms of grants and subsidies. The current state of knowledge does not permit us to estimate the quantitative effects of such a system. But it is possible to assess on a qualitative basis the advantages which would accrue to less developed countries by the different commodity groups and by groups of countries.

Assessing Advantages of System

Two aspects of preferences must be taken into account when assessing the advantages they confer on less developed countries. The first is the reduction of the effective protection enjoyed by producers in NAFTA countries over producers in less developed ones. The second is the extent of the effective preferences afforded to the less developed over developed exporters. It will be recalled from earlier discussion that the effective protection afforded to the production of a commodity by a tariff is determined by the value added in the processing (if any) of that commodity and also by the tariff structure. The effective protection may be much greater than the nominal value of the tariff. Following this argument, a preferential tariff reduction may result in a much greater fall in effective protection afforded to domestic producers than is apparently indicated by the actual size of the tariff cut. Similarly, the margin of preference received by the less developed producers may be greater than the number of percentage points by which the tariffs applied to them are reduced below the remaining tariffs on intra-NAFTA trade or the MFN rate. Although this analysis is unnecessary for the following qualitative assessment of the potential advantages of the preference system, it should be borne in mind as an important consideration to be allowed for when evaluating the possible effects of tariff cuts. Quite small tariff cuts may involve substantial reductions of effective protection and afford a substantial margin of effective preference.

In assessing the effects of preferences on a commodity basis it is useful to distinguish five groups of commodities of export interest to less developed countries. They are (1) commodities which do not compete with industries in the developed countries; (2) primary commodities, especially agricultural produce, which compete directly with producers in developed countries; (3) primary commodities which compete with synthetic commodities produced in developed countries; (4) directly competitive semi-processed and processed primary commodities; and (5) directly competitive manufactured commodities.

The commodities falling into the first group, mainly tropical products, would not require preferential treatment. Currently, most of the tariffs and other barriers to the imports of such commodities are imposed by individual developed countries on a discriminatory basis favouring specific less developed countries associated with the barrier-imposing country. The preference systems currently extant (fundamentally, only the Commonwealth system is of importance in this connection, although the Portuguese, American and Danish arrangements would also be affected) could be phased out if all barriers on trade in these commodities were eliminated and the markets of the NAFTA countries were open to all less developed countries on a non-discriminatory basis.[37] The benefits currently enjoyed by the favoured countries would pass to those developing nations able to compete effectively with them for their markets. To the extent that the resultant competition reduced world market prices further gains—increased sales—might result, although (depending on elasticities of demand and supply) increased competition may equally result in a fall in revenues from sales of these commodities. In addition, limited trade expansion might result from the removal of the remaining non-discriminatory barriers to trade in the commodities in this group. For example, sales to Scandinavia of bananas increased following the removal of the substantial tariff barriers on imports of that fruit.

The agricultural products of the second group are, for the most part, precisely those commodities for which the less developed countries currently have a comparative advantage. Producers in the developed countries are also heavily protected against outside competition. Besides benefiting from tariffs and quantitative restrictions they also receive large subsidies. Less developed producers of such commodities as sugar and oil-seeds would stand to benefit substantially from free access and preferences for these

[37]This is true for all commodity groups and some form of compensation would have to be devised for those countries currently enjoying preferences, as discussed in an earlier chapter.

products. Progress in the liberalisation of trade in agricultural produce has been slower than in any other field and the vested interest groups formed by farmers in developed countries are so strong that even in NAFTA this sector would probably continue to be heavily subsidised. In the first instance it is improbable that preferences, or even freer access, would be extended by NAFTA members to imports from developing countries of commodities in this group. The most which could be conceded at first would be an increase in the ratio of imports to production. Later, as the need for mobility of factors of production developed consequent upon the expansion of trade among NAFTA members, it is possible that the participating countries might find it in their own interests to give adjustment assistance to agriculture. In this way agriculture could be integrated into the overall economic structure of the developed countries, instead of being increasingly divorced from economic realities, as at present.

For the foreseeable future the less developed world faces a food-grain shortage even while the USA is paying farmers billions of dollars a year to keep grain land out of production and almost all developed countries are subsidising farmers to produce crops (on potential grain bearing land) which could be imported at a much lower cost. Freer access and preferences for imports of such crops from less developed countries would release land which farmers could be subsidised to use for growing grains for export to the Third World as part of NAFTA members' aid programmes. Viewed in the kindest light, the new International Wheat Agreement can be regarded as a faltering step in this direction.

The prospects for the commodities in group three, those in competition with substitutes, especially synthetic substitutes, is somewhat more complicated. This is because many of the synthetics industries are also treated by the developed countries as "infant-industries". Here the relevant question is whether or not the less developed producers of natural raw materials could compete with NAFTA synthetics industries after the end of the preference period when the synthetics industries could be assumed to have reached their most efficient scale of operation. Where commodities were able to compete with synthetics over the long run, preferences would raise the prices that could be charged over the preference period. For commodities unable to compete with fully mature synthetics industries, preferences would prolong the period during which they could sell in NAFTA markets on a competitive basis. If the long run price of some synthetics were only marginally less than the natural products for which they are substitutes, the NAFTA countries might be well advised to consider whether the resources invested in the manufacture of synthetics could not be employed more profitably elsewhere. If such marginal synthetics industries were to be scrapped, preferences would provide a long run competitive advantage for less developed producers against producers of synthetics in non-NAFTA developed countries. This is an important point. For factors of production in developed countries are much more mobile and have many more opportunities for alternative employment than factors in less developed countries, where the running down, for example, of a jute or rubber industry would cause widespread hardship.

Most raw materials in group four go through several stages of processing before they are ready for use as consumer goods or industrial inputs in a final manufacturing stage. At present most of these processing industries are located in the developed countries where they have been established under substantial protective barriers. The actual protection is greater than is reflected in tariff levels because of the escalated nature of tariff structures in industrial countries. It is useful to reiterate earlier discussion with an example. Most developed countries import cocoa beans at zero or very low tariffs whereas cocoa butter or paste typically carries a tariff of some 15 per cent *ad valorem*. If we assume that a third of the cost of cocoa butter represents processing costs, then the effective protection of the industry processing cocoa butter from cocoa beans is 45 per cent. The result is that whereas all cocoa beans are imported from less developed countries most developed countries are either self-sufficient in cocoa products or import their residual requirements from other developed countries. The bulk of world trade in processed cocoa products is between developed countries, mostly under free trade or customs union arrangements. This situation is typical for many of the exports of less developed countries. In a very real sense such industries as the jute processing industry in Dundee, in Scotland, can be regarded as depriving the very much poorer workers of Pakistan and India of income and employment and their countries of foreign exchange earnings.[38]

[38]An extreme case is the French overseas departments of Martinique and Guadeloupe, both large sugar producers. They are forced by the French Government to import all their requirements of refined sugar from France. They export all their raw sugar to France and reimport it from France at inflated prices.

The potential effect that free access alone to NAFTA markets could have on the commodities in group four is exemplified by a comparison of the Malaysian and Bolivian tin industry. Malaysia receives Commonwealth preference on exports of refined tin to the UK. Bolivia, on the other hand, does not receive preferential treatment from any developed country. Britain imports substantial quantities of tin from both countries; from Malaysia in the form of refined tin ingots and alloys; but from Bolivia only in the form of crude ores, which are then smelted and refined in the UK. The economies of tin smelting and refining in the UK, in an environment of trade preferences, made it profitable for the UK tin companies to finance the establishment of a smelting industry in Malaysia, but not in Bolivia. Malaysia is fortunate, however, that metals receive more generous treatment in most developed countries' tariffs than other primary commodites. The Commonwealth preference system still maintains tariffs and quotas against other processed commodities large enough to prevent the establishment in other less developed Commonwealth countries of competitive processing industries for quite a large number of products.

Setting up a NAFTA preference system would encourage the fairly rapid establishment of processing industries in the participating less developed countries, directly replacing the equivalent protected industries in NAFTA producing for their respective domestic market and for export (often back to less developed countries) and also replacing NAFTA imports from non-NAFTA developed countries. The industries concerned, often vertically integrated, could be encouraged to invest in setting up processing plants in less developed countries, as happened with Malaysian tin.

There are two significant factors favouring preferences for products in group four that are not present in the first three groups. First, the establishment of processing industries in less developed countries would stimulate a large and continuing expansion of demand for processing machinery and related capital goods (for example, power and packaging equipment) produced in and exported by NAFTA countries. Secondly, the labour which would become redundant in NAFTA countries would be semi-skilled and skilled production line workers who could easily be absorbed into the expanding industries benefiting from the expected increase in trade among the NAFTA countries themselves.

The short term prospects of less developed countries for increased exports of group five commodities—manufactured goods, with or without preferences—are not very good. Manufactured products currently amount to about 20 per cent of the total value of all exports from developing countries. Some nine countries account for around 80 per cent of these. Almost half (by value) of the Third World's manufactured exports, moreover, are textile products. The competitive position of textile exporters from developing countries is such that if the developed nations simply dropped the discriminatory protectionist measures of the international textiles arrangement, the export earnings of the less advanced economies concerned would be substantially augmented. Preferences would make only a marginal difference. No other manufactured product is exported by less developed countries in significant quantities.

The move towards freer market access involved in a removal of quantitative restrictions, particularly on textiles, would represent a further unfolding of the spirit of free trade on which the proposal for NAFTA is based. It represents, not an increase in discrimination, but a move towards non-discrimination. If all countries in NAFTA were to liberalise policies on imports of such commodities the burden of adjustment required to absorb the increased flow of them from the developing world would be spread more evenly. Under the rules of GATT, members of a free trade area are only required to extend to developing nations the same terms as they impose on all non-members. NAFTA should go further and offer the same terms as they do to each other. In this respect the timing of preferences would be crucial. It might be considered preferable to reduce barriers to imports of textiles and other manufacturers from less developed countries faster than they are removed on trade between NAFTA members, thus extending additional preferences in the short-run. The state of underdevelopment can in fact be described in one sense as the inability to produce competitively priced manufactured commodities. In general, preferences for commodities in group five would not be of great assistance to less developed countries taken as a whole. If developing countries were to be enabled to take advantage of preferences they would have to be accompanied by substantial flows of capital and technical assistance in production and marketing techniques.

Although the short term foreign exchange gains from preferences for manufactured products would probably be small, after the

87

complete elimination of trade barriers between NAFTA members the potential benefits would be even less. Initially exporters have to compete with domestic producers for each country's market; and some might be high cost, inefficient producers. Once the free trade area was fully established, however, Third World exporters would have to compete with the most efficient producers of the NAFTA countries, producers with vast markets able to reap fully the maximum possible economies of scale. This contrasts with the prospects for producers of processed commodities. For instance, a coffee exporting country, in current circumstances, might send raw coffee beans to, say, fifteen developed countries, each with its own roasting plants and firms making instant coffee. Preferences based on zero tariffs would mean that one large coffee roasting and instant coffee making industry in the coffee growing country could benefit from all possible economies of scale.

The fact that the short term gains from preferences would probably not result in more than a small increase in total NAFTA imports of manufactures from less developed countries is no justification for the maintenance of widespread and high protection from such imports. The removal of this protection would substantially increase the sales of the producers of the few exports from the South currently in this group and preferences could induce businessmen in less developed countries to invest in plants producing other simple manufactured products. One example of this possibility is the establishment of watch and electrical apparatus industries in the Virgin Islands following the extension, in 1957, of preferential entry into the USA of imports from those islands.

It is impossible to say, without extensive empirical work, how much each individual less developed country would benefit from NAFTA arrangements for trade with less developed countries. But it is possible, on the basis of qualitative assessment, to derive some indication of the distribution of potential benefits on a group-by-group basis according to their interests in the commodity groups listed above.

As far as non-competing primary commodities are concerned, the group of countries which would stand to gain from the elimination of trade barriers would be those not at present receiving preferences on these items. They would be Latin American countries and some in Asia. The gains of these countries would be mainly at the expense of countries presently receiving preferential treatment. Although this is true for all traded products, the potential gains and losses following the absorption of the Commonwealth (and other NAFTA countries') preference systems into a NAFTA scheme would be quantitatively most important in this group. As mentioned previously, a form of compensation for the losers would have to be devised.

No significant concessions are expected for the competing products, particularly agricultural crops in group two. A maintenance of the *status quo* is the most which could be hoped for in the early stages. It is not possible to assess, even on a crude basis, which countries would gain from preferences for natural products competing with synthetics in NAFTA countries.

All less developed countries stand to benefit from free trade and *a fortiori* from preferences for processed primary products in proportion to the value of their exports of primary products and the degree of processing which their particular exports undergo before final use.

The potential beneficiaries of preferences on exports of manufactures are those countries already exporting significant quantities of such products, namely Hong Kong, India, Israel, Mexico, the Philippines, Pakistan, Taiwan, Argentina and Brazil. In addition those less developed countries which already have well established manufacturing sectors could conceivably benefit. These are Rhodesia, Kenya, the Magreb countries and the UAR in Africa; Thailand in Asia; and Chile, Colombia, Jamaica, Panama, Peru and Uruguay in Latin America.

The availability of potential benefits is, of course, no guarantee that the potential beneficiaries will be able to take advantage of them. This is especially true in the cases of processed commodities and manufactures which would depend upon the availability of capital, skilled labour and technical expertise. The countries that would benefit are not necessarily those which the NAFTA countries would most like to assist on grounds of need. The remedy[39] for this problem would be for NAFTA governments to encourage, perhaps with tax concessions, private enterprise to invest capital and technical "know how" in those countries most needful of such assistance to enable them to take advantage of preferences.

---

[39]This would be apart from the use of explicit aid policies to distribute income to those countries which would remain poor in spite of the advantages of the preference system.

Summary

This chapter has been concerned with outlining an ideal basis for the commercial policies of the members of the proposed Atlantic-based free trade area towards less developed countries. It has been based on the twin objectives of moving towards freer world trade and of assisting less advanced economies in their efforts to develop. The adoption of such commercial policies would be based on duty-free entry for tropical products and industrial goods from less developed countries into NAFTA countries.

The move towards freer access would in itself simply be an extension of the move towards freer trade which would be the underlying spirit of NAFTA. To the extent that some countries (particularly those of the EEC) remained outside NAFTA, the extension of freer access would constitute preferential treatment among NAFTA members and by NAFTA members towards developing countries. The preferential treatment for the Third World could be augmented initially by removing barriers on their trade more rapidly than the barriers on intra-NAFTA trade were removed. These arrangements would necessitate dismantling the protection enjoyed by NAFTA industries over less developed competitors and would require a structural re-organisation of the economies of NAFTA countries additional to that which would be required by the establishment of the free trade area itself.

In the UK there are already semi-judicial bodies like the Monopolies Commission, the Restrictive Practices Court and the Prices and Incomes Board where vested interests are required to justify policies that are in conflict with consumer interests. There is no reason why an additional body, a Tariffs Board, should not be created to oblige industries to justify their claims for the continuance of protection by tariffs and quantitative controls rather than subsidies to finance uncompetitive production. The subsidies could be voted on an annual basis. And each year subsidised producers could be required to make out a case as to why they should continue to receive cost-reducing subsidies rather than grants designed to facilitate the running down of their productive capacity. In this way the burden of maintaining protected industries would fall on the consumers and taxpayers of NAFTA nations rather than on less developed countries. Consumers in NAFTA would thus be more clearly aware of their interest in seeing uneconomic industries closed down than they seem to be at present of the harmful effects of tariffs and quantitative restrictions.

Finally, what are the prospects for less developed countries in the absence of a NAFTA preference system? First, as argued in Chapter 2, the prospects for less developed countries under GATT are not very hopeful. Secondly, the politically feasible possibilities within UNCTAD are not very bright either. An increase in the number of commodity agreements would increase restrictions on world trade. Supplementary financial measures are unlikely to be of any significance due to the improbability of adequate funds being forthcoming in a period of disenchantment over capital aid. The protectionist, safeguard restrictions likely to be imposed on any UNCTAD preference scheme for semi-manufactures and manufacture would vastly reduce its value. UNCTAD's ineffectiveness is due to calls for concessions from developed countries not matched by any immediately obvious benefit to developed countries. By contrast, the concessions implicit in a NAFTA preference system would be balanced by, and complementary to, the benefits that the NAFTA countries would expect to derive from free trade among themselves. Thirdly, less developed countries could combine into producer groups exerting monopoly power over the markets for individual commodities, a development which would be detrimental to the interests of developed countries. Fourthly, a very real possibility is that the less developed world, in its associations with developed countries, would break up into preferential trading blocs. The four probable blocs would be (1) a modified version of the Commonwealth system, (2) an association of Asia with Australasia and possibly the Soviet Bloc, (3) an expansion of the association of African countries with the EEC and (4) an association of Latin America with the USA. Discussions are already taking place on the feasibility of the last of these. It was to some extent in response to the undesirability of this possible development that President Johnson expressed the willingness of the USA to explore with other developed countries the possibility of a preference system embracing all less developed countries.

5 CONCLUSIONS

The starting point of this study has been that the less developed countries of the world require increased inflows of foreign exchange to finance the imports needed to sustain efforts to achieve faster rates of economic growth. It has been argued that present international arrangements discriminate against the interests of less developed countries and that current developments do not hold out much hope for improvement. It has been suggested that the countries which would form the proposed open-ended, Atlantic-based free trade area—the countries which already constitute the source of the bulk of less developed countries' receipts of foreign exchange—could accommodate the Third World's interests in such a way as to provide increased assistance and at the same time benefit themselves from the arrangements. Unlike other proposals, it would call for no major change in the trade policies of NAFTA members, all of which have already (in Chapter IV of GATT) conceded non-reciprocity to developing countries and all of which have some element of discrimination in their trade relations. The change of attitude towards protection that the proposed NAFTA preference system would require of NAFTA members would be marginal to that required by the formation of NAFTA itself.

The limitation of GATT is that the interpretation and implementation of its principles, rules and regulations favour the developed signatory countries. The role of GATT as a negotiating centre for multilateral tariff reductions based on bargaining power means that the voice of less developed countries is a small one in arguments for reorganising world trade. The achievements of GATT have been concentrated on lowering barriers to trade in sophisticated, manufactured products where less developed countries possess little present, or short term potential, export interest. This tendency was exemplified in the results of the recently concluded Kennedy Round negotiations.

The basic weakness of UNCTAD is that it is regarded by the governments of developed countries as little more than a forum in which the less developed countries can air grievances. As a result, any proposal made at UNCTAD favouring less developed countries which would require trade policy changes based on unilateral concessions on the part of developed countries is unlikely to be implemented in any meaningful way. The main value of UNCTAD derives from its role as a research and public relations organisation, documenting and drawing attention to the grievances and needs of less developed countries. It has not been equipped—by the developed countries—to negotiate actual changes in trade policies.

This paper has proposed that member countries of NAFTA could assist less developed economies by encouraging them to increase exports by encompassing them in the free trade area arrangements and, in addition, by extending preferential treatment on selected imports from developing countries. The proposed preferential system is far-reaching. Without some such arrangement, however, the establishment of NAFTA would increase discrimination on products entering NAFTA trade which are competitive with Third World exports. The system would not increase discrimination among NAFTA members; it would only increase discrimination against non-members. The proposal assumes that the developed countries would be sufficiently anxious to assist less developed countries to be willing to abolish the mass of restrictions presently imposed on imports from poor countries and go even further by granting them preferential treatment. Availability of opportunity is no guarantee, though, that the less developed countries would be able to take advantage of these moves, especially where industrial products are concerned. To help them do so, private enterprise in NAFTA could be encouraged to invest in the establishment of production facilities in less developed countries.

The preference system would include all NAFTA members and its benefits would be extended to all participating, less developed countries on a non-discriminatory basis. It is envisaged that initially the scheme would take the form of an extension of the Commonwealth system, except that reciprocity from the less developed countries would not be required. The removal of existing trade barriers on a non-discriminatory basis would alone result in a significant increase in the export earnings of less developed countries. Preferences would add to this. To be of any value in respect to intra-NAFTA trade, the concessions made to less developed countries by NAFTA members would have to be afforded at a more rapid pace than the reduction of barriers to trade between themselves. Preferences would cease to be of much value once the barriers to intra-NAFTA trade were completely eliminated. They would only be of some continuing value as long as some developed countries (or less developed countries) with competing exports remained outside NAFTA.

As members of the proposed Atlantic-based free trade area would be drawn from the developed participants in GATT and UNCTAD, the question arises as to why the interests of less developed countries are more likely to be accommodated within NAFTA than they have so far been in the two established institutions. There are three reasons for expecting this to be the case. In the first place, the spirit behind the NAFTA movement is based on belief in the benefits to be gained from free trade and the concessions called for in the proposed preference system would represent a more extensive diffusion of this particular spirit. Secondly, if NAFTA was to be successfully established, its members would be better off and consequently able to bear the cost of the preference system more easily, which contrasts with the UNCTAD scheme that incorporates no *quid pro quo* for developed countries. And thirdly, the extension of preferences by NAFTA as a group would ensure that the burden of accommodating those preferences would be shared as broadly as possible. The fear of market disruption has in the past militated against any single developed country making unilateral concessions, the argument being that the wider the market area the less any single group of domestic producers will suffer and consequently the less will be the problems of adjustment. In addition, such action would reverse the tendency for the world to break up into discriminatory trading blocs bent on protecting the interests of producers within each bloc.

Lastly, the question remains as to why prospective NAFTA countries should go beyond freer market access and extend preferential treatment. The motive behind the suggestion is that it would compensate less developed countries for the past discriminatory trade policies of developed countries. It would also provide the rich nations with a method for assisting poor countries at a time when they have become disenchanted with the efficiency of ordinary capital aid programmes.

Part III

HARMONISATION ISSUES
UNDER FREE TRADE

by

Hans Liesner

I THE HARMONISATION ISSUE

The proposal that trade barriers among a group of countries be abolished raises a wide variety of important questions. Some are concerned with the overall economic gains—to a particular country or to the group as a whole—expected to accrue from the removal of tariff barriers. Others relate to effects upon particular commodities or industries in the member states. Yet others are to do with the consequences of the formation of the free trade scheme for economic relations with third countries. Furthermore, the problem arises how far existing national economic circumstances, institutions and policies are compatible with free and unrestricted trade. This last problem has come to be discussed by economists under the general heading of "policy harmonisation". The purpose of the present study is to consider the harmonisation issue in the context of what would be at first a North Atlantic free trade area (NAFTA), proposals along these lines being at present advocated as a fresh approach towards liberalising world trade.

The subject matter of the paper is therefore the extent to which economic conditions, institutions and policies in the various countries taking part in the scheme would have to be changed if the abolition of trade barriers is to achieve the ultimate aim of raising real outputs and incomes by inducing greater specialisation and the wider exploitation of economies of scale and if, despite the removal of trade restrictions, the member countries are to be able to balance their external accounts without abandoning other policy goals such as price stability, overall full employment and a "reasonable" rate of economic growth.[1] The study will thus be concerned, on the one hand, with questions related to the (long run) efficiency-increasing effects of the free trade scheme, to be considered under the heading "Structural Policy Harmonisation" and, on the other hand, with (short run) questions of balance of payments stability, to be discussed

[1] As the subsequent discussion will show, this way of formulating the problem in effect prejudges the form the free trade agreement will take. More specifically, it assumes that the Atlantic countries would opt for a free trade area rather than an economic union approach. (See Pages 103-4.)

under the heading "Balance of Payments Policy Harmonisation".[2]

Before proceeding further it may be as well to consider these two aspects in a little more detail. Structural harmonisation issues concern questions of economic efficiency. The problems which arise have therefore to do with the distribution of resources in the partner countries. There are some obvious questions to be considered which may help to give more concrete meaning to the concept: How far is it possible for rates of indirect and direct taxation to differ in the member countries of a free trade scheme? Is it feasible for the partners to continue the pursuit of policies aiming at some kind of economic balance between different regions within their countries? To what extent is it necessary to co-ordinate anti-monopoly legislation in the different countries and/or to institute a common policy to prevent agreements among industrialists in the partner countries? Is it necessary to adapt the transport policies of the member countries? In what way do government procurement policies have to be changed? Can governments continue to control the rate of exploitation of natural resources or to subsidise domestic users? Most of these issues will be considered in some detail below, but the general meaning of structural harmonisation should now be reasonably clear.

Balance of payments policy harmonisation, rather more obviously, relates to the implications of free trade arrangements among a group of countries for the balance of payments stabilisation policies of the partners. The problems which arise are thus "macro-economic" in character. They concern the ability of the nations taking part in a free trade scheme to use various instruments—such as fiscal or monetary measures, "incomes policies", or exchange rate variations —to control the balance of payments.

The distinction between structural and balance of payments policy harmonisation does not rule out the possibility that a particular problem may raise both structural and balance of payments harmonisation issues. (The best example of a case in point is perhaps the common agricultural policy of the European Economic Community [EEC].) It nonetheless appears to constitute a useful device for setting out the questions. The subject of harmonisation in an

[2]These terms are used in Harry G. Johnson, "The Implications of Free or Freer Trade for the Harmonisation of Other Policies", in Johnson, Paul Wonnacott and Hirofumi Shibata, *Harmonisation of National Economic Policies under Free Trade* (Private Planning Association, University of Toronto Press, Toronto, 1968). The present study owes much to Professor Johnson's paper.

Atlantic-based free trade scheme will accordingly be considered under these two headings.

A number of preliminary points need to be made to put subsequent discussions into proper perspective.

1. *Approach and Scope of Study*

To begin with it should be made clear that the present paper is aimed at "the general public". No claim is made that the ground is being covered exhaustively. First, most of the discussion is conducted in fairly general terms. Technicalities, over which experts may quarrel, are disregarded. Secondly, the paper does not mention all the harmonisation issues likely to arise. Trade between countries embraces many thousands of different items. The production as well as consumption of these items is affected by a host of circumstances, some of them "natural", such as the prevalence of certain climatic conditions, others the direct or indirect outcome of particular institutional arrangements, government policies and so on. In general one may presume that these circumstances differ from country to country. It does not follow that the abolition of trade barriers should necessarily be accompanied by measures to create equal circumstances. Indeed, it is generally contended by economists that actual harm would frequently be done by equalising the "starting points" of the producers and consumers of a given commodity in the different member countries of a free trade scheme, because one may be removing the very cost differences from which the advantages of freer trade will flow.

At the same time, it is not possible to give a definite indication of the harmonisation issues which remain. As the experience of existing free trade schemes—such as the Benelux arrangement (between Belgium, the Netherlands and Luxembourg), the EEC and the European Free Trade Association (EFTA)—has shown, harmonisation issues are liable to "crop up" quite unexpectedly, though in view of the complexity of modern economies this is not perhaps very surprising. It is therefore highly unlikely that even much more careful and detailed research than has in fact been undertaken in connection with the present study would reveal all the harmonisation issues with which a NAFTA arrangement might be faced. The paper can thus claim to do no more than to outline some of the underlying principles—on the basis of which many apparent harmonisation issues turn out to have little substance—and to give an indication of a number of areas in which *prima facie* some degree of harmonisation may be called for. In this context the experience of the European forerunners, and especially that of the EEC and EFTA, is most valuable. Frequent reference will hence be made to these.

One further point should be made. Relatively simple analysis may suggest that, at first sight at least, a harmonisation problem will arise with regard to a particular practice adopted by a particular government. It is generally, however, far more difficult (a) to assess the economic impact of the policy measure in question—there may or may not be indirect effects on other products or markets—and (b) to come to a reliable estimate of the quantitative significance of the forces involved. The experience of existing free trade schemes has shown that very often the quantitative significance of a lack of harmonisation appears to be relatively small. But this cannot be accepted as a general rule. Detailed and painful research is often required in order to establish just what the position is. The present analysis will attempt, where possible, to give some indication of the quantitative importance of the points under dicussion. There will be many important issues though which can only be examined qualitatively.

2. *Membership and Commodity Coverage*

Some assumptions need to be made regarding the scope of the free trade arrangement envisaged. This matter is discussed more fully in the parallel study[3] by Mr David Robertson, of Reading University. In the present context it is possible to be very brief. With respect to membership the general assumption is that the free trade scheme would initially embrace the United States, Canada, Britain, some or all of the remaining EFTA countries, and possibly the EEC. On the other hand, harmonisation problems raised by an extension of the free trade arrangements to Australia, New Zealand and Japan are referred to only occasionally. This does not mean that a radically different approach would be required if the Pacific countries were to join, but rather that economic policies and institutions peculiar to these countries have not been considered.

The question of the scope of the free trade grouping does not, however, relate only to the issue of membership. Consideration

[3]David Robertson, "Scope for New Trade Strategy", in Harry G. Johnson (ed.), *New Trade Strategy for the World Economy* (Allen & Unwin, London, 1969; University of Toronto Press, Toronto, 1969).

must also be given to the commodity coverage of the arrangement. Here two extreme cases might be cited. On the one hand, there can be an arrangement which creates free trade conditions for only one industry. The Canada-USA Automobile Agreement, providing for free trade in cars and accessories between the two countries, is the example which naturally springs to mind.[4] The European Coal and Steel Community (ECSC), creating a common market in coal, iron ore, scrap, and steel, might also be mentioned. At the other end of the spectrum, there would be the abolition of all trade barriers among the member countries and therefore free trade in all goods and services.

The extent of commodity coverage has important implications for the scope and complexity of the harmonisation issues likely to arise. On first consideration any increase in the number of commodities or industries included in the free trade scheme may be expected to be accompanied by the appearance of more harmonisation issues. In some respects this is a valid argument. In particular, there are certain industries—agriculture and the service industries spring readily to mind—which in many countries are characterised by an especially large degree of government regulation and interference. The exclusion of such industries from the free trade scheme may make the harmonisation problem considerably easier. There are also, however, strong counter arguments. A modern economy is a complex interlocking edifice. It is ultimately not possible to create conditions suitable for a state of free trade for one sector without in some way affecting other sectors or, indeed, the whole economy.

The ECSC provides numerous examples of the difficulties which partial integration as applied to commodity coverage can cause. Time and again the proper functioning of free trade in the integrated sectors pre-supposed adjustments being made in other industries, such as the transport sector, or in overall government stabilisation policies. But these adjustments would have had further, and often undesirable, repercussions.[5] It is therefore not surprising that one of

[4]For a brief account of this agreement see *A Possible Plan for a Canada-US Free Trade Area* (Canadian-American Committee, Washington D.C. and Montreal, 1965), pp. 64-65.

[5]Cf. James E. Meade, Hans Liesner and Sidney Wells, *Case Studies in European Economic Union: The Mechanics of Integration* (Oxford University Press, London, 1962) Study III, especially Ch. 2, 4 and 5. It should be said that some of the harmonisation issues encountered in the ECSC stemmed from the particular approach of economic integration adopted in that Community and would not be likely to arise in a rather looser free trade scheme for the commodities concerned.

the factors persuading the six ECSC member countries to proceed to the formation of the general common market of the EEC was the difficulty of satisfactorily operating a free trade scheme restricted to just a few, though important, commodities.

As far as NAFTA is concerned, it is assumed that initially the free trade scheme would be confined to industrial goods and basic materials. Some special arrangements might be made for increased trade in agricultural products. But the nature of such arrangements, or the implications of a subsequent extension of the free trade provisions to the agricultural sector, have not been considered in this paper.[6]

3. *Form of Free Trade Arrangement*

Some assumptions must be made about the kind of free trade scheme that would be adopted. The main possibilities would appear to be "conditional most-favoured-nation (MFN) tariff cuts", a free trade area, a customs union or an economic union. In practice the distinctions between these different approaches are not always as clear-cut as they may appear on paper, especially when it comes to the last three, but for present purposes the following brief categorisation should suffice.

A member of a conditional MFN scheme will have reduced the tariffs applied to a range of products in return for equivalent concessions by the other members. The situation is thus very similar to that which exists after the conclusion of a round of tariff-cutting negotiations under the General Agreement on Tariffs and Trade (GATT) (like the recent Kennedy Round), except that in the case of the conditional MFN scheme the tariff cuts have been restricted to a certain, and possibly quite small, group of countries. The conditional MFN scheme could, but need not, involve the abolition of tariffs over a smaller or larger segment of trade. It may therefore not qualify as a free trade scheme at all. For this reason, and also because of the incompatibility of conditional MFN cuts with cherished GATT principles, it will be excluded from further consideration.

At the other end of the spectrum, providing for maximum in-

[6]Cf. Maxwell Stamp and Harry Cowie, "Britain and the Free Trade Area Option", in Johnson (ed.), *op. cit.*, p. 204. The problem of agriculture has been dealt with separately under the Atlantic Trade Study Programme in Brian Fernon, *Issues in World Farm Trade* (The Atlantic Trade Study, Trade Policy Research Centre, London, 1970).

tegration among the member countries, there is the economic union. All commodity trade restrictions are abolished. Labour and capital can move freely within the union. Trade in services is also free. And there is a common currency and a common tax system. The participants attempt, in effect, to create a single economy. In the EEC many hope that the Community will ultimately become an economic union. So far, though, the six countries have travelled but a short distance on what will undoubtedly prove a long and arduous road.

A rather less far-reaching commitment to economic integration is found in the free trade area and the customs union. Both approaches concentrate on the abolition of barriers such as tariffs and quantitative restrictions on trade in goods, sometimes with the exception of certain sectors, such as agriculture. The main difference between the customs union and the free trade area is that in the former the abolition of mutual trade restrictions among the partner countries is accompanied by the adoption of common barriers towards third countries. This means, first and foremost, that the member countries adopt a common external tariff; and secondly, that any other trade barriers, such as quantitative restrictions, are also unified. A free trade area, on the other hand, is characterised by the retention of national—and therefore generally different—tariffs and other trade barriers towards third countries. It follows that a free trade area arrangement must include the common adoption of some provisions —usually referred to as "origin rules"—which deal with the consequences of different third country trade barriers (cf. Pages 144-146 below).

The choice between the various approaches to free trade is dictated by numerous considerations. Although most of these are not relevant to the present discussion, the harmonisation issue is involved in an important way.

The best way of tackling the problem might be first to look at the role of harmonisation in the context of the economic union. As pointed out above, in that case the goal of the participants is to build a single economy. The introduction of common economic policies and of common institutional arrangements and practices forms an essential feature of the establishment of the union. Policy harmonisation becomes an aim in itself. Important political consequences follow because the determination and administration of common economic policies in effect pre-suppose the existence of a supranational decision-taking unit. It is therefore not surprising that countries attempting to create an economic union are generally also aiming at some form of political union.

There are clearly many countries, however, which on the one hand wish to obtain the advantages of free trade, but which on the other are not interested in, or indeed are fearful of, the political consequences of the economic union type of approach. They will look at policy harmonisation measures in quite a different light—as a necessary consequence of the freeing of trade, probably to be determined on an *ad hoc* basis as and where problems arise, and with some room for give and take. Such countries are likely to choose one of the other forms of free trade schemes—a free trade area or a customs union. From the point of view of harmonisation the customs union in one way implies a somewhat greater commitment than does the free trade area, because the introduction of the customs union's common external tariff (together with various attendant steps) is in itself a significant harmonisation measure. On the other hand, as already mentioned, the free trade area requires common origin rules.

Because of the closeness of the links between the form of a particular free trade scheme and the nature and extent of policy harmonisation it is necessary to make some definite assumption about the form of the proposed free trade arrangement among the Atlantic countries. This is clearly an important question, but in the present context there is no need to go into details. The economic union type of approach is likely to be eliminated because the political implications would probably not be acceptable to any of the prospective members, especially perhaps countries other than the USA. Of the two remaining possibilities (the free trade area and the customs union) the choice is likely to fall upon the former. In view of factors such as divergent customs administrations, the constitutional position in the USA regarding the determination of commercial policy and the system of Commonwealth preferences, the problems associated with the adoption of a common external tariff as required in a customs union would prove pretty difficult. The prospective partner nations will probably wish to sidestep these problems by opting for a free trade area. In what follows it will accordingly be assumed that an Atlantic-based scheme would take the form of a free trade area.

2 STRUCTURAL POLICY HARMONISATION: SOME BASIC PRINCIPLES

A brief account has been given of the meaning of structural harmonisation. It was argued that structural harmonisation issues primarily relate to efficiency and the distribution of resources in the member countries of a free trade scheme. Provision of a broad outline of the principles which guide the economist's approach to structural harmonisation is now necessary.

1. *Introduction*

One preliminary point must, however, be considered. The policies and practices which give rise to structural harmonisation issues in a free trade area—preferential purchasing of domestic supplies by public authorities, the pursuit of regional policies, the levying of internal taxes and so on—do of course operate before free trade is introduced. In principle the problems for international trade which result from these policies are present as soon as commercial relations between the partner countries come into being. What is the special association between structural harmonisation and free trade?

The answer falls into two parts. First, it is clear that the presence of harmonisation issues, even under conditions of restricted trade, is in fact recognised (though the term harmonisation has on the whole been associated with free trade situations) and a set of rules to deal with some of the more obvious problems has been evolved and incorporated in the instrument governing international trade, namely the GATT. Many of the GATT rules, however, have been observed to only a very limited degree. Moreover, there are a number of important practices—preferential government buying of home-produced commodities is perhaps the best example—which GATT does not deal with at all.

The second part of the answer is bound up with the basic purposes of free trade schemes. As has been mentioned on more than one occasion, the underlying economic aim of a free trade grouping, such as the Atlantic countries are presumed to be establishing, is to attain a more efficient distribution of resources in the partner countries. For instance, if Britain were to take part in a NAFTA arrangement, it would be expected that industries which can only produce at relatively high cost under the shelter of the tariff would be forced into a decline, at least relatively speaking, with more of the products in question being imported from partner countries. Other stronger industries would expand (with the help of the resources released by the first group of industries) and their exports would grow, replacing the products of less efficient industries in the other NAFTA countries. Moreover, as a result of the growth of output, the second group may also be able to reap economies of large-scale production, thus making even better use of the resources it employs.[7]

The acceptance of a free trade policy on the part of a group of countries, anyway as far as commercial relations with each other are concerned, may then be taken to indicate that the countries have come to attach rather more weight to economic efficiency arguments than they have done hitherto—possibly because changes in economic conditions, such as the increased availability of economies of large scale production, have added to the efficiency gains to be obtained. It is thus likely that nations which adopt a free trade scheme will in general become increasingly concerned about policies and practices which have effects similar to those of tariffs. In other words, the structural harmonisation problem, though it exists for any country involved in international trade, is rendered far more urgent by the freeing of trade.[8]

2. *Basic Principles of Structural Harmonisation*

At the beginning of this study an attempt was made to outline the meaning of structural harmonisation. Typical harmonisation questions were listed in order to provide an idea of the kind of issue likely to arise. Some may have expected to see at the head of that list a question which was in fact omitted altogether—a question relating to wages.

[7]This account of the redistribution of resources following upon the establishment of a free trade area is of course grossly over-simplified. In particular, the assumptions on which the argument rests have not been brought out. Some of the most critical assumptions are, however, referred to below (Pages 109-111). The question also arises which are each partner country's "weak" industries and which are the "strong" ones. A tentative answer to this question, as far as Britain is concerned, is given in Stamp and Cowie, *op. cit.*, Ch. 5.

[8]Even a significant *reduction* in tariff barriers will bring other trade restrictions more into the limelight. For instance, in the course of the Kennedy Round, non-tariff barriers were the subject of much discussion and it appears to be agreed that in any further tariff negotiations non-tariff restrictions must be given more attention.

It may help if the point is put in a rather extreme form. One of the potential member countries of NAFTA is Japan. The layman's first reaction to the possibility of Japan's participation is to question the feasibility of free trade between countries with such divergent money wage levels as Japan and Britain, let alone Japan and the USA. "Unless steps were taken to bring wages into line", it might be argued, "surely Japanese exports would be able to undersell British firms on the UK's home market in virtually every product line, thus causing widespread depression and unemployment and an impossible balance of payments position." The argument used to demonstrate that this fear is unfounded goes to the core of the economist's analysis of international trade, and it is this analysis which must be used to investigate structural harmonisation issues.

Beginning with a grossly over-simplified example, let it be assumed there exist only two countries, Britain and Japan; that only two products, chemicals and textiles, are produced and consumed; and that the only resource used in the production process is labour. For reasons that need not be gone into at the present juncture, Japanese labour is assumed to be less efficient than British labour in the production of both textiles and chemicals. In other words, in Japan more units of labour (man-hours, say) are needed to produce one unit of textiles or of chemicals than in Britain. However, the difference in labour productivities between Britain and Japan is less marked in the case of textiles than it is in the case of chemicals. In the case of textiles, for instance, the average British workman may per unit of time produce, say, 50 per cent more than his Japanese equivalent, whereas in the case of chemicals the efficiency of British labour may exceed that of Japanese labour by a factor of 3 to 1.

Assume it is proposed that there should be free trade between Britain and Japan, provided that wages paid in the two countries are made equal. Reflection will suggest that if this condition were in fact carried out, there could not possibly be balanced trade between the two countries. As the British use less labour per unit of output of either product than the Japanese do, but payments per unit of labour are the same (and no other resources are employed), the money prices of both products—chemicals as well as textiles— would be lower in Britain than they are in Japan. If transport costs are disregarded, neither British nor Japanese consumers would wish to purchase either of the two goods from Japanese firms and Japan would import both textiles and chemicals, exporting nothing in exchange.

Clearly, the situation is not a tenable one. In the two-country/ two-product economy, balanced trade can exist only if each country exports one commodity and imports the other. For this to happen, Japanese wages must be lower than British ones, to an extent which ensures that Japanese costs of one of the products are, in the general case, lower than the costs of the same good in Britain. For instance, if Japanese wages were one half of those in Britain (which very approximately is the existing relationship), Japan would produce textiles more cheaply than Britain does, because output per man in Japanese textile making is assumed to be two-thirds of that in the British industry, whereas Britain would still be in a position to under-sell the Japanese in chemicals, because in that industry her superiority in terms of output per man more than offsets the lower Japanese wage level. Two-way trade would now be possible, with Japan exporting textiles to Britain in exchange for imports of British chemicals. On the other hand, if Japanese wages were only a quarter of those in Britain, balanced trade would once again be ruled out, because the Japanese would now be able to under-sell British firms in both lines of production. (There is plainly a range within which Japanese wages may lie given the relative productivity levels for the two industries. This range extends from Japanese wages equal to one-third of those in Britain to Japanese wages equal to two-thirds of those in Britain.)

It is abundantly clear that the example outlined in the preceding paragraphs is an exceedingly simple one, far removed from the complexities of the modern economy. Because of its very simplicity, however, the example should help to illustrate a number of important principles.

With regard to the immediate point at issue—the significance of different wage levels in the countries taking part in a free trade scheme—the proposition can be derived that without reference to other cost elements, such as the productivity of labour, inter-country comparisons of wages are not really very meaningful and that it is certainly not legitimate to insist on equality of wages as a pre-condition for free trade.

This proposition may also be illustrated by referring to wage differences between the UK and her single most important trading partner—the USA. Average wages in the US are far higher than those in the UK; for manufacturing, for instance, the US earnings figure is more than twice the British. Despite these wage differences

American firms sell a wide variety of goods on the British market (and in the absence of tariff barriers imports from the USA would undoubtedly be considerably larger still). The reason why the high US wage does not prevent American goods being sold in the UK lies in the higher average productivity of US labour. Although accurate estimates are very difficult to obtain, it is clear that man-hours used per unit of output are generally much lower in the USA than they are in the UK, thus counteracting the effect of the wage differential. Insistence on equal money wages in NAFTA would in these circumstances lead to hopelessly uncompetitive prices for most British goods.

How can anyone be certain, though, that relative wage and price levels are such that the balancing of trade flows will in fact occur? Full discussion of the issues raised by this question must be deferred until the problem of balance of payments policy harmonisation is reached in Chapter 4. For the present it may be sufficient to remember that the nations which would form NAFTA are already heavily engaged in mutual trade, so that *average* wages and prices may be presumed to be in approximate equilibrium relative to one another. All the same, this does not rule out two possibilities. (a) When trade barriers are abolished, some countries may find their exports growing faster than their imports do, and vice versa for other countries. And (b) the prices of *particular* commodities may diverge to a substantial degree, though before free trade is instituted tariffs assure the more expensive product at least a share of its home market. If (a) were to occur, balance of payments equilibria would come to be disturbed, and thus once again there would be encountered the problem of balance of payments policies in a free trade grouping. The divergence of particular prices, point (b), raises quite different issues, issues which go to the heart of structural harmonisation. In order to clarify the problem the simple example of free trade between Britain and Japan outlined above may be used again.

It was postulated earlier that in Britain both textiles and chemicals are produced more efficiently than they are in Japan. The difference in efficiency, however, was assumed to be more marked with respect to chemicals than it is with respect to textiles. It follows from this that if Britain were to shift a given quantity of labour from producing textiles to producing chemicals, she would obtain more chemicals per unit of textiles foregone than would be the case if the same operation were performed in Japan. Similarly, if labour resources were shifted from chemical production to textile manufacture, the increase in textile output per unit of chemicals foregone would be less in Britain than in Japan. (The economist describes this situation in terms of the concept of comparative advantage. He would say that Britain has a comparative advantage in the production of chemicals and Japan a comparative advantage in the manufacture of textiles.) Consequently, Britain would save resources if she moved some of her resources into the production of chemicals and satisfied at least part of her consumption of textiles out of imports from Japan. Similarly, Japan would make best use of her scarce resources if she increased her output of textiles, at the expense of the production of chemicals, and relied on imports from Britain for a greater part—perhaps the whole—of her supply of chemicals.

In principle the effect of free trade between Britain and Japan is, of course, to bring about this pattern of specialisation and thereby permit resources to be saved. As seen above, provided relative wage levels are consistent with balanced trade, the prices of the two commodities in the two markets will be such as to enable British producers of chemicals to raise output and increase sales to the Japanese market and Japanese producers of textiles to step up production and raise exports to the British market.

The crucial question is whether free trade will have this effect in practice. The answer depends on a number of factors. But in the present context the important issue is the relationship between costs and prices. The free trade argument rests on the assumption that the relative prices of goods produced and consumed in the countries concerned give a fairly accurate indication of relative costs of production. If relative prices fail to correspond to relative costs, international trade will not produce the pattern of specialisation required.

The point may best be clarified by reference again to the simple example of free trade between Britain and Japan. The assumptions made about labour productivities imply that in Britain textiles will be more expensive relative to chemicals than they are in Japan. If in Japan the price of a unit of textiles were equal to that of a unit of chemicals, then in Britain the price of textiles would be twice that of chemicals. Suppose, however, that for certain reasons the British government wishes to lower the relative price of textiles and, therefore, imposes a tax on the production of chemicals, the proceeds of the tax being devoted to the subsidisation of the production of textiles. The outcome will be that the relationship between the prices of chemicals and of textiles will no longer reflect the relationship between the respective costs of production. This in turn will affect international trade between Britain and Japan. As long as the price of chemicals stays below that of textiles, the direction of trade— Britain exporting chemicals in exchange for textiles—will remain the same, but the volume of trade will decline. If the tax and subsidy payments are large enough, though, the price of British chemicals will exceed the price of textiles and trade between Britain and Japan will take the form of Britain exporting textiles and importing chemicals. Thus, instead of specialising on the goods she can produce relatively efficiently, Britain does the opposite.

In economists' jargon, the tax and subsidy policies pursued by the British government distort the comparative cost position and consequently the volume and possibly even the direction of international trade.

At this point it is essential to realise that the distortion of comparative cost conditions is due not to the fact of government taxation and subsidisation as such, but rather to the different treatment of the two commodities. One, chemicals, is subject to the tax and there is no subsidy; the other, textiles, is not subject to tax and the producers receive a subsidy. If, on the other hand, the UK were to impose a tax on both commodities, at some common rate, or if producers of the two products were to qualify for a subsidy, again at the same rate, relative costs and prices would in principle remain unaffected and so would trade between Britain and Japan.

What is true of taxes and subsidies also applies to other factors influencing the relationship between the costs and prices of commodities. As far as the pattern of trade is concerned, the existence of such factors does not matter, at least at a straightforward level of analysis, if their effect on the relationship between costs and prices is more or less the same for all the commodities produced within a given country. On the other hand, such factors do matter if they affect different commodities in different degrees.

These conclusions are clearly of direct relevance to structural policy harmonisation. As shown earlier, structural harmonisation is concerned with such questions as the significance, in the context of free trade schemes, of different transport policies being pursued or some regional policy measure being retained. It can now be seen that the essential question to ask in these cases is not whether a particular practice (tax, or transport regulation, or regional measure, or whatever it may be) differs from practices applying to similar goods in the partner countries, but rather whether it differs from the practices applying to the other goods produced within the same country. If it does, a structural harmonisation problem exists; if it does not, no harmonisation issue arises.

The subsequent discussion of particular harmonisation issues will provide ample opportunity for illustrating the application of this principle. Before considering specific cases a few qualifications need to be dealt with.

First, the argument has implicitly been based on the assumption that economic relations between countries consist entirely of trade. Put another way, no allowance has been made for international migration of labour or for capital transfers between countries. As will be shown later (on Pages 114-15), the possibility of factors of production moving between countries opens up a different aspect of the structural harmonisation issue.

Second, the conditions giving rise to structural harmonisation issues may also have implications for the balance of payments. For instance, if Britain were to impose a heavy tax on the consumption of textiles, this would not only affect the relative prices facing consumers and thus distort their choice of goods, but—assuming that textiles are partly or wholly imported—would also disturb the UK balance of payments. Moreover—and this is probably the more important point—the fact that some particular practice may turn out not to raise structural harmonisation problems, because it appears to leave the comparative cost position unchanged, by no means rules out its relevance to balance of payments policy harmonisation. The *general* price level may be higher or lower than it would be in the absence of the practice. Unless other determinants of the balance of payments, especially the exchange rate, are appropriately adjusted, this will affect the country's external balance.

Thirdly, although inter-country comparisons of the position of particular goods with respect to some tax or government regulation or other policy may be inadmissible in the first stage—when it is asked whether a structural harmonisation problem exists—they may nonetheless serve a useful purpose at the subsequent stage, when the member countries of a free trade scheme have to reach a solution of the problems they have found.

This is a large topic. Very briefly the argument runs as follows.[9] There are at least three sets of reasons why countries pursue policies which give rise to structural harmonisation issues. (1) Sometimes it may be a result of administrative convenience. Government revenue, say, may be raised relatively easily by heavy taxes on certain commodities. (2) Sometimes it may be a question of the deliberate pursuit of a policy goal, such as balanced regional development. (3) And sometimes it may merely be a matter of slow and cumbersome legislative and administrative processes. The problem giving rise to the practice may long have disappeared, but the authorities have not yet "found time" to rearrange their policies accordingly.

Harmonisation issues in the last category are not perhaps likely to be very important. In any case, their solution should be straightforward. Problems arising under the first heading should similarly not prove too hard to resolve, at least in principle, given the range of alternative measures open to most modern governments (though in practice this optimism may not always be justified). Distortions deliberately created to meet a policy requirement (the second category) are likely, on the other hand, to lead to considerable difficulties. It must be assumed (a) that the clash between resource allocation, as determined by the price mechanism, and the achievement of the particular policy goal was recognised by the authorities; (b) that the choice in favour of the policy goal was deliberate; and (c) that this preference will not be affected by membership of a free trade scheme.

Inter-country comparisons may prove to be helpful at this point. They will indicate to what extent similar policy objectives are pursued in the partner countries. If it turns out—as may often be the case—that other partners do pursue similar aims, the best solution may well be for the member countries not even to try to assert the pre-eminence of the free trade argument. For example, if all the partner countries of a free trade scheme impose heavy taxation on alcoholic beverages, because they wish to discourage consumption, it would appear mistaken for these countries jointly to try to remove these special taxes on the grounds that they interfere with the optimum allocation of resources. On the other hand, if the cross-country comparison were to reveal that only one or a few partners were concerned about the adverse effects of high alcohol consumption, the problem would be far more difficult to resolve.

[9]For further details see Johnson, *op. cit.*, pp. 12-13.

So far this analysis of the principles of structural policy harmonisation has been confined to questions related to the movement of goods between the member countries of a free trade scheme. In addition to goods being traded among countries, though, there may be transfers of factors of production. Capital may be shifted from one country to another. There may also be migration of labour. As the significance of factor mobility for policy harmonisation is an important aspect of the overall problem, the basic economic principles concerning the distribution of factors between countries should be accorded some attention.

Simple economic theory suggests that if maximum economic efficiency for the world as a whole is to be achieved, factors of production should be distributed between countries in such a way that at the margin the contribution any given factor makes to output (in economists' jargon, the factor's "marginal product") is the same in each country. If certain very restrictive assumptions are fulfilled, universal free trade will bring about this optimum state of affairs and no factor movements will be required. In the general case, however, unrestricted trade alone will not result in marginal products being equalised. The achievement of maximum world output therefore demands that mobile factors move from locations where their contributions to output are relatively low to those where they are greatest. *Mutatis mutandis* the creation of limited free trade conditions—that is, the establishment of free trade areas—is unlikely to bring about an equalisation of marginal products of factors in the member countries. Output in the area as a whole may thus be expected to benefit if factors are free to move from locations of low marginal products to those of high marginal products.

Many objections can be advanced against the statement that world output—or the total output of a free trade area—will be maximised if at the margin factor contributions to output are the same in all the countries concerned. The statement rests on a number of premises unlikely to be fulfilled in practice. It disregards many of the forces making for long run economic growth. It overlooks that non-economic issues play an important part in any arguments about migration, especially migration of labour.[10] Nonetheless, free trade arrangements often include provisions stipulating that obstacles to the transfer of factors be removed. This is true of

[10]For an analysis of the economic issues see Meade, *Trade and Welfare* (Oxford University Press, London, 1955), Parts III and IV.

Benelux and the EEC and the Stockholm Convention's Article 16, dealing with establishment, implies a limited degree of factor mobility within EFTA. (The EFTA countries are also bound by their acceptance of the capital liberalisation programme of the Organisation for Economic Co-operation and Development [OECD].) It may therefore be expected that a free trade arrangement of the NAFTA type would in due course aim at least at a certain measure of freedom of factor movement, particularly perhaps with regard to capital.

Full integration of factor markets, on the other hand, is exceedingly unlikely. This makes it very hard to determine the limits of any analysis of policy harmonisation concerning factor movements. In the present context discussion will be confined to policies and institutions which *prima facie* appear likely to *worsen* the distribution of factors; that is, to encourage the transfer of factors from locations where their contributions to output are relatively high to those where they are relatively low. The possible adoption though of measures to improve the distribution of factors among the free trade countries will generally be left to one side.

3 STRUCTURAL POLICY HARMONISATION: SOME PRACTICAL CASES

Having considered some broad general principles which should guide the approach to structural harmonisation the analysis will now turn to the kind of harmonisation issues which the member countries of a NAFTA arrangement may in fact have to face, though as was pointed out earlier, the treatment will be selective rather than exhaustive.

Because of their bewildering variety, harmonisation issues are not easy to classify in any very satisfactory manner. For purposes of exposition three broad groups of policies and practices will be distinguished:

(A) Practices which have effects similar to those of tariffs, in that particular domestic producers of import substitutes are afforded some protection against rival suppliers in partner countries;

(B) Policies which result in differential charges of some kind or another being imposed on the production and/or consumption of commodities in the partner countries; and

(C) Other institutional and/or administrative factors influencing relative costs and prices.

As may become clear later on, in a number of cases the assignment of a particular problem to one of the three categories is rather arbitrary. The classification scheme is accordingly far from perfect. It should nevertheless help the argument along.

(A) PRACTICES WITH EFFECTS SIMILAR TO THOSE OF TARIFFS

It has long been recognised that many countries protect domestic industries not only by means of imposing customs duties, but also by various other devices, frequently referred to as non-tariff barriers.[11]

---

[11]In principle this term could be interpreted as almost synonymous with "practices giving rise to structural harmonisation problems", but in fact it has tended to be confined to a much narrower, though nonetheless rather imprecise, meaning: viz. obstacles to trade, other than tariffs, for the benefit of particular domestic producers.

A typical list of such barriers would include (a) methods of classifying and valuing goods for customs purposes which increase the effective level of protection; (b) impediments to trade associated with steps taken to prevent dumping; (c) import quotas; (d) the restrictive effects of state trading and of government procurement policies; and (e) measures to assist particular domestic industries.[12]

In the present context some of these devices do not require further discussion, as the assumed abolition of tariffs among the free trade area countries would render them inoperative. This obviously applies to obstacles to trade arising in connection with (a) and in large part also to those related to (b). Dumping can only take place if the products concerned cannot readily be returned to the country of origin. As transport costs generally form only a very small fraction of the value of commodities, the main obstacle to re-entry is the exporting country's tariff, which will be reduced to zero for inter-area trade.[13] In practice governments may not always be willing to rely on these safeguards.[14] But the scope for direct anti-dumping measures, and therefore for impediments to trade associated with them, should be much reduced in a free area.

There is similarly no need to discuss import quotas. It can be assumed that the partner countries would make the abolition of quantitative restrictions part and parcel of the establishment of the free trade area just as the member countries of the EEC and of EFTA have done. In any case, trade among the Atlantic countries is already virtually free from quota restrictions, the main exceptions being trade with Japan, trade in coal and trade in agricultural products.

The remaining non-tariff barriers listed above—government procurement, state trading and assistance to particular industries —would not disappear with the establishment of the free trade area. They form the three items to be discussed in category (A).

[12]For an up-to-date discussion of non-tariff barriers in the Atlantic area see William B. Kelly, "Non-Tariff Barriers", in Bela Balassa and Associates, *Studies in Trade Liberalisation: Problems and Prospects for the Industrial Countries* (Johns Hopkins University Press, Baltimore, 1967).

[13]It may be noted that both the Rome Treaty and the Stockholm Convention explicitly provide for duty-free readmission of goods in order to prevent dumping (Articles 91 and 17 respectively).

[14]There are clearly commodities for which transport costs are not negligible; more important, perhaps, because of various imperfections there may not be a market for "dumped goods" in the country of origin.

1. Public Procurement

Modern governments play an important part in economic affairs. Not only do they attempt to influence the development of the economy in various ways. They also constitute large purchasers of goods and services. Among the goods governments buy mention might be made of such diverse items as equipment and materials for the armed forces, office supplies for civil servants, uniforms and equipment for the police and educational supplies. The services obtained include the construction of roads, schools and hospitals and the carrying out of various kinds of research.

Many of the goods and services purchased can be obtained from a wide range of firms, some of them the exporters of other countries. The possibility arises that in placing their contracts, governments grant a measure of preference to domestic as against foreign suppliers, thus affording the former an element of protection (generally in addition to any customs duty imposed on imported goods). In other words, public procurement (as government purchases of goods are often called) and public contracting (the purchase of services) may give rise to trade restrictions similar in their effect to tariffs.

In the present context only public procurement will be pursued. It is to be assumed that an Atlantic-based free trade arrangement will, at least to begin with, be confined to goods trade and that trade in services will not be included. There is hence no need to discuss the problems which public contracting may create for the working of a free trade area.

The quantitative importance of public procurement is hard to estimate in precise terms because purchases of *goods* by the public sector are not normally separately distinguished. However, UK and US national income data suggest that in these two countries a significant part of total goods production—perhaps something of the order of 10 per cent—is absorbed by the public sector (including the nationalised industries).

To what extent do governments in fact discriminate in favour of domestic suppliers when making their purchases? Evidence on this point is fragmentary. What there is suggests that discriminatory policies are by no means uncommon. Moreover, it is clear that discriminatory procurement occurs at central as well as at local/state government level, and that equivalent practices are sometimes adopted by publicly-owned enterprises and corporations.

The best-known example is undoubtedly the preference in favour of domestic suppliers which US federal agencies are required to adopt by the terms of the 1933 Buy American Act. Broadly speaking, other things being equal, US goods will be purchased unless their prices exceed the prices of imported supplies, including customs duty, by more than a certain percentage margin, a margin which can range from only 6 per cent to 50 per cent and more.[15] On occasion this general preference has been reinforced by more specific action amounting in some cases to an outright prohibition to buy from abroad. In the summer of 1967, for instance, the US Congress ruled that funds from the 1968 budget could not be used for the construction of naval vessels in foreign yards, thus preventing the US Navy from placing a contract for the construction of a certain number of minesweepers with British shipyards.

Discriminatory procurement policies are also adopted by many other industrial countries, though in general fewer details are available. In Canada the federal authorities permit a premium of approximately 10 per cent on products of Canadian origin.[16] Preferential purchasing practices are also common at the provincial level (see below). The position in the EEC is not always clear. In some countries, though, the authorities appear to work on the basis that, at least in the case of certain commodities, domestic suppliers should be awarded the contract unless the goods are not produced in the country.[17] In the UK there is no general preference margin on government contracts. Ordinary commercial criteria apply to a wide range of government purchases. But there are also important exceptions. A government order stipulates that purchases of computers are to be made from British firms if there is no "undue price differential", the British product is technically suitable and, too, the delivery date is acceptable.[18] The term "undue price differential" is clearly open to varying interpretations. Given the

[15]For details see Kelly, *op. cit.*, pp. 278-279.

[16]Cf. Albert Breton, *Discriminatory Government Policies in Federal Countries* (Private Planning Association, Montreal, 1967), p. 9.

[17]Cf. European Parliament, Session 1965-1966, Document 1 (March 22, 1965). The draft directives and decisions discussed in this report deal with public contracting rather than procurement, but the introductory discussion of discriminatory practices contains several references to procurement issues. In Kelly, *op. cit.*, pp. 280-281, there are a number of quotations from the report.

[18]*Government Purchasing in Europe, North America and Japan: Regulations and Procedures* (Organisation for Economic Co-operation and Development, Paris, 1966), p. 105.

circumstances of the case it is unlikely though to be taken to mean a zero preference margin. Certain nationalised industries will buy from foreign suppliers only if the foreign product is available on substantially better terms. Government purchasing departments are also encouraged to allocate public contracts as far as possible to producers in development districts to help alleviate the regional unemployment problem. (However, any discrimination resulting from this practice would clearly tell against other British as well as foreign firms.) Preferential procurement practices can also be found in other EFTA countries and in Japan, although amongst the EFTA governments there are also some which expressly require government purchasing to be based on purely commercial criteria.

The consequences of the pursuit of discriminatory public procurement policies for the working of a free trade scheme should be fairly obvious. Like tariffs, such policies serve to place the firms or industries concerned in a relatively advantageous position within the countries concerned. The efficiency gains expected to result from removal of the "obvious" trade barriers—in the main, tariffs—are thus unlikely to become available in full. Given the size of government procurement it is accordingly not surprising that discriminatory procurement policies have constituted an important harmonisation issue for existing free trade schemes.

The Benelux countries recognised the problem at an early stage and in 1956 agreed on a protocol under which discriminatory practices were not to apply to supplies from partner countries. Article 14 of the Stockholm Convention *inter alia* provides for the "progressive elimination", with respect to other EFTA countries, of preferential procurement practices by the end of the transition period (December 31, 1966). A little earlier—in October, 1966—the EFTA governments agreed on an "authoritative interpretation" of Article 14, a step which in effect amounted to a renewed resolve to carry it out.[19] They also agreed on certain practical measures to facilitate the implementation of the Article, such as the adoption of certain guide lines concerning the methods used in public tendering and the exchange of "lists of public undertakings responsible for major procurement programmes", together with information regarding the goods normally bought.

The Rome Treaty does not deal with discriminatory public

[19]For details see *EFTA Bulletin*, European Free Trade Association, Geneva, March-April, 1967, pp. 2-6.

procurement as such. But the general prohibition of discrimination on the basis of nationality, expressed in Article 7, is generally acknowledged to extend to public purchasing. Up to the time of writing, however, no specific action appears to have been taken to put Article 7 into effect, though the EEC Commission is known to have been working on the issue for some time. (The Commission's attempt to obtain the member governments' agreement on a harmonisation of public *contracting* policies—see Footnote 17, Page 119—has similarly not been successful so far.)

What, then, should be the rules concerning public procurement in a NAFTA arrangement? General economic reasoning, together with the example of EFTA in particular, clearly point towards the adoption of a strict non-discrimination rule as far as supplies from other partner countries are concerned, though as in the Stockholm Convention and in the Rome Treaty there would obviously have to be provision for special treatment of defence procurement or for cases raising issues of public health or morals. Following another EFTA precedent an exception might also be made for contracts connected with government-sponsored industrial research, provided the "development nature" of such contracts was clearly established.

At the same time, there is little doubt that a strict non-discrimination rule would not be readily approved by all the prospective NAFTA countries, especially perhaps the USA and Canada. On present evidence, preferential procurement is more widely accepted in these countries than elsewhere.[20]

An institutional factor greatly adding to the seriousness of the problem is the federal character of the American and Canadian constitutions. The federal authorities may simply lack the power to enforce a non-discrimination rule, which they had agreed to as part of a free trade scheme, at the lower levels of government. EFTA has encountered this issue; so far it appears to have been dealt with satisfactorily, but the evidence is only fragmentary.

Because of these difficulties some observers have suggested that it would be too ambitious to seek agreement on an outright prohibition of discriminatory public procurement practices and that it might be more realistic to try to lay down a commonly accepted

[20]Particularly illuminating in this context is the fact that Canadian provincial governments, in awarding contracts, frequently discriminate in favour of suppliers from the home province and against suppliers from other Canadian provinces, though perhaps not to the same degree as against foreign suppliers.

maximum margin of preference.[21] This solution is not likely though to find favour with countries which expressly pursue a non-discriminatory policy, quite apart from more general objections. It might not be unduly optimistic to hope for an acceptance of non-preferential practices among the central government agencies (subject to the exceptions mentioned earlier). This would solve a substantial part of the problem and might in due course encourage the lower levels of government to follow suit.

2. State Trading

In highly developed Western economies, goods production and trade are usually in private hands. In most countries, all the same, goods can be found which are produced and/or traded by a state agency. Moreover, this agency is frequently the sole producer and/or trader. Government monopoly positions often extend to imports; in other words, the government's trading agencies have the exclusive right to import the commodities concerned.[22] For example, a number of European governments—in the EEC as well as in EFTA —are monopoly producers, importers and traders (up to the retail stage) of tobacco products. Other commodities which are sometimes state traded in the above sense include alcoholic spirits, ethyl-alcohol, salt, matches and lighters.

The exclusive right to import is the feature of state trading which generally receives attention[23] in discussions of non-tariff barriers and which most obviously raises the question how far the operations of state monopolies are compatible with the proper functioning of a free trade scheme. There are clearly a number of ways in which the exclusion of other importers can be used to give artificial encouragement to the sale of the domestic product—the simple refusal to stock foreign goods, the application of excessive margins to imported supplies, limitations on advertising of foreign products and so on.

[21]Cf. Johnson, op. cit., p. 25. On the other hand, A Possible Plan for a Canada-US Free Trade Area, op. cit., p. 37, suggests a common free trade area procurement policy. This would seem even more difficult to achieve than a simple rule of non-discrimination towards products from partner countries.

[22]This right is sometimes combined with a similarly privileged position with regard to exports, an aspect of state trading which is probably less important quantitatively than direct control over imports and which will therefore not be examined in the present context.

[23]Cf. Kelly, op. cit., pp. 276-278, and Gerard Curzon, Multilateral Commercial Diplomacy (Michael Joseph, London, 1965), pp. 290-294.

The evidence suggests that these and other devices have in fact been applied quite commonly.

Although the appropriate figures are not readily to hand, it seems unlikely that in the NAFTA area state trading in the sense of exclusive government import rights is quantitatively very important, though there may be countries of which this is not true. For this reason, the issue will not be pursued in any detail in this study. Suffice it to say that in a NAFTA arrangement, as has been done in the EEC and in EFTA, an attempt would have to be made to ensure that the government agencies in question did not retain policies serving to restrict foreign supplies. At the same time, they should be left free to pursue their legitimate fiscal and social aims. In practice it may not be entirely straightforward to achieve this objective. In many cases the sheltered domestic producers use inputs supplied by the agricultural sector, with the result that the thorny issue of agricultural protection is at least indirectly involved. On the other hand, consumer interests can presumably be relied upon to press for relatively liberal practices.

Although discussion of state monopolies is often confined to those which can directly control imports, their operations raise other, wider problems which may conveniently be considered under the general heading of state trading.[24] Private producers are in principle guided by considerations of profitability; they will maintain or perhaps expand the output of goods which yield a profit to them, and reduce or even cease production of commodities on which they make losses. The re-allocative and therefore the efficiency-raising effects of freer trade depend on this process. When considering in Chapter 2 the pattern of specialisation brought about by the hypothetical creation of a free trade arrangement between Britain and Japan— and finding that in the conditions postulated Britain would come to satisfy an increased proportion of her consumption of textiles out of imports, simultaneously raising her exports of chemicals—it was taken for granted that British textile producers, when faced with

[24]At this stage the discussion is concerned only with those state-owned industries which produce internationally traded goods. The policies pursued by state-owned industries producing commodities not normally traded (like electricity, gas and rail transport) may also be relevant to the working of free trade schemes. For the prices charged will affect the costs of goods that can be traded. The problem is in principle the same as that raised by different indirect taxes. This is examined below (Pages 131-138). Quantitatively the effect of differential charges for commodities such as gas and electricity is in general probably rather small. The question of transport is briefly touched upon on Pages 149-152.

falling profit margins, would reduce output, whilst producers of chemicals, now confronted with a larger market, would raise production. If both textiles and chemical production are in private hands, this is a reasonable assumption to make. The case is considerably weaker when the possibility of state ownership is introduced. The reason is that if the state owns an industry, it can in principle ward off the consequences of economic forces acting upon that industry in a way not normally open to private owners. The matter may be of only academic interest if government ownership of an industry with improved prospects is assumed, because in these circumstances the public policy adopted may not perhaps vary so much from that which would be pursued by private owners. The situation may be quite different though if the industry owned by the government faces a contraction in demand. The losses incurred would force private owners to reduce and possibly to cease production. But this is not likely to be true if the industry is run by the state. In other words, the reaction of the government to one of its own industries failing to earn sufficient profits is not necessarily to make the appropriate adjustment in output, because it can generally meet the shortfall out of general taxation.

The consequences of this situation for the working of the free trade scheme are easy to see. The country's relatively inefficient industry ("textiles") does not in fact decline, at least not to a sufficient degree. This in turn means that the efficient sector ("chemicals") is held back because it cannot obtain the resources it requires to realise its full expansion potential. The overall efficiency gains of free trade will thus at best be only partially obtained.

It will be clear that this outcome in no way depends on the ability of the nationalised sector directly to control imports—all that is needed is government willingness to meet losses.

The problem is rendered more difficult because the original decision in favour of state ownership of an industry may have been prompted by the view that it would not be to the benefit of the community if the operation of the industry were determined on the basis of "normal" rules of profitability. Failure to adjust output in the face of mounting losses may thus reflect not so much narrow protectionist motives, but a genuine conviction that the country's true interests—economic or social or political—are at stake.

Having set out the problems created by the existence of government-owned industries in general terms, what needs next to be considered is how far these issues have in fact been of importance in existing free trade schemes. Unfortunately it will not be possible to take the matter very far in the present context, because the necessary information is frequently not readily available.

As seen above in connection with government monopolies which enjoy exclusive rights over imports, in the EEC as well as in EFTA there are a number of cases of state-owned industries. Once the discussion is extended to include industries not directly controlling imports, further examples can readily be found in both trading areas. In France, as well as in Britain, the coal industry is in state ownership. Crude steel production is wholly government-owned in Britain and in Austria and virtually so in Italy. There are also numerous cases of the government owning one or more units within otherwise privately controlled industries. In these circumstances, though, the problems described above are probably less likely to arise.

When it comes, however, to the question how far the operations of these industries have thrown up the kind of problem discussed in general terms above, there is no ready answer. The issue is not specifically dealt with in the EEC and EFTA treaties and while it has occasionally been referred to in publications of the relevant organisations, there is no evidence that it has received systematic attention. The answer may, of course, be that there has been no need for action. But in view of the complexity of the issues involved (it would certainly not be sufficient to take the financial results of state-owned industries at their face value) it seems unlikely that this conclusion could be reached without pretty thorough investigations. There is no report of these being pursued. It is also relevant to refer to the apparent absence of any real action on the part of the High Authority of the ECSC in the case of the nationalised French coal industry, despite the existence of *prima facie* evidence that the position and practices of the industry have not accorded with the requirements of French membership of a common market for coal.[25]

It follows that the experience of the free trade schemes already in being in Western Europe does not tell how problems connected with the operations of state-owned industries (other than direct control over imports) should be tackled in a NAFTA scheme. It is, of course, easy enough to suggest that in principle the industries concerned should operate on the basis of strictly economic criteria.

[25]Cf. Meade, Liesner and Wells, *op. cit.*, pp. 232-235.

But there can be much room for argument what exactly these criteria are in each case and how they should be applied. Moreover, as was pointed out earlier, insistence on the application of economic criteria to state-owned industries may lead to a clash between the aims of raising efficiency through freer trade and equally legitimate social and/or political objectives.

How far would the problems discussed arise in practice? It is impossible to answer this question with any degree of certainty, except that it is not difficult to think of one case which may raise the various issues in a pretty acute form. One of the major examples of a state-owned industry in a prospective NAFTA arrangement would be the British coal industry. This industry is already faced with serious adjustment problems. In a free trade setting though it would very likely find the going even harder because of competition from relatively low-priced American coal which at present is kept out of Britain by a prohibition of all coal imports. In the event, there would probably be strong pressure on the British Government—not least because of the importance of coal mining for the development regions—to adjust to this situation not so much by further cutting output (as private owners would presumably be forced to do), but rather by reducing prices in order to match the lower quotations for US coal and running up losses in consequence. It is unlikely that US coal mining interests would stand idly by.

3. Measures to Assist Particular Industries

The last of the non-tariff barriers to be considered in the discussion of structural harmonisation issues is government assistance to selected industries; that is, measures adopted by governments with the specific purpose of improving the relative position of a particular set of producers. This matter can be dealt with fairly briefly, not because it is unimportant, but because the issues are generally fairly straightforward (even though pretty complex analysis may be required to establish in what way and to what extent an industry does in fact benefit from a given set of measures).

Before the question is taken any further it should be made clear that at the present stage the matter under review is assistance given on an industrial as opposed to a regional basis; that is, government support received by the producers of a given commodity, wherever within the country in question they may be located, and not the assistance which the producers of a particular region may obtain, no matter what they produce.[26]

The scope of the present section is further reduced because in a number of the cases that could be included under the heading "government assistance" the method used by the authorities to aid the industry is closely related to issues discussed elsewhere in this study. It seems more appropriate to consider such cases in the alternative context. In particular, government assistance which primarily takes the form of discriminatory taxation is briefly referred to in the section dealing with taxation (see Page 131).

Despite these limitations on the scope of the present discussion there is still a fairly wide range of cases. The most important of these (and the only one to be considered in detail) appears to be government assistance to the shipbuilding industry, a practice which is found in virtually every industrial country with access to the sea. This assistance takes a variety of forms. In some countries, notably the USA and Canada, the shipyards *inter alia* receive direct subsidies, whilst other countries, like the UK and West Germany, concentrate more on cheap credit facilities. Widespread use is also made of special tax arrangements, of subsidisation of inputs and of various other devices. The quantitative significance of the aid is often difficult to establish. But a few figures are available. The EEC Commission estimated in 1965 that government aid to the shipyards amounted to 16 per cent of contract value in France, 14 per cent in Italy and between 3 and 5 per cent in West Germany (the German figure refers only to federal and not to state aid). The amount of the American subsidy can exceed 100 per cent of the world market price.[27]

Both the Rome Treaty (Articles 92-94) and the EFTA Convention (Article 13) in principle prohibit government aids which interfere with trade among the member countries. Articles 92 to 94, though, allow a number of exceptions (among them regional unemployment which is discussed on Pages 152-155 below) and EFTA's Article 20 (which deals with adjustment problems) has similar implications, although the scope for exceptions appears to be considerably narrower. Not much detail is readily available on the action taken

[26]In practice these two kinds of government aid may not always be so easy to disentangle. The authorities may decide to support industry A because its production facilities are predominantly located in an area of high employment and so on.

[27]These figures are taken from European Parliament, Session 1965-66, Document 103, November 22, 1965, German edition, p. 16 and p. 23.

127

by the EEC under Articles 92 to 94. What there is suggests that the Commission has frequently agreed to the continuation of aid, at least on a temporary basis. EFTA has been considering the problem. Nothing very definite has yet emerged.

Special mention should be made of the EEC's attempt to harmonise government aid in the shipbuilding sector. For technical reasons it is generally held to be impractical to protect national shipyards by means of tariffs (which explains the widespread use of other protective devices, such as those mentioned above). A rigorous enforcement within the EEC of the prohibition of government aids would hence leave the Community's shipyards without protection from third countries, thus placing them in a disadvantageous position relative to other Community industries which are sheltered by the common external tariff. The Commission has accordingly proposed that the six governments should agree on a common form and a common level (10 per cent has been suggested) of support for national shipbuilders, thus creating a reasonably undistorted market within the Community without removing all protection towards third countries. So far the Commission's proposals have not been accepted by the member governments.

In a NAFTA arrangement the problem of government assistance for specific industries is not likely to be easily soluble. In principle prohibition on the lines of the EFTA Convention would appear to be appropriate. But governments would probably claim that in at least a few instances the aid is not intended merely to serve narrow protectionist purposes and that wider issues—relating to matters such as defence requirements and/or "infant industry" protection—are involved. Exceptions would thus have to be permitted.

In the shipbuilding sector NAFTA would face problems very similar to those encountered by the EEC. The removal of government aids would imply the extension of free entry to non-members and the only practical answer would probably be the adoption of common aid measures. Given the fact, however, that at present national support measures appear to differ very substantially both in form and especially in their quantitative significance, agreement on such harmonisation measures would probably be very hard to obtain. In other words, some governments may well not be prepared to abolish assistance for their shipyards even *vis-à-vis* other NAFTA countries. This would be particularly likely were Japan to become a NAFTA member.

(B) DIFFERENTIAL CHARGES

The structural harmonisation issues so far dealt with in this study, though diverse in nature, have in one sense been of a relatively straightforward character—the practices discussed restricted trade in a fairly evident way, just as tariffs do. In the present section, by way of contrast, it is necessary to consider policies and practices whose effect on trade is often rather more difficult to establish. Moreover, the solution to the problems found is by no means always obvious.

In simple models of the economic system consumers pay prices which are equal to the production costs of the firms making the goods (plus charges for distribution and so on) and differences in costs per unit of two commodities should therefore be reflected in similar differences in the prices paid by consumers. In practice prices are frequently not equal to costs, either because of monopoly elements in production and/or distribution, or because the imposition of a charge or levy by the government or its agencies. The significance for free trade schemes of the latter of these two factors will be outlined in this section.

At least four kinds of charges should be considered in a harmonisation study, namely: (1) internal taxes imposed by the central and local governments; (2) employers' social security contributions; (3) tariffs on imports from third countries; and (4) levies imposed by government agencies, such as state-owned enterprises. In the present context, attention will primarily be directed to the problem of taxes. Social security contributions and external tariffs will be dealt with only to the extent necessary to give the reader a "feel" for the issue. The charges made by state-owned industries have already been very briefly referred to earlier (see Footnote 24, Page 123).

1. Taxes

In one way and another modern governments are large spenders. In many countries government expenditure accounts for more than one quarter of the gross domestic product. Hand in hand with large-scale state spending goes heavy taxation, in the form of both direct and indirect taxes. As examples of the former, one might cite income tax and levies on the profits of companies ("corporation tax"); of the latter, excise duties and sales and value-added taxes.

Even a cursory glance at the tax systems employed by different countries will indicate substantial differences in the approach to the problem of raising taxes. In the first place, there are considerable variations in the contributions to total government revenue consisting of direct and indirect taxes respectively. In France, for instance, the two are virtually equal, whereas in the Netherlands and in the USA the ratios of direct to indirect tax revenues are about two to one (though in the case of the USA the position might be rather different if state and local taxes were included).[28] Secondly, the ways of raising both direct and indirect taxes are similarly anything but uniform. In the case of personal income tax, there are appreciable divergencies in the overall level of the tax and in the degree of progressivity. In the case of indirect taxes there are particularly marked differences in the spread of taxation. Some countries, like most of the EEC member states, have adopted broad-based indirect tax systems under which most, if not all, commodities are subject to tax. Others, especially the UK, rely for their indirect tax revenue on levies—usually at relatively high rates—on a narrow group of commodities. In other words, given a set of income earners in the NAFTA countries placed in comparable positions on the income scale (a term that would have to be defined rather carefully) it would be found that their liability for personal taxation differed from country to country and that the taxes which they paid on the articles consumed would show very sharp variations. Business firms in comparable circumstances would similarly be found to be liable for substantially different tax payments on their profits.[29]

What are the consequences of such differences in taxation for the working of a free trade scheme? In recent years this question has been examined by many economists and a voluminous literature now exists, some of it of a highly technical nature. Only the bare outlines of the issues involved will be considered here, together with the main conclusions. The customary distinction between direct and indirect taxes will be retained. It is convenient to deal with the latter first.

[28]Cf. Douglas Dosser, "Fiscal and Social Barriers to Economic Integration in the Atlantic Area", in Bela Balassa and Associates, *op. cit.*, Table 8:4.
[29]For a careful attempt to make such comparisons (which are clearly much more meaningful than an inspection of nominal rates only), see Dosser, *op. cit.*, pp. 217-233 and Appendix Tables 8:1—8:6. With reference to profits taxes see also Peggy B. Musgrave, "Harmonisation of Direct Business Taxes: A Case Study", in Carl S. Shoup (ed.), *Fiscal Harmonisation in Common Markets* (Columbia University Press, New York and London, 1967), Vol. II.

(i) Indirect Taxes

One might best begin by briefly considering a tax practice which raises the question of compatibility with free trade conditions in a very obvious form—that of specific indirect taxes which apply to imports but not to comparable home produced goods.[30] Such taxes are clearly very similar in their effect to tariffs. It is, therefore, not surprising that free trade agreements like the Stockholm Convention and the Rome Treaty demand their removal. They are also contrary to GATT.

It is, in fact, difficult to find examples of indirect taxes which only apply to imports. In a slightly less blatant way, however, particular indirect taxes can and have been used to afford some protection to certain domestic industries. For instance, in a number of countries motor vehicle taxation is based on technical specifications which in effect favour the domestic product against at least certain types of imported car (in practice mainly American).[31] Again, the French Government in 1959 introduced, though apparently as a temporary measure, depreciation provisions discriminating in favour of investment goods of French origin.[32] In the USA the excise on distilled spirits is levied in such a way that spirits of less than 100 per cent are taxed as if they were 100 per cent proof. Because spirits, such as Scotch whisky, are normally imported in bottles, and therefore at 86 per cent proof, the effective tax rate is higher (by about 16 per cent) than that on US produced spirits, since US distillers can have their product taxed at a stage before dilution to less than 100 per cent proof has been effected.[33]

Although NAFTA countries are likely to be faced with a number

[30]In other words, the present discussion is not concerned with taxes which are levied on imports in lieu of similar indirect taxes imposed on home-produced substitutes. The issues raised by that kind of taxation are discussed on Pages 132-135 below.

[31]For details see Kelly, *op. cit.*, pp. 301-303.

[32]Cf. Clara K. Sullivan, "Indirect Taxation and Goals of the EEC", in Shoup (ed.), *op. cit.*, Vol. II, p. 48.

[33]Cf. Kelly, *op. cit.*, pp. 303-304, and H. G. Grubel and Johnson, "Nominal Tariff Rates and US Valuation Practices: Two Case Studies", *Review of Economics and Statistics*, Department of Economics, Harvard University, May, 1967, pp. 140-142. The proof gallon ruling also applies to the import duty on spirits and results in the effective rate being raised above the nominal rate. But in a free trade area context this factor would cease to be significant. It should be added that until a recent change in the law, much of the advantage which the domestic producers derived from the tax arrangement was offset by certain cooperage and labelling regulations which in effect discriminated *against* the domestic product.

of specific tax practices similar to those just described, much the more important question concerns inter-country differences in "general" indirect taxes. To put the problem rather bluntly, is it possible to create undistorted free trade among a number of countries if these countries continue to impose different indirect taxes? If the answer to this question is in the negative, the founders of free trade schemes will clearly face some very knotty issues. Agreement on common taxes would obviously not be easy to achieve. Governments would also be very reluctant to accept the resultant restrictions on their freedom of action over expenditure and overall stabilisation policies.

In order to deal with this question the basic principles of structural harmonisation briefly outlined in Chapter 2 need to be recalled. It was then argued that the influence upon international trade of an indirect tax (or other "artificial charge") imposed on a given commodity in a particular country must be judged not by reference to the tax position of similar goods in the other countries, but by reference to the generality of the tax within the first country. If in that country taxes of the same height are imposed on the whole range of goods and services produced, *relative* costs and prices within the country are, in the general case, not affected by the tax and trade with other countries will not be distorted. On the other hand, if the tax only applies to one particular commodity, or more generally, if there are differences in the tax burdens borne by different commodities within the country, then a distortion of relative costs and prices exists and the pattern and volume of international trade will be affected. Put another way, what matters from the point of view of international trade, and therefore of structural harmonisation, is the extent of deviations of particular indirect taxes from the average level of such taxes within any given country. It is not the average level itself that counts.

If indirect tax systems were on the whole reasonably uniform, the matter could almost be left here, at least as far as the present discussion is concerned. But indirect taxes are not uniform. Furthermore, the extent to which the tax burden on particular commodities diverges from each country's average will in general vary from country to country, as it certainly does in the prospective NAFTA countries.

In order to assess the significance of this state of affairs for free trade, two alternative ways of treating taxes on internationally traded commodities should be briefly discussed. Under the first system, countries exempt their exports from the payment of the tax and impose on imports a compensating import duty equivalent to the tax borne by the corresponding home-produced goods. Under the second, all home produced goods, whether for export or domestic consumption, are subject to tax and no "equalising" tax is levied on imports. In the first case one speaks of taxing foreign trade goods according to the "destination principle"; in the second, according to the "origin principle".[34]

Although exceptions can be found, it is generally true to say that indirect taxes are applied on the destination principle. In Britain, for example, no purchase tax is payable on exports of goods (like motor cars) which are subject to the tax when sold at home, and imports of the relevant articles are taxable. The same holds for excise duties and, at least in principle, for turnover taxes levied in many continental countries like the Netherlands, Austria and Italy.

The effect of the application of the destination principle is that consumers' choice between home produced and imported supplies of a certain good is not affected by national differences in taxation, because indirect tax is imposed at the same rate—that of the country of consumption. That is to say, under the destination principle producers of a given commodity in different countries can in general be said to enjoy equal access to national markets. This conclusion is not affected by the lack of uniformity in indirect tax rates found in many countries. To take conditions in the UK as an example, it applies just as much to clothing, tax on which is 12.5 per cent, as it does to alcohol, which attracts a much heavier excise duty.

At first sight it may thus appear that with the destination principle countries have found a way of neutralising the effect of inter-country differences in indirect taxes and that in this particular field there is therefore no need for free trade areas to introduce harmonisation measures. Unfortunately the matter is not so easily settled. Whilst under the destination principle indirect taxes are neutral with respect to the distribution of production between countries, this is

[34]It has been repeatedly shown in the literature that if taxes are uniform within countries, it does not matter, as far as the pattern of international trade is concerned, whether the countries use the destination or the origin principle, provided all goods are treated on the same basis as far as any particular tax is concerned. (Moreover, different principles may be applied to different taxes.) In view of the general inequality of indirect taxes, however, this conclusion is only of academic interest.

not true with regard to consumption. If Britain levies a light tax on clothing and a heavy one on alcohol, whereas in another NAFTA country the opposite is the case, consumers in the two countries will have different incentives to consume the two commodities (British consumers having a stronger incentive than consumers in the other country to purchase clothing rather than alcohol). It follows that consumers in both countries would gain from a re-distribution of consumption, more alcohol being consumed in Britain and more clothing in the other country. But this is prevented by the differential tax arrangements. Despite the abolition of trade barriers there is a distortion in the distribution of consumption between the two countries. The pattern and volume of trade are not "optimal".

If countries are unwilling to change their tax systems and yet wish to avoid such distortions, they could switch from the destination principle to the origin principle. Under the latter system the relative prices paid by consumers for different commodities would be equal throughout the free trade area, transport costs apart. The result would be, however, that indirect taxes would cease to be neutral with respect to production—the comparative cost position would be distorted, as was shown in the course of the discussion in Chapter 2. (At that stage taxation was implicitly assumed to be according to the origin principle.)

Economic analysis does not provide any guidance on how to choose between distortions in the pattern of production and those affecting consumption. In practice, though, governments have generally decided to place the distortions on the consumption side. In many federal countries like the USA, Canada and Australia, the states or provinces impose differently structured indirect taxes, which are in effect applied on the destination principle. The same is true of many important indirect taxes in Benelux. Moreover, the Neumark Report,[35] on which the EEC's tax harmonisation programme is based, viewed with some equanimity the continued existence, in the six member countries, of sharply divergent excise duties on commodities such as tobacco and alcohol, provided the destination principle continued to be applied to such taxes.[36]

[35]*Rapport du Comité fiscal et financier* (European Economic Community, Brussels, 1962) appearing in translation as *Tax Harmonisation in the Common Market* (Commerce Clearing House, Chicago, 1963).

[36]Nonetheless, eventual unification of excise duties has remained a goal of the EEC's tax harmonisation programme.

Several reasons lie behind the general preference for the destination principle. One deserves special mention. Governments frequently use the tax system to discourage particular activities; in other words, distortions may be deliberately created in order to influence the pattern of production and/or consumption. Observation suggests that this applies especially to consumption taxes. The general adoption of the destination principle can thus, in part, be interpreted as reflecting government determination to ensure that national policies relating to the consumption of particular commodities continue to be effective.

It follows that attempts to reduce the distortions on the consumption side by all the partner countries adopting the same set of indirect taxes—a possible way out of the dilemma—may run into strong opposition, because a partial or even complete sacrifice of accepted national policy goals may be involved. Moreover, the revenue implications of any such harmonisation would probably not be generally acceptable.

It may be concluded, then: (a) that inter-country differences in the overall level of indirect taxation certainly do not call for any harmonisation measures and (b) that it may be a mistake for the builders of free trade schemes to attempt to remove the distortions which necessarily arise when the divergencies of specific tax rates from national averages differ from country to country (or state to state), especially when it is a matter of different consumption taxes.

Two further points should be mentioned. In the first place, in the discussion of the destination principle it was implicitly assumed that the necessary border tax adjustments—the exemption of exports from indirect taxation and the imposition of compensating taxes on imports equivalent to those borne by domestic products—do not give rise to any special problem. In the case of single stage indirect taxes (that is, indirect taxes which, like British purchase tax, are levied at one given point in the production/distribution chain) this assumption is broadly speaking justified, particularly if, as is often the case, the tax is levied close to the point of consumption—at the wholesale or, better still, at the retail stage. Value-added taxes of the French type are similarly reasonably well suited to the application of the destination principle.[37] When it comes though to cumulative

[37]There is some evidence, however, that with both kinds of taxes export exemptions generally fail to cover the whole of the tax paid, though the quantitative significance of this factor is probably small. Cf. *Report on Border Tax Adjustments* (OECD, Paris, 1964).

turnover taxes of the kind all EEC countries except France have been using until very recently, the position is much less straightforward. Such taxes are generally levied (usually at a relatively low rate—4 per cent would be a fairly representative figure) at every transaction which a commodity passes through on its way from the raw material input stage to the final retail stage. Experience has shown that the cumulative amount of tax, though generally in excess of the standard rate, is impossible to calculate with exact precision. As a result there is of necessity an arbitrary element in the rates of export rebate and of compensating import duty applied. This may in turn give rise to allegations of "hidden subsidisation of exports and indirect protection against imports", allegations which may be given particular weight in a free trade context.

Secondly, continued reliance on the destination principle in practice implies the retention of tax frontiers. Otherwise compensating import duties may largely be avoided. But the existence of tax frontiers is likely to lead to administrative delays for international trade of a kind not found in internal trade. Moreover, the very fact that tax frontiers still exist, so that the baggage of international travellers continues to be subject to inspection, will bring home to the "man in the street" that integration is not complete.

To many observers these considerations may seem of relatively minor significance. There is no doubt, all the same, that they have played an important part in determining the EEC's approach to the harmonisation of indirect taxation.[38] That approach is characterised by the pursuit of three aims:[39] (a) to remove any element of distortion consequent upon inaccurate border tax adjustment; (b) to bring about a complete abolition of tax frontiers (except perhaps with regard to a few commodities traditionally used as large revenue raisers, such as tobacco and alcohol); and (c) to avoid certain internal disadvantages of cumulative turnover taxes.[40] The first and third objectives are to be achieved by the adoption in all member countries of a value-added tax system roughly on the lines of the French one (though with many differences on points of detail); the second, by

[38]Cf. Shibata, "Tax Harmonisation in the European Free Trade Association", in Shoup (ed.), *op. cit.*, Vol. II, pp. 444-451.

[39]Of these, only the first is specifically referred to in the Rome Treaty. In general the tax clauses of the Treaty (Articles 95-99) left the matter of tax harmonisation wide open.

[40]These disadvantages primarily relate to the effect of cumulative taxes upon industrial structures and upon investment. See Shibata, *op. cit.*, pp. 447-449.

changing from the destination to the origin principle (again with the possible exception of tobacco, alcohol and so on). It is intended that the first step should be taken by January 1, 1970. The timing of the second step is as yet uncertain, because the EEC countries hold that a switch to the origin principle *de facto* requires at least a close approximation, if not complete equalisation, of the tax rate, a requirement which raises a number of far-reaching issues. It should be added that in West Germany the switch to a value-added tax has already taken place (on January 1, 1968) and that the French value-added tax has also been brought into line with the detailed tax specifications agreed with the other EEC members.

The EFTA position differs from that of the EEC in at least two important respects. (a) The indirect tax systems employed by the member countries at the time the Stockholm Convention was negotiated gave rise to far fewer difficulties in connection with the operation of the destination principle than was the case in the EEC. Only Austria used a cumulative multi-stage turnover tax. (b) Because of other features of the free trade scheme adopted, notably the absence of a common external tariff and the exclusion of agricultural goods, the possibility of doing away with customs posts *de facto* does not arise in the EFTA context. In consequence there has been little pressure for any major harmonisation measures concerning indirect taxation.[41] The Convention confines itself to requiring that border tax adjustments should not exceed the appropriate amounts (Article 6 and Article 13, together with Annex C) and in most member countries existing practices by and large appear to meet this requirement.

Two exceptions should nonetheless be noted. As mentioned earlier, Austria is the only EFTA country employing a cumulative turnover tax. Predictably this has led to doubts whether the border tax adjustments applied by the Austrian authorities always accord with the rules of the Convention. The Austrians have stated that they intend to go over to a value-added tax system before long, a move which in part reflects EFTA pressure, though other considerations were probably rather more decisive.

The other indirect tax harmonisation case to be mentioned concerns the British export rebate. Among the measures adopted by the new Labour Government in October, 1964, to bring about an improvement of Britain's balance of payments was the introduction

[41]For an account of the EFTA position see Shibata, *op. cit.*

137

of a scheme under which exporters would qualify for refunds of certain indirect taxes previously applied under the origin principle —purchase tax on stationery, taxes on fuel oil and on petrol and motor vehicle licence duties. These taxes are payable by manufacturers and traders and clearly add to their costs, though the extent to which the prices of particular export commodities are affected must in the last resort be a matter of conjecture. It is probably for that reason, and also because of administrative convenience and the relatively small quantitative significance of such taxes for final prices (the British rebate varied from about 1 to about 3 per cent), that countries have generally been content to apply the origin principle to such taxes. The UK's decision to pay a rebate on exports[42] therefore meant that British policy was at variance with practices in the other EFTA countries. Pressure was brought to bear on the British Government to withhold the rebate from exports to EFTA. After some negotiation a compromise was agreed. UK exporters to EFTA could not both claim EFTA treatment and qualify for the rebate. But the other EFTA members remained uneasy. The matter was finally settled when the UK Government decided in November, 1967, after the devaluation of the pound sterling, that the rebate be generally withdrawn.

In the light of the preceding discussion the question of harmonisation of indirect taxation in a NAFTA scheme can be dealt with quite shortly. Apart from Austria—where the position is in any case due to be changed—the NAFTA countries do not employ cumulative turnover taxes and are thus likely to avoid the difficulties which the EEC has encountered in connection with the application of the destination principle. Furthermore, as in EFTA pressure to remove tax frontiers will probably be weak. In these circumstances there would not appear to be any need for far-reaching harmonisation measures, provided that governments are content to accept continued distortions on the consumption side. Past experience suggests that this will be the case. The operation of the free trade area will probably reveal tax harmonisation problems in specific sectors. But their solution is not likely to raise major issues of budgetary and/or social policy.

---

[42]No attempt was made though to introduce the other part of the destination principle—a compensating import duty. Technically the rebate was therefore equivalent to a small and variable export subsidy.

(ii) *Direct Taxes*

As the earlier discussion implied, the quantitative significance of direct taxation on average exceeds that of indirect taxation. The question of the harmonisation of direct taxes is therefore an important one. Moreover, the rates of tax differ substantially between the countries in the Atlantic area, both in the case of the profits tax and in that of personal income tax. The information does not lend itself to being summarised in a few figures, because of the wide variety of assumptions that can be made about the nature of the source of profit (direct investment, investment in a subsidiary company, portfolio investment) and the personal circumstances and position on the income scale of the individual income recipient. The available figures are anyway frequently out of date. Even so, in the case of profits tax one may hazard the generalisation that in Belgium, Luxembourg, Italy and Sweden, effective tax rates are on the whole significantly lower than they are in West Germany, the UK, the USA and Canada, with France and the Netherlands occupying somewhat intermediate positions.[43]

The significance of differences in profits taxes for the working of a free trade area is a complex and in some ways a controversial subject. Here it will be dealt with in brief.[44] Three points require discussion: first, the effects of different profits taxes upon relative costs and prices; secondly, the effects upon investment and the growth of firms; and thirdly, the effects upon international migration of capital.

In terms of a simple example, the first point raises the following issue. Suppose that two countries intend to free mutual trade from all barriers and that the profits of corporate business in the first country, A, are taxed at 50 per cent, whereas profits earned in country B are taxed at only 25 per cent. Is the continued existence of different profits tax rates likely to result in trade between the two countries being distorted?

No simple answer is available. Neither economic theory nor statistical research supply any clear evidence about the relationship between profits taxes and prices. Traditional economic theory would suggest that taxes on profits do not affect prices—that is,

[43] Cf. Dosser, *op. cit.*, Appendix Table 8:2.

[44] For instance, any distinctions between different kinds of business taxes (corporation tax, profits tax, dividend tax) will be disregarded and so will distinctions between different kinds of investment (branch investment, investment in subsidiaries and so on). For a lengthy discussion of business tax harmonisation problems see Musgrave, *op. cit.*

139

that profits taxes are not "passed on" to consumers—but there is much doubt about the applicability of the theory. The results of empirical research—mainly in connection with conditions in the USA—are equally unsatisfactory, because the conclusions reached by different writers are sharply at variance with each other.[45]

The point at issue at this stage is the connection, if any, between profits taxes and prices. In order to show though that trade is distorted it would have to be established not only that there is a relationship between the level of profits taxes and prices, but also that this relationship is significantly different for the various internationally traded goods produced within any of the free trade countries; that is, that comparative costs are distorted. The preceding paragraph suggests that there is not much hope of reaching hard and fast conclusions in this matter.

A second way in which differences in profits taxes may disturb the working of the free trade scheme is through the effects of such taxes upon investment. Unless such taxes are wholly passed on to consumers they will bring about a reduction in the earnings of companies and thus in the amounts available for retention within the company sector or for dividend distribution. In consequence, the cost of funds to finance investment is likely to be raised and their availability diminished. If in the member countries of a free trade scheme rates of profits tax differ significantly, these consequences of business taxation would place producers in the high tax country in a relatively disadvantageous position. This is likely to be especially true of firms employing highly capital intensive processes[46] and during a time of rapid industrial change, such as the period of transition to free trade conditions.

At the same time one must beware of laying too much stress on the factors just mentioned. In the long run the incidence of the profits tax is not likely to be confined to the company sector and shareholders. It will probably extend to all the factors of production employed by the company sector. The tax will therefore at least partially fall on consumption. Also, the investment behaviour of business enterprises depends upon a host of influences and there

[45]Cf. Dosser, *op. cit.*, p. 225, and also R. J. Gordon, "The Incidence of the Corporation Income Tax in US Manufacturing, 1925-62", *American Economic Review*, American Economic Association, Menasha, Wisconsin, September, 1967.

[46]Cf. Bertil Ohlin, "Aspects of Policies for Freer Trade", in R. E. Baldwin, *et al.*, *Trade, Growth and the Balance of Payments: Essays in Honour of Gottfried Haberler* (North-Holland Publishing Company, Amsterdam, 1965), pp. 80-90.

may be considerable danger in concentrating attention on only one element—the rate of profits tax. Post-war experience would certainly not support any simple generalisations about relative levels of company taxation in different countries and relative volumes of investment undertaken in company sectors. The case for the harmonisation of direct business taxes to create "equal conditions" for industrial investment is consequently not as strong as may appear at first sight.

As the third point to be considered in the discussion of profits taxes there is the effect upon inter-country capital movements. Put in very general terms, the argument is that the attainment of maximum efficiency in the free trade area requires that gross (that is, before tax) returns to capital should be the same in the various countries, whereas the owners of capital will look at net returns (see Chapter 2, Pages 114-115). If capital can be freely transferred within the area, substantial divergencies in national rates of profits tax may induce capital movements which worsen, rather than improve, the international distribution of this factor of production. There would also very likely be indirect effects upon commodity trade. In such conditions some measure of policy harmonisation may be required.

The obvious form of such harmonisation would be an equalisation, or at least substantial approximation, of profits tax rates in the different countries. In practice this may be difficult to achieve, because of budgetary and other considerations. The free trade member countries may then fall back on an alternative approach to the problem—the provision of appropriate double tax arrangements. Such arrangements can be so designed as to remove at least a large part of the distorting effects of differential profits taxes upon capital flows, though in practice this is likely to remain a second best solution.[47]

Having briefly examined the effects of differences in direct business taxes upon the working of a free trade arrangement in general terms it is necessary to turn next to the relevant experience of the EEC and of EFTA.

There is not much to report. The EFTA Convention—which in any case provides only indirectly for some degree of freedom for capital transfers (see Page 115 above)—makes no explicit reference to direct taxes. Action among the member countries has been confined to an attempt, so far abortive, to arrive at a multilateral double

[47]Musgrave, *op. cit.*, pp. 311-314.

taxation agreement. The Rome Treaty refers to direct taxes only in connection with double taxation (Article 220), though the very general provisions concerning the "approximation of legal and administrative provisions which have a direct bearing upon the functioning of the common market" (Articles 100-102) are clearly relevant. The Neumark Report discussed the issue at some length and went on to propose a harmonisation of corporation tax rates in the six EEC countries (50 per cent on undistributed profits, 15-25 per cent on distributed profits). There has been much subsequent discussion among the six member countries and the Commission on this proposal and on various other aspects of national differences in profits taxes. So far very little has been seen by way of concrete action.

In the light of the general considerations outlined earlier it is unlikely that in an Atlantic-based free trade area the problem of divergent profits taxes can simply be disregarded. On the other hand, one may assume that at least to begin with the freeing of capital movements is not likely to be a primary aim of the proposed association. In any case, many, though not all, of the prospective member countries are already linked by bilateral double tax conventions. Initially, NAFTA might well concentrate on urging the completion of the network of such agreements, and, possibly more importantly, on pressing for modifications of agreements which permit or perhaps even encourage distorted capital flows. Only practical experience could tell whether further harmonisation measures would be required.

The problem of personal income taxes can be covered speedily. International differences in personal income tax rates are not likely to affect trade in any obvious manner. The only matter of concern is the effect upon labour migration. This is a very complex issue. Decisions to move between countries are presumably influenced by comparisons not only of the burdens of taxation, but also of the level of benefits obtained as a result of government expenditure. In other words, the critical factor is the difference, between one country and the next, in the excess of taxation over benefits (or *vice versa*). How far such differences exist, and what influence they have on labour mobility, is plainly very difficult to say. In general, though, they are not likely to be important. The matter appears to have received little attention in the EEC, partly no doubt because the Neumark Report did not attach much significance to it, and none in EFTA. It is unlikely to become a serious issue in NAFTA.

2. *Other Charges*

Having considered the question of taxation in some detail, the problems raised by other charges can be dealt with much more quickly, because the approach to the issues raised by the existence of such charges will in principle be the same as that adopted over tax matters. All that need be done is to indicate where the question is likely to arise and what kind of solution seems appropriate.

(i) *Social Security*

As the information provided by Professor Douglas Dosser,[48] of York University, shows, there are substantial differences between the NAFTA countries in national social security contributions payable by employers. However, such contributions are usually at uniform rates *within* any one country. In addition, it is generally argued that they should properly be regarded as a part of the wage bill, withheld from wage earners to provide benefits to labour in an alternative form. In other words, employers' contributions and direct wage payments are considered to be alternative forms of payments to labour.[49] In the general case, therefore, a proposal to even out differences in employers' social security contributions in a free trade area comes to much the same thing as the suggestion that free trade cannot function if there are substantial differences in money wages—a question which was discussed in Chapter 2. Social security contributions paid by employees are even less likely to affect comparative costs.

If free mobility of labour is part of a free trade scheme the matter is less straightforward, partly on analogy with differences in personal incomes taxes (see above), but particularly because social security contributions are, at least nominally, payments into an insurance fund. The question arises how far benefits are transferable between countries. This issue has been important in the EEC, because of the Community's aim to establish a free Community labour market. But it has naturally not been encountered in EFTA and is not likely to be in a NAFTA scheme.

[48]Dosser, *op. cit.*, Appendix Table 8:9.
[49]*Ibid.*, pp. 238-239, and N. Andel, "Problems of Harmonisation of Social Security Policies in a Common Market", in Shoup (ed.), *op. cit.*, Vol. I, pp. 354-355.

(ii) *External tariffs*

National tariffs are usually far from uniform. Moreover, if the tariff schedules of any group of countries which are not members of a free trade scheme are compared, it will certainly be found that the extent to which the tariff rates for particular goods diverge from the average for each country will differ from country to country. In so far as imported supplies are used as inputs by domestic industry, this variability of tariff rates therefore represents another instance of differential charges.

The issue is an important one, not least because the policy adopted to deal with it has commonly been taken to constitute the dividing line between alternative approaches to free trade. A customs union, like the EEC tackles the problem by the adoption of a common external tariff. Rates of duty for individual goods will become the same for all member countries. A free trade area, like EFTA, permits the partner countries to retain their national tariffs, but attempts to prevent the occurrence of serious distortions by excluding from the free trade scheme commodities with a high content of imports from third countries. It is thus necessary for the member countries to agree on a set of rules—commonly known as the origin rules—to determine whether or not particular commodities qualify for free importation into other partner countries.

As the experiences of Benelux, the EEC and EFTA have shown, the negotiation of a common external tariff and the drawing up of a set of workable and not unduly restrictive origin rules can both raise some serious and difficult issues. At this juncture, however, attention will be confined to a brief account of EFTA's origin rules—which are clearly particularly relevant in the present context because the Atlantic countries are assumed to opt for an arrangement of the free trade area kind.

According to Article 4 of the EFTA Convention, a commodity sold by one member country to another member country will qualify for "area treatment" (that is, be traded free of duties and so on) if it meets *any one* of three conditions:

(a) that is has been wholly produced within EFTA,
(b) that it has been produced by one of a number of stated processes (no matter what the origin of the inputs may be), and
(c) that the value of inputs imported from third countries does not exceed 50 per cent of the export price.

144

Moreover, a Basic Materials List contains a number of materials which are deemed to originate within the area whether or not this is in fact the case and which therefore do not enter into any calculations of non-EFTA import content.

It may be noted that these rules do not refer to the tariffs which member countries may impose on third country imports, despite the fact that the whole problem arises because of different national trade barriers. This omission is in part rectified in Article 5, which deals with the difficulties—"trade deflections"—which an industry in a member country may encounter because its rival in another EFTA country benefits from particularly low duties on non-EFTA inputs. The Article establishes a procedure for dealing with particularly urgent cases of trade deflection, but otherwise simply provides for the problem to be reviewed in the light of experience. The indications are that no serious difficulties have in fact arisen and that in consequence there is no need for any general amendment of the origin rules.

On the basis of EFTA's experience it appears that a similar set of rules may well be an appropriate starting point for NAFTA. It has been suggested though that the provisions could be further simplified by stipulating that where the national tariffs of member countries differ by less than a stated margin, the goods in question be deemed to originate within the area, analogous to the commodities contained in EFTA's Basic Materials List.[50] This proposal appears to constitute a useful addendum to rules of the EFTA kind. In the case of certain commodities, though, different national procedures in the matter of classification and valuation for customs purposes may raise some practical difficulties.

Because of different characteristics of the national tariff structures of the prospective NAFTA countries some further adaptation of EFTA's origin rules may well turn out to be necessary. In one way NAFTA's problems should be simpler than those faced by EFTA. Provided that the free trade arrangement comprises the two North American countries and at least the major part of EFTA, the proportion of imports from other partner countries will generally be higher than was the case when EFTA was created and the significance of different national tariff barriers towards third countries will therefore generally be less.[51] This does not mean that origin rules

---

[50] *A Possible Plan for a Canada-US Free Trade Area, op. cit.*, p. 24.
[51] The important exception is the USA.

can be dispensed with. But the sectors for which different national tariffs on non-NAFTA imports could be important would be fewer in number and the drawing-up of appropriate rules correspondingly less difficult.

(C) OTHER INSTITUTIONAL AND ADMINISTRATIVE FACTORS

Having dealt with practices similar in their effects to tariffs and with differential charges, it is necessary to discuss structural harmonisation issues which cannot very readily be considered under these two headings. Not surprisingly there are here a rather heterogeneous collection of questions. Among the problems that should be discussed are anti-monopoly policies, transport, regional policies, establishment rights, "technical barriers" (largely the question of standards), policies towards natural resources and public investment. It would take far too long to examine all these issues in detail. Attention will be focussed on the first three.

1. *Anti-Monopoly Policies*

The economist's arguments demonstrating the benefits resulting from free trade usually assume that markets are competitive. That this assumption must in practice be heavily qualified can be demonstrated by reference to conditions in many countries.[52] On the one hand, there have been numerous examples of agreements between firms serving in one way or another to diminish competition and thus to prevent or at least to retard the progress of more efficient enterprises. On the other hand there have been the cases of single firms which, having attained a strong monopoly position, pursue policies designed to keep out potential rivals in order to protect their monopoly profits.

The effects of such actions on the part of business enterprises are very unlikely to be purely domestic in character. In any event, one of the chief aims is frequently to reduce the impact of competition from imported supplies and/or on export markets. Indeed, the conclusion of agreements with enterprises in other countries is in many cases an important part of the restrictive arrangements.

[52]Cf. D. Swann, "Cartels and Concentrations: Issues and Policy", in G. R. Denton (ed.), *Economic Integration in Europe* (Weidenfeld & Nicolson, London, 1969), pp. 172-177. Restrictive practices which directly affect international trade are discussed, with special reference to the EEC, in D. L. McLachlan and Swann, *Competition Policy in the European Community* (Oxford University Press, London, 1967), Ch. 6.

It is clear that monopolistic practices in general, and those affecting international trade in particular, can frustrate the working of a free trade scheme in an important way. If the abolition of trade barriers is to lead to a redistribution of resources within the member nations, the more efficient producers must, in one way or another, exploit their superior position and expand at the expense of less efficient firms elsewhere. But agreements between firms, especially perhaps with those in other countries, may retard or even prevent this process. Again, single firm monopolies may use the large profits earned on their "safe" lines or markets to maintain their positions with respect to products or markets in which they face strong competition from more efficient producers in other countries.

In these rather general, qualitative terms the problem can thus be set out relatively easily and, as already indicated, it is not difficult to find examples cited in the literature. It is quite another matter, though, to attempt to assess the quantitative significance of restrictive practices in relation to that of tariffs and of other trade barriers. The question is clearly a very important one for countries forming free trade schemes, but unfortunately there is no answer. The multitude of examples tends to convey the impression that the issue is indeed of great significance. On the other side of the argument one may refer to the obvious point that the abolition of trade barriers should in itself serve to increase competition. Moreover, in the post-war period anti-monopoly laws have been passed in many countries. The problem, then, should have gradually become less serious, although it must be remembered that restrictive practices involving transactions with other countries have generally been looked upon rather more kindly by legislators than have those affecting primarily domestic markets.

So far this discussion has mainly been concerned with the possibility that monopolies and restrictive practices may seriously impede the operation of a free trade scheme. The matter is further complicated by the argument that inter-firm agreements, and perhaps particularly monopolies, may confer benefits (primarily through lower costs) which outweigh the disadvantages. National legislators are familiar with the issue, but its significance is clearly not confined to the domestic economy.

The authors of the Rome Treaty undoubtedly thought the problem of restrictive business practices an important one and so included a number of provisions (Articles 85-90) designed to ensure that the Community would be reasonably competitive. Progress towards the implementation of these provisions has, however, been only slow. Initially, after introducing a notification system for restrictive practices, the EEC Commission devoted most of its attention to vertical agreements (agreements between a producer and his suppliers and/or his customers), particularly those providing for exclusive distribution channels. More recently there has also been some action concerning horizontal cartel arrangements—those between producers of the same commodity. Much thought has been given to the way in which agreements and particularly mergers may lead to greater efficiency. There is hope that changes in national company and tax laws may be brought about so as to encourage the formation of "European companies". These developments cannot hide the fact all the same that the general impact of the Community's provisions has so far remained pretty slight.

The EFTA Convention (Article 15) similarly recognises that restrictive practices may interfere with the working of the free trade area. In the crucial matter of implementation the authors of the Stockholm Convention were rather more hesitant than those of the Rome Treaty. They provided for complaints to be addressed to the EFTA Council, which would then attempt to find a solution, and, more significantly, for a review and possible strengthening of Article 15 in the light of experience. For various reasons (of which the absence of restrictive practices is not likely to be one) such complaints have not been forthcoming, with the result that the Association has had no material to work on. It is consequently suggested that if the EFTA governments wish to see Article 15 put into operation, they will have to take the initiative and institute enquiries concerning restrictive practices (one of the possible ways of strengthening Article 15 provided for in the Convention), instead of waiting for complaints to be made. So far they have preferred to remain inactive.

Despite the difficulties of assessing the relative importance and the net effects of restrictive practices it is unlikely that the founders of NAFTA could simply overlook the problem. Something on the lines of Article 15 of the EFTA Convention would appear to be required. The experience of EFTA suggests, however, that a complaints procedure is not sufficient and that some definite provision for enquiry by the NAFTA authorities should be made. If these enquiries reveal the existence of practices which *prima facie* have an adverse effect on trade in the Association, the member countries will have to decide how to consider such cases in detail. In view of the complexities of the issues involved, and the conflicting arguments of efficiency and equity, this is not likely to be an easy problem. The institution of legal proceedings against offending businesses would clearly have to be left with the member governments (this is also the procedure in EFTA). In some countries amendments of national anti-trust laws may be required.[53]

2. Transport

The carriage of commodities within a common market raises structural harmonisation issues for at least two (related) reasons.

In the first place, transport charges clearly affect delivery prices and hence relative prices received by producers and/or paid by consumers. As the determination of relative prices is of crucial significance for the attainment of the efficiency gains of a free trade scheme (see Pages 109-112 above), it is important that transport charges should not be such as to distort the price structure. This means, in general terms, that freight rates should reflect costs of carriage (admittedly a very elusive concept). Among the reasons why freight charges may fail to meet this requirement and may thus have a distorting effect, two stand out as probably the most important:

(a) The pursuit of pricing policies by government-owned carriers, chiefly the railways, which have the object of deliberately discriminating among products and among customers; and

(b) The widespread practice of transport undertakings to base their rates on "what the traffic will bear"; that is, on the competitive position of the carrier in particular markets.

The second way in which harmonisation issues may be encountered in connection with transport arises as a result of the possibility that the free trade scheme is extended to the provision of transport services. This would mean the establishment of a free market for the commodity "transport", so that the carriers of country A would have free access to the transport market in B and *vice versa*. As all governments interfere in the working of the transport

[53]An alternative—and perhaps preferable—approach to the problem of restrictive practices in a NAFTA arrangement would be for the member countries to change their domestic laws so that trade within the association comes to be treated on the same basis as domestic trade. The question of investigating specific cases would then be left to national institutions. Some co-ordination of the way in which they approach their task would probably be required.

industry, though in very different ways and to different degrees, such a proposal would be virtually impossible to implement unless government regulations were at least in large part equalised.

The quantitative significance of the first of these two points will clearly vary with the characteristics of individual goods. In the case of commodities with a relatively low ratio of value to volume and/or weight (typically, coal or sand and gravel) freight charges, and therefore distorting elements in freight rates, will be far more important than they are in the case of commodities with a relatively high ratio of value to volume or weight. The issue of transport rates has accordingly been a particularly important one in the ECSC.[54] The goods for which that Community created a common market—namely coal, iron ore, scrap and steel—are all of a relatively bulky nature. Even in the ECSC, however, the quantitative significance of distortions in delivery prices due to distorted transport rates has rarely exceeded a figure which, by comparison with average tariff levels, one would regard as fairly moderate. This does not mean that the ECSC was wrong in paying so much attention to transport, but rather that, for commodities in general, the issue is probably of secondary importance.

The harmonisation of transport rates and conditions has nonetheless been a major problem in the EEC. In part this simply reflects the fact that the ECSC had unearthed a great many distorting features in transport conditions, features which an organisation like the EEC was unlikely to overlook even if their importance for relative goods prices might sometimes be small. Some progress in the removal of discriminatory railway charges has been achieved. Much the most important reason though for the EEC's concern about transport has been the Community's aim to establish a common transport market; that is, to extend free trade to the carriers themselves. In consequence the Six have become involved in some very difficult issues. Despite repeated attempts by the Commission to find solutions, progress towards the goal of freeing transport markets has been very slow.[55]

In sharp contrast to the experience of the EEC, transport has not been an issue in EFTA. The Convention does not explicitly refer to transport (though distorting transport charges could be said to be

[54]Cf. Meade, Liesner and Wells, *op. cit.*, Study III, Ch. 5.
[55]Cf. Liesner, "Policy Harmonisation in the EEC and EFTA", in Denton (ed.), *op. cit.*, pp. 320-323.

indirectly prohibited by the terms of Articles 14 and 15). No harmonisation problems have been reported. These facts first and foremost reflect the deliberate exclusion of transport services, together with services generally, from the free trade provisions. The second group of harmonisation issues distinguished at the beginning of the section was therefore side-stepped. Other reasons have probably been the geographical position of the EFTA countries (much of the traffic goes by sea, with perhaps a relatively undistorted pattern of rates, and another significant portion has to be carried through third countries, whose charges the Association would hardly be able to control) and the fact that bulky commodities, with the possible exception of steel, were not likely to figure very prominently among the goods traded between the EFTA countries.

EFTA's experience suggests that with respect to transport no elaborate harmonisation provisions are called for in a NAFTA arrangement. Even so, it is unlikely that the issue can be avoided entirely. To begin with, studies of the implications of a USA-Canada free trade area have drawn attention to the existence of various distorting conditions, such as discriminatory freight charges for bulky commodities, double taxation of vehicles crossing international borders and heavy subsidisation of rail transport in Canada.[56] Secondly, trade in bulky commodities, and particularly in coal, may potentially be of greater importance than it has been in EFTA, with the result that both international and internal freight charges for such commodities may require inspection. It has also been suggested that geographical distances in NAFTA are much greater than they are in EFTA and that this increases the significance of transport charges and therefore of possible distorting elements. Whether the last point really amounts to very much is a matter of considerable doubt, in view of such data on international transport rates as are readily available.[57]

One specific issue which has been raised is the policy on ocean freight rates pursued by the Atlantic Shipping Conference, an organisation of shipowners agreeing charges for liner freight transport across the Atlantic. Rates for freight carriage to North America are generally significantly lower than those from North America, a fact

[56]Cf. *A Possible Plan for a Canada-US Free Trade Area, op. cit.*, p. 36, and J. M. Munro, *Trade Liberalisation and Transportation in International Trade* (Private Planning Association, University of Toronto Press, Toronto, 1969).

[57]Cf. C. P. Kindleberger, *Foreign Trade and the National Economy* (Yale University Press, New Haven and London, 1962), pp. 12-15.

which has given rise to complaints that US exports are being discriminated against.

In the case of transport, as in many others, NAFTA might best
approach the problem of harmonisation on the basis of a *de minimis*
understanding. The member countries would then avoid becoming
involved in disputes on what are in fact very minor issues (though in
many cases even the collection and assessment of the necessary facts
is likely to be a complicated matter). Of major issues there may well
be relatively few, but these may not be easy to solve.

3. *Regional Policy*

Since the last war governments have paid much attention to the
problem of disparities in income levels between different parts of
their countries. They have adopted a wide range of measures to aid
the development or rehabilitation of relatively poor regions. The
question arises whether policies aiming to reduce regional disparities
—"regional policies"—are compatible with the attainment of the
aims of free trade schemes and if not what changes in national
policies appear most appropriate.[58]

A brief account of the kind of regional policy measures governments have tended to adopt may be useful. In most countries the
emphasis has been placed on achieving a better regional balance of
industry. This in turn can be brought about both by "negative"
actions (measures which prevent producers from settling or expanding in high income areas) and by "positive" actions (measures which
attract producers to low income areas). By and large the latter have
been favoured relative to the former. The chief tools have been
government help to private industry—through grants, loans and
preferential tax treatment—and the provision of government
finance to help the development of the infrastructure—the building
of roads, schools, power stations and so on.

It is clear that in some ways such measures constitute, within a
country, the opposite of policy harmonisation—what has been called
a planned differentiation of policy.[59] It does not follow that regional
policies are necessarily undesirable from an economic point of view.
Indeed, strong arguments can be advanced that in many cases the
country as a whole will benefit economically from a preferential

[58]For detailed discussions of the problem see R. M. Bird, "Regional Policies in a
Common Market", in Shoup (ed.), *op. cit.*, Vol. I, and Gavin McCrone, "Regional
Policy in the European Communities", in Denton (ed.), *op. cit.*, pp. 194-219.

treatment of economic activity located in certain regions, though the possibility that an overall loss will be incurred should not be overlooked.

In what way is the situation altered by the country's participation in a free trade scheme? The fact that regional policies constitute government interference in the market suggests that conflict with the aims of free trade may well arise, especially as the reasons for the adoption of regional aid measures are generally not purely economic. But the free trade argument cannot be assumed to be the over-riding one, just as it is not within the country. The main task of policy harmonisation is therefore to ensure that national measures are such as to affect trade with other countries relatively little.

This requirement raises some formidable practical issues which cannot be discussed at the present juncture. One basic, though simple, point may briefly be made.

Although it may sometimes be difficult to do so in practice, a distinction should be drawn between regional policy measures which distort the structure of comparative costs of existing or potential industries in a development region as compared with comparative costs in the rest of the country (and in the remainder of the free trade area) and those which do not. A rather extreme example of the first kind of policy would be a production subsidy to a specific manufacturer in a development area. On the other hand, general assistance to a region, particularly perhaps in the form of infrastructure investment, would probably have little if any effect on the comparative cost position and thus provide an example of measures of the second kind. Although the case of regional policy is not quite analogous, the earlier discussion of comparative costs (Chapter 2 above) would suggest that as far as the functioning of free trade schemes is concerned the first group of measures is far more likely to have adverse effects than the second group. The case for policy harmonisation is consequently far stronger in the first case than it is in the second. Fortunately the fact that discrimination in favour of producers in poor parts of the country will tend to tell against other producers in the same country as well as those of the other free trade partners is likely to push governments into non-distorting forms of assistance, although it is not difficult to think of exceptions.

Two further points should be made before considering how the

[59] Cf. Ohlin, *op. cit.*, p. 90.

EEC and EFTA have tackled this problem. In the first place, only the way in which regional policy measures may affect trade between countries has been examined. No mention has been made of the consequences for movements of factors of production, especially of capital. These consequences may be quite important. But as free factor mobility is not likely to be a primary aim of the formation of NAFTA they will be disregarded in the present context.

Secondly, it has been suggested that the creation of free trade conditions may in itself serve to accentuate national problems of regional imbalance. The likely result of free trade is that industries which even before the removal of trade barriers found it difficult to keep going will decline further and that "prosperous" industries will be further stimulated. In so far as there are regional differences in the locations of these industries, disparities in income levels between different parts of the country may widen. The problem of ensuring that national policy measures do not interfere in any serious way with the operation of free trade schemes may thus be rendered more urgent by the effects which free trade itself brings about.

It is clear that this is not a conclusive argument. The consequences of the freeing of trade upon different industries could be such as to help even out regional imbalances. Experience in Western Europe, however, appears on the whole to support the pessimists.

The EEC tackles the problem of regional policies in two distinct ways. First, the Rome Treaty recognises that regional assistance may be compatible with the aims of the common market, but it provides for the examination and possible rejection of specific measures which the member countries may have introduced in the past or wish to introduce. Secondly, the authors of the Treaty thought it important that the Community as a whole should help to even out regional disparities. Two of the financial institutions established by the Treaty—the European Social Fund and the European Investment Bank—may *inter alia* provide assistance to poor regions, the former by aiding schemes to encourage labour mobility, the latter by helping to finance development projects.

The implementation of the Treaty has been very slow. It is true that both the European Social Fund and the European Investment Bank have made grants and loans. But the far more difficult part of the Community's policy—the examination and co-ordination of the policies pursued by the member states—has progressed very little beyond the carrying out of detailed studies. Furthermore, prospects for more rapid advance in the near future are not good. Indeed, some observers speak of a process of competitive escalation of regional policy in the Six, particularly with regard to the attractions offered to US capital investment.

The EFTA Convention refers to regional problems in explicit terms only in connection with difficulties of adjustment to free trade conditions (Article 20). As general government aids are prohibited by the terms of Article 13, it thus appears at first sight that the freedom of action of governments in the matter of regional policy is strictly limited. For reasons which are not entirely clear it has so far been accepted nonetheless that the prohibition clause does not extend to regional policies.

The upshot is that the situation is somewhat indeterminate. It is likely to remain that way until the pressure of events forces the member governments to define the limits of national action rather more precisely. A particular case—the British Government's proposal to assist in the erection of aluminium smelter plants in development areas—is at present under review. Casual examination suggests that this is very much an instance of help to a particular industry (see Page 153 above), so that the issue of compatibility with free trade conditions is likely to arise in a pretty acute form.

It is clear that in a NAFTA scheme member governments must be allowed to pursue regional development policies. The means they employ should, however, be such that no obvious and direct distortion of comparative costs is created. Appropriate provision should perhaps be included in the agreement establishing the free trade scheme.

CONCLUSION

A number of structural policy harmonisation issues which may arise if a NAFTA scheme were established have now been examined. In view of the wide variety of problems discussed it is rather difficult to draw up an adequate set of conclusions. But the following four points might usefully be made:

(1) The NAFTA countries cannot avoid the issue of structural policy harmonisation. Given the complexities of the modern economy and, in particular, the many ways in which governments intervene in the market, an effective freeing of trade among the Atlantic countries would require a good deal more than a mere

abolition of tariffs. It follows that the agreement that would establish NAFTA should contain the ground rules for "fair competition" among the member countries, as does the EFTA Convention. In view of the somewhat mixed record of EFTA in the matter of policy harmonisation one cannot, of course, be certain that a free trade area treaty will always prove an efficient instrument for tackling harmonisation issues. On the other hand, the general circumstances in which EFTA has operated have hardly been conducive to a speedy solution of the problems encountered. In any case, EFTA has certainly been more successful in this field than has the GATT.

(2) Whilst the ground rules for structural harmonisation would probably have to be included in the treaty, there appears to be little case for laying down elaborate and detailed harmonisation provisions. The drawing up of such clauses is not likely to be at all easy, and experience may show that the real difficulties arise elsewhere. Rather, what is required is readiness on the part of the member governments to partake in a continuing process of jointly identifying harmonisation issues and to make adjustments in national policies when the need arises.

(3) It is unlikely that it would be possible or even advisable for NAFTA to strive for perfectionism in this complex field. An attitude of "give and take" would seem far more appropriate. Moreover, the adoption of a *de minimis* clause, by analogy with that implied in origin rules, may be helpful, though any formal proposition to that effect would probably be impossible to agree.

(4) A special difficulty which the NAFTA countries will face relates to the federal character of the constitutions of two important members—Canada and the USA. Although for reasons of space the point has not on the whole been explicitly raised in the course of this chapter, many of the harmonisation issues discussed touch on policies pursued at the provincial/state government level. The central authorities may simply lack the power to bring about the appropriate changes at the lower levels of administration. This factor alone would probably make it impossible for NAFTA to adopt an approach to harmonisation similar to that suggested in the Rome Treaty, quite apart from other objections.

4 BALANCE OF PAYMENTS POLICY HARMONISATION

As was stated at the outset, the formation of a free trade scheme raises not only issues concerned with long-run efficiency—the kind of problems we have discussed in Chapter 3—but also the question of short-run balance of payments stability. More specifically, the problem arises how far the member countries of the free trade arrangement can retain their ability to achieve balance of payments stability whilst pursuing their own national targets with regard to the overall employment level, the degree of price stability and the rate of economic growth and how far they can continue to enjoy command over the various tools which may be employed to achieve these ends.

For two reasons the examination of balance of payments policy harmonisation will occupy very much less space than did that of structural harmonisation questions. First, the issues involved, though often very complex, are less diverse and sometimes perhaps also more familiar. Secondly, when it comes to the application of the analysis, not a great deal of material is available, confining discussion to setting out the basic principles. At the same time it should be stressed that the brevity of treatment must not be taken to indicate that the question of balance of payments policy harmonisation is of relatively little importance. On the contrary, as the concluding remarks will indicate, the issues involved in the present discussion may well have a greater significance for real incomes in the member countries of a free trade scheme than those raised by structural policy harmonisation.

The first point to note is that in the general case the aim of balance of payments policy is not affected by a country's participation in a free trade scheme. In a world in which the main currencies are freely convertible no special significance attaches to the bilateral payments position of a free trade country *vis-à-vis* its partners. The goal continues to be equilibrium in the overall balance of payments.

At the same time, it is plain that the formation of free trade groupings may well give rise to balance of payments disequilibria. Before the abolition of trade barriers the degree to which the prospective partners restrict imports is likely to differ. Moreover, effects upon trade with third countries will hardly be uniform. Again, structural harmonisation measures may have important balance of payments consequences, as can be illustrated in connection with Britain's adoption of the EEC common agricultural policy should she join the Community. It is clearly very improbable that these and other forces will cancel each other out, with the result that payments imbalances are likely to appear as a free trade scheme is being implemented.[60] In addition, it must be borne in mind that membership of a free trade scheme increases the sensitiveness of the balance of payments to changes in internal economic activity and in relative price levels.

In order to examine in what way, and to what extent, the formation of a free trade scheme affects the means at the disposal of the member countries to attain the goal of balance of payments stability it is necessary first briefly to review the main tools available to a country not committed to free trade. Here three types of measure may be broadly distinguished.

First, governments may preserve equilibrium in the balance of payments by appropriate adjustments of trade controls like tariffs and quantitative restrictions, or of controls over other items in the balance of payments, principally capital movements.

Secondly, governments may seek to tackle balance of payments disequilibria in a more indirect fashion by adjusting the level of domestic costs and prices through varying the level of economic activity. Two broad sets of measures—monetary policy (variations in interest rates and in the supply of credit) and fiscal policy (adjustments in government expenditure and taxation) are commonly employed for this purpose. It is important to remember though that monetary policy may also have a direct effect on the balance of payments by influencing the direction and size of capital flows, especially those of a short-term character.

Finally, a government may tackle a balance of payments disequilibrium by an adjustment of the country's exchange rate. This could take the form of moving the rate from one fixed level to another (as happened in the case of the devaluation of the pound sterling in November, 1967, or that of the appreciation of the West

[60]Stamp and Cowie, op. cit., p. 46, indicated that membership of NAFTA may raise Britain's receipts from exports considerably more than her expenditures on imports.

158

German currency in March, 1961). Alternatively, the authorities could allow the currency to "float"; that is, leave the rate to be determined by demand and supply in the foreign exchange market.[61]

It is important to note that in general the tools described not only act upon the balance of payments, but they also have domestic effects. These are not necessarily compatible with the country's domestic policy targets. Much the most important point that arises in this context relates to the adjustment of domestic costs and prices through variations in economic activity, particularly in cases of balance of payments deficit. A deficit country seeking to reduce its price level relative to that of others in order to improve its balance of payments is likely to find that the process is a very slow one and that the loss of potential output and employment is considerable. For surplus countries the speed of adjustment is less of a problem. Such countries will probably be reluctant to see price stability endangered, but on balance their difficulties appear more manageable.

Because of the disadvantages of using internal deflation as a balance of payments stabilisation device deficit countries may attempt to resort to an additional tool: an incomes and prices policy; that is, the institution of a measure of control over important determinants of costs and prices. Thus, in a period of balance of payments strain the authorities would try to keep increases in incomes and prices below those in other countries in order to improve the relative competitive position of the country and therefore the balance of payments.

The post-war period has seen many examples of conflicts between internal and external stability. This difficulty, however, has by no means been the only constraint on the use of balance of payments correctives. In the case of trade controls, for instance, developed

[61]Several other forms of exchange rate flexibility could be added to this list. For instance, the government could cease to fix the parity but still intervene in the foreign exchange market (possibly in collaboration with other governments) to prevent undue exchange instability. Exchange rates could be permitted to fluctuate within a given range—say, 10 per cent—of the parity. Or the authorities could opt for a "sliding parity" (or "crawling peg"): the exchange rate could be moved in the desired direction by a continuing process of small adjustments, until balance of payments equilibrium was restored. (Cf. Meade, "Exchange-Rate Flexibility", *Three Banks Review*, Manchester, June, 1966). Each of these methods raises its own problems in the context of balance of payments policy harmonisation, but these cannot be explored at the present juncture.

countries have increasingly moved away from the early post-war policy (enshrined in the instrument governing world commercial policy, the GATT) of resorting to quantitative restrictions in order to rectify balance of payments deficits. International criticism of the UK Government in connection with the import surcharge, imposed in October, 1964, to help remove the large payments gap, showed very clearly that countries have almost reached the position of regarding trade barriers as unalterable in an upward direction. In other words, since the early post-war years there has been a significant degree of harmonisation of trade policies. Variations in other payments controls (for instance, those on capital movements) have remained more acceptable, though on balance there has undoubtedly been a substantial degree of liberalisation.

Exchange rate changes have also been rare, largely because of the nature of the international monetary system that has evolved. Post-war governments have regarded them as measures of last resort and not as normally available tools. Resistance to the use of floating exchange rates has been very strong. Few governments appear even to have given serious consideration to the possibility of setting rates free. The Canadian dollar was allowed to float during the 1950's, but this is the only instance of an important currency not being fixed. Adherence to fixed exchange rates has meant that countries have been forced to adopt policies keeping relative costs and prices reasonably closely in line with one another.

The post-war world has witnessed a far-reaching liberalisation of international capital movements, with the result that the efficacy of monetary measures in inducing flows of capital to deficit countries has greatly increased. Lack of confidence in the ability of governments to maintain existing parities has meant though that as a balance of payments stabilising device monetary policy has tended to be least effective when it was most needed—in cases of serious and lasting balance of payments disequilibria, such as that experienced by the UK since 1964.

Moreover, the rapid response of short-term capital flows to interest differentials has created considerable problems for governments attempting to use monetary policy for the control of domestic activity. Many countries, particularly perhaps those with federal constitutions, traditionally place much reliance on monetary policy for internal stabilisation purposes and they have often been unable (or unwilling) to forgo the use of monetary measures even though this conflicted with balance of payments stability. For instance, countries with excess domestic demand have often resorted to high interest rates in order to dampen inflationary pressure, but these then served to attract large inflows of capital and to produce substantial payments surpluses—and *ipso facto* deficits for other countries.

The upshot is that even without a commitment to free trade, countries have lost a great deal of their freedom of action over balance of payments and domestic policies. Much policy harmonisation has already taken place. In recognition of this fact the major Western countries periodically review and confront their internal and external policies through the OECD and other international organisations.

In what way does membership of a free trade scheme alter the situation? At first blush one may be tempted to pick on policy with regard to trade controls as an instance of an important difference, drawing a sharp distinction between the policy of the non-member country, able to resort to trade controls, and the free trade country, which cannot do so. This approach is subject to important qualifications. As was pointed out earlier, developed countries are *de facto* severely constrained in their use of trade controls. In addition, the instruments establishing free trade schemes generally include an escape clause permitting temporary resort to quantitative restrictions in the case of balance of payments deficits, with the result that the *de jure* position of the free trade country is not as different from that of the non-member country as might be thought.

The use of other balance of payments controls, especially those relating to capital transfers, has remained rather more acceptable, as was pointed out earlier. If the free trade scheme extends to capital transfers, member countries will lose their ability to apply control measures, though escape clauses may again be provided. In principle free trade countries could, of course, confine their balance of payments control measures to transactions with third countries. But various institutional and practical factors raise a number of awkward problems.

On balance it seems fair to conclude that membership of free trade schemes makes it more difficult for the countries concerned to rely on controls over trade and payments and that greater weight must be put on the remaining tools.

As regards exchange rate policy, a strong case can be made for the proposition that free trade schemes should not include the unalterability of exchange rates among any balance of payments harmonisation policies and that, on the contrary, member countries should largely rely on the exchange rate mechanism for overcoming balance of payments disequilibria. The arguments behind this proposition are (a) that as already mentioned free trade will further reduce countries' ability to resort to trade controls; (b) that countries may also lose some of their freedom of action with regard to fiscal policies (a point to be discussed shortly); and (c) that reliance on "internal adjustments" may in any case interfere with the attainment of other policy objectives. For at least two reasons it can also be argued that use of the exchange rate mechanism should take the form of adopting floating exchange rates. Various difficulties arise in connection with adjustments of exchange rates from one fixed level to another. Secondly, the potency of monetary policy (over which free trade countries are less likely to lose command) for internal stabilisation purposes is greatly enhanced when exchange rates are free.

The counter arguments tend to fasten on the fact that exchange rate changes in turn raise many problems. More important in the present context is the point that free trade supposedly removes many of the differences between domestic and international trade, yet *within* countries exchange rates are always fixed. The short answer to this is that within a country automatic forces of adjustment are much stronger than they are between countries. Furthermore, national governments have at their disposal a variety of instruments to solve balance of payments disequilibria between regions, instruments which free trade countries are reluctant to cede to a supranational authority just because they do not wish to accept the far-reaching degree of policy harmonisation that would be implied.

So far governments have shown little willingness to accept the free exchange rate argument. It is true that both in EFTA and in the EEC exchange rate changes have taken place. But this does not signify any real shift in official positions.

If free trade countries retain their preference for fixed exchange rates they will be forced to rely on monetary, fiscal and incomes policies. Free trade may imply though that these instruments, too, become subject to additional constraints. This is perhaps particularly obvious in the case of fiscal policy. As was pointed out at an earlier stage (see Pages 129-143), there may be a need for some harmonisation of national taxes and thus a corresponding diminution in countries' freedom to adopt independent fiscal measures. In a free trade area kind of arrangement, however, this process is not likely to be taken very far.

Constraints on incomes policies stem from the greater mobility of labour which may accompany the creation of the free trade scheme and from a tendency of national wage bargains to become more closely aligned, though both these factors are much less likely to be significant in a loose free trade grouping than in an economic union. Much more important, incomes policies have not so far been very successful, largely due to problems of implementation.

On the other hand, unless restrictions on capital flows increase, the efficacy of monetary policy in stimulating equilibrating capital transfers should be unimpaired and quite possibly enhanced. Additionally, the existence of close economic links among the member countries is likely to encourage governments and/or central banks to pursue policies of mutual assistance by means of large-scale loans.[62] The correction of temporary balance of payments disequilibria may therefore be accomplished without undue difficulty, subject, of course, to the proviso that countries do not attempt also to use monetary policy for internal stabilisation purposes. More serious disequilibria, on the other hand, may call for unpalatable adjustments of domestic activity levels.

The general conclusion to be drawn from this discussion is that free trade does make it more difficult for the member countries to pursue divergent macro-economic policies, but that the additional degree of policy harmonisation required is probably small in relation to what countries have in any case been forced to accept as a result of their attitudes towards controls, towards the exchange rate mechanism and towards monetary policy. It can be argued as well that in the long run freer trade may increase "the natural competitive pressures for preserving the alignment of national price and cost levels" and thus help to prevent the emergence of balance of payments disequilibria.[63]

This discussion of balance of payments harmonisation has so far proceeded on a general plane. The question naturally arises how

[62]This assumes, of course, that the deficits of some member countries are matched by the surpluses of others and that the free trade grouping as a whole is more or less in balance with the rest of the world. If this is not the case and if, for instance, all member countries were to run balance of payments deficits, mutual assistance is less likely to help.

[63]Johnson, *op. cit.*, p. 35.

existing free trade schemes, notably the EEC and EFTA, have tackled the problem. The relevant section of the Rome Treaty (Articles 104-109) opens with the statement that member countries will pursue economic policies which, whilst preserving a high level of employment and price stability, will safeguard equilibrium in the balance of payments and confidence in the national currency. The tools which member states may employ to achieve these ends include exchange rate policy, trade controls *vis-à-vis* third countries, and, in the last resort and subject to Community approval, "protective measures" (in practice probably quantitative restrictions) against other members. The scope left for independent action is consequently fairly wide. At the same time, members are enjoined to co-ordinate their economic policies in order to facilitate the attainment of the basic aims, and a high-level committee—the Monetary Committee—was established to promote this co-ordination.

The EFTA Convention deals with balance of payments and overall economic policies in Articles 19 and 30. Article 19 permits member countries in balance of payments difficulties to introduce quantitative restrictions against other members, though this is intended to be a strictly temporary tool. Article 30 stresses the need for member countries to pay attention to their mutual inter-dependence when devising their general economic policies.

Having briefly considered the relevant provisions of the Rome Treaty and of the EFTA Convention, one should proceed to the much more important task of discussing: (1) how balance of payments difficulties have in fact been tackled in these two free trade schemes; (2) how far the individual country has found that because of its membership of one of these organisations its freedom of action with regard to alternative tools has been circumscribed; and (3) to what extent the absence of trade barriers has resulted in a sacrifice of other policy desiderata. There are a number of actual cases that could be examined, notably Italy's balance of payments difficulties in 1963-64 and the UK's long drawn-out crisis which has persisted since 1964. Also relevant is the work of the EEC's Monetary Committee and of EFTA's Economic Committee (established in 1964 to help facilitate the co-ordination of economic policies envisaged in Article 30).

Unfortunately the matter cannot be pursued very far at the present stage. Research into these questions is difficult, partly because the reasons for government actions are often hard to establish; more

164

fundamentally, because a full analysis must be based on a comparison of what did happen with what would have happened in the absence of the free trade commitment. Not a great deal of work of this kind appears to have been done elsewhere. It certainly could not have been undertaken in connection with this paper.

Nevertheless, a few rather general observations can be made. First of all, as already indicated, members of both economic groupings have resorted to exchange rate changes in order to rectify balance of payments disequilibria. West Germany and the Netherlands appreciated their currencies, though by only small amounts, in March, 1961. The UK and Denmark devalued in November, 1967. A little earlier Finland had devalued her currency. Much the most important of these exchange rate changes was that of the pound sterling. It is far too early to say whether and to what degree the other member countries of EFTA will experience balance of payments and/or other difficulties as a result of the British action.

Yet it is clear that since 1961 the EEC countries have moved significantly in the direction of abandoning the exchange rate mechanism. The official position in Brussels and in the member capitals has been firmly to reject the possibility of further exchange rate changes. In addition, the introduction of the EEC's common agricultural policy, with prices throughout the Community fixed in terms of "units of account" (that is, dollars) has made it more difficult for a member country to alter the parity of its currency. In the event of a devaluation, for instance, the prices of agricultural goods would automatically rise in the country concerned in proportion to the exchange rate adjustment. Whilst agricultural exports would benefit from this, upward pressure on the general price level, and thus erosion of the price advantage gained by devaluation, would become harder to combat. Contributions to the Community fund to finance the common agricultural policy would also increase in proportion to the devaluation.[64]

Thirdly, one should mention the opposition which Britain encountered among her EFTA partners to the introduction of the import surcharge in October, 1964. As already pointed out, the international reception of Britain's move was generally hostile, but

[64]Despite the attitude adopted in Brussels and the technical difficulties referred to, there have been two further important exchange rate changes in the EEC since this paragraph was written—the devaluation (by just over 11 per cent) of the French franc in August, 1969, and the 8.5 per cent appreciation of the German mark in October, 1969.

in EFTA criticism was particularly strong. On the surface much of the trouble stemmed from the fact that the UK had acted *ultra vires* because the balance of payments measures stipulated by the Convention are quantitative restrictions and not additional tariffs (to which Britain replied that quantitative restrictions entail a far greater degree of government interference in international trade flows and are therefore less desirable). Beneath the legal point, however, was clearly the more general feeling that resort by the major EFTA country to a measure which directly and significantly affected trade with the other member countries was incompatible with the proper functioning of the free trade scheme and indeed raised the question of the future of the Association in an acute form. Pressure from EFTA was instrumental in bringing about a cut in the surcharge after only six months and also its final removal in November, 1966.

It is not easy to draw any very definite conclusions from the preceding discussion for balance of payments policy harmonisation in a NAFTA arrangement. If the member countries were prepared to resort to the exchange rate mechanism they would avoid the need for policy harmonisation in this field. It must be assumed though that the preference for fixed exchange rates will continue to prevail. Countries will as a result be forced to keep their price levels closely in line. Unless incomes policies can be made to work more effectively, this implies in turn that countries must be prepared to make the appropriate adjustments in internal activity.

In view of the probability that international capital transfers will continue to be fairly free monetary policy will remain an important weapon to stabilise balances of payments. As pointed out before, however, many governments find it difficult to forgo the use of monetary policy for internal stabilisation purposes, a difficulty which may be increased in so far as tax harmonisation limits the use of fiscal policy. It is therefore likely that monetary policy will continue to be subject to conflicting requirements.

Just as in the EEC and in EFTA the interdependence of the economic policies pursued in the member countries may well lead to pressure for the establishment of machinery for closer consultation about problems of balance of payments and overall economic policy.

Provided the member countries start the operation with reasonably balanced external accounts and major disturbances do not occur, or at least take effect only relatively slowly, adjustments in payments balances in the way indicated should not give rise to undue difficulties, imperfect though the mechanism may be. There are nonetheless many reasons why payments imbalances may not be small and/or transitory. Two deserve special mention.[65]

In the first place, member nations may be unable to maintain the required degree of internal stability. Of particular importance in this context is clearly the role of the USA. Because of its relative weight, and the importance of its foreign trade for other countries in particular, the behaviour of the US economy is even now of great importance for the course of events in the rest of the world. In view of the increased interdependence of the countries taking part in a free trade scheme major fluctuations of the US economy would almost certainly imply unacceptable burdens of adjustment for NAFTA members. In other words, reasonable economic stability in the US may be regarded as an essential prerequisite for the success of a NAFTA scheme. The post-war record suggests that the chances for this condition being met are reasonably good.

The second point is of rather a different nature. At the beginning of this chapter it was suggested that the establishment of free trade conditions may be an important source of balance of payments disequilibria. Various sizeable shifts in the determinants of the balance of payments will take place. Only by accident will the results cancel out. It is true that it will take some time to implement the abolition of trade barriers and other accompanying changes. Nonetheless it cannot be ruled out that by the end of the transition period some of the member countries will find themselves in positions of "structural" balance of payments disequilibrium.

It is probable that such disequilibria can finally be removed only through an adjustment of relative price levels. If this adjustment is to be brought about by changes in internal activity, the pursuit of domestic policy goals may be placed in real jeopardy. In particular, deficit countries may sustain a considerable loss of real income and growth potential.

The point is perhaps particularly well illustrated in connection with Britain's possible membership of the EEC. For a number of

[65]The optimism expressed in the text could be challenged on many other grounds. One might mention the threat to the international monetary mechanism stemming from lack of confidence in the dollar and also the consequences of the continued pursuit in the world as a whole of inconsistent balance of payments targets. Some of the issues raised are discussed in Sir Roy Harrod, *Dollar-Sterling Collaboration* (The Atlantic Trade Study, Trade Policy Research Centre, London, 1968).

reasons, in particular, the consequences of accepting the common agricultural policy, joining the EEC would probably have an adverse effect upon Britain's balance of payments by a substantial margin—£500m is generally considered to be a minimum figure. If exchange rates are regarded as unalterable, the country would be forced to bring about the necessary improvement in the balance of payments by other means. The discussion of this chapter suggests that most of the weight would have to be placed upon downward adjustments in internal activity. The resulting loss of real income may well outweigh, at least for a considerable period of time, any gains in efficiency which the country may obtain through the abolition of tariffs and structural harmonisation measures.

So far the indications are that in a NAFTA arrangement balance of payments effects would be rather less marked. In this area, though, forward estimates are notoriously difficult to make. Member countries should therefore stand ready to resort to the exchange rate mechanism in case structural balance of payments problems of the kind described arise.[66] Otherwise the purpose of the whole exercise may largely be frustrated.

[66] If the possibility of using floating exchange rates is ruled out, careful consideration should be given to one of the alternative forms of exchange rate adjustment mentioned in Footnote 61 (Page 159). In a free trade context these would have several advantages over the traditional method of shifting the rate by a relatively large amount from one fixed level to another.

Part IV

AMERICAN CAPITAL
AND FREE TRADE

by

M. D. Steuer

1 PROBLEM OF FREE TRADE AND AMERICAN INVESTMENT

Economic integration with the rest of Western Europe, through membership of the European Economic Community (EEC), summons up for many people in Britain a favourable image of their country playing an active role among roughly equal or lesser powers and eventually aspiring to the leadership of them. The EEC as a whole is large. Its components, though, are not overpowering in size. The prospect of free movement of goods, and perhaps labour and capital as well, between Britain and the Continent of Europe is one which appears manageable, although it might be distressing for certain sectors. By contrast, the idea of a multilateral free trade association, which has been conceived as a new approach towards the further liberalisation of world trade, and which calls for a form of economic integration with the United States, summons up for many people a very unfavourable image of Britain being dominated by an unmanageable competitor.[1] These two images have heavy emotional overtones which may be quite unrealistic and disturbing to rational judgement.

The free trade association proposal is limited; its objective is the free flow of goods between member countries, but nothing else. The harmonisation of policies and practices required at the formal level, to safeguard against the benefits of free trade being frustrated, would be small and the institutional arrangements need only be minimal.[2] These facets of the proposal may be appreciated. And the prospect of easier access to the big American market, as well as to

[1]How Britain's trade might fare in such a free trade association is analysed in Maxwell Stamp and Harry Cowie, "Britain and the Free Trade Area Option", in Harry G. Johnson (ed.), *New Trade Strategy for the World Economy* (Allen and Unwin, London, 1969; and University of Toronto Press, Toronto, 1969).

[2]For a discussion of the policy harmonisation problems in a free trade association embracing Western Europe and North America see Hans Liesner, "Harmonisation Issues under Free Trade", Part III of this volume. Also see Johnson, Paul Wonnacott and Hirofumi Shibata, *Harmonisation of National Economic Policies under Free Trade* (University of Toronto Press, Toronto, 1968).

The institutional arrangements of such an association are discussed in David Robertson, "Scope for New Trade Strategy", in Johnson (ed.), *op. cit.*

the markets of other member countries, would be exciting and welcome. But the prospect of easier American access to the United Kingdom market touches off a whole gamut of fears. Even when the proposal is seen for what it is, it is nevertheless the case that for many people it appears to be a necessary consequence that Britain will be dominated by US size, wealth and economic power.

Americanisation of Britain?

Worry over loss of British autonomy to the USA, while not yet a popular national issue, has been expressed in the press, on television and in some books. *The American Take-Over of Britain*, by two skilled *Daily Express* journalists, Mr. James McMillan and Mr. Bernard Harris, is a good recent example.[3] These writers, and those of similar persuasion, plainly feel that the current existing economic and political arrangements have led, or are leading, to economic domination by the USA. How much worse the situation, and how much more rapid the deterioration, they might say, if Britain was to enter a multilateral free trade association with the USA! While existing tariff walls, on both sides, have not protected British industry, the removal of these walls can only speed and intensify the process. Such is the assertion that is commonly made.

The Americanisation of Britain is a catch-phrase. What does it mean? A comprehensive answer would cover a wide territory. It would cover the role of the mass media, the demonstration effect of American wealth, international politics, the history of the two countries and so on. Both the causes and the effects require careful study, however ready are one's emotions and intuition to provide snap answers. A key factor in the view of the authors mentioned, and several others, is extensive US direct investment in Britain. Direct investment entails ownership. And ownership gives decision-taking power. Many firms operating in Britain are American-owned. Some of these were British firms and were taken over by a US parent firm. Others are new establishments. It is this aspect of American economic influence in the UK, and its relation to the proposal for a multilateral free trade association, which is the subject of this study.

In order to appraise the economic significance of US direct

---

[3]James McMillan and Bernard Harris, *The American Take-Over of Britain* (Leslie Frewin, London, 1968). The best known work in this category is Jean-Jacques Servan-Schreiber, *Le Défi Américain* (Editions Denoel, Paris, 1967; Hamish Hamilton, London, 1968).

investment in Britain, and the likely influence of a free trade arrangement on this investment, it is necessary to explore both topics. As already indicated, closer ties with the USA, while being unequivocally welcomed by some, for many others suggests a spectre of economic domination. Perhaps domination could come through the agency of more American investment in the UK. The proposal calls for a freer flow of goods: more American goods in evidence in Britain and more British goods in evidence in America. It certainly does not follow that there will be more foreign investment in the UK. But that may be a consequence which should certainly be considered.

If there is more US investment in Britain (or less investment) as a result of forming a free trade association including the USA, it is an open question as to whether that investment is desirable or undesirable. Those who are sure that the investment is bad usually make a central argument of the fact that many familiar products are produced by subsidiaries of American parent firms located in Britain. This is not an argument at all. In a very loose way it suggests the extent of US production abroad. But it does not do so in any statistical sense. In popular writing, the foreign ownership of firms producing well-known household products seems to be of particular significance, similar to the dangers of foreign ownership of "key sectors". Neither notion rests on a quantitatively measurable concept of significance. Even a sober analysis, however, of the extent, trends and characteristics of US investment in Britain says little in itself. To that one can still legitimately say, "So what?" Unless foreign investment beyond a certain size (what size?) is bad in itself, like poverty and disease, it is necessary to go on to examine the consequences of foreign ownership.

The heart of the present study is a consideration of the economic consequences of foreign investment. British public discussion is more used to considering in a serious way the effects on Britain of UK investment in other countries. The Reddaway Report, commissioned by the Confederation of British Industry, is a recent example which emphasises balance of payments effects.[4] Here will be considered the effects on the external accounts of the inward flow of investment. These effects, and others, are related to the level of income and growth of income in Britain. Another broad area of

[4]W. B. Reddaway *et al.*, *Effects of United Kingdom Direct Overseas Investment: Final Report* (Cambridge University Press, Cambridge, 1968).

discussion is the state of technology and the part in it played by foreign investment. Competition and industrial relations may also be influenced by the presence of foreign subsidiaries. These areas will also be considered. Regional policy and development, too, can be sensitive to the foreign firm. On all these questions, the behaviour of the foreign firm, and the nature of parental control, is something that needs to be clarified. A better understanding of the process and consequences of inward American direct investment is the primary objective. It is hoped that this will be an improvement on vague fears of economic domination.

At every stage, on a topic of this kind, there is uncertainty. There are effects one can only speculate over and relationships one can only reason about. Professor Robert Solow, of the Massachusetts Institute of Technology, once remarked in a lecture at the London School of Economics: "It is not my job to predict the behaviour of the British economy in fifty years time, but I don't mind making a guess about the past". This study confronts a similar situation. It is therefore especially important to raise, as a final question, the regulation and control of inward investment. Though it is not possible to be sure how a free trade area initiative, which would have to be taken by North Atlantic countries, and hence NAFTA, would affect the volume of American investment, or how a given volume of investment would affect the economy, one need not passively accept any outcome. The flow of inward investment is subject to policy decisions and it is important to consider the various policy choices.

2 EFFECT OF A FREE TRADE TREATY ON AMERICAN INVESTMENT

There are several avenues for exploring the relations between trade flows and investment flows between countries. Examining these can provide considerable insight into the likely effect on the volume of American direct investment in Britain of simultaneously removing British and American tariffs on each other's goods. One such avenue is that of traditional pure theory as developed by a number of economists.[5] In this approach precise economic models, based on a range of simplifying assumptions, are examined. The most important assumption is perfect competition. Competitive firms are assumed to maximise profits and consumers to maximise utility. In equilibrium the price of internationally traded goods is everywhere the same, after allowing for transport costs and tariffs. Investment is allocated to countries so as to equate after-tax profits at the margin. If such a hypothetical set-up is made mathematically explicit, answers can be obtained as to what happens to trade and investment when tariffs are removed. The answers are not easy to derive in dealing with a complex and inter-connected system in which the relevant factors simultaneously interact with each other. It is also the case that some small and apparently insignificant changes in the assumptions of the model can quite strongly influence the results.

Limitations of Traditional Analysis

International trade allows countries to import goods which require relatively more of the factor of production which is scarce in the importing country. In the same way, exports will be relatively intensive in the abundant factor. In the absence of trade the reward to the scarce factor, be it labour or capital, will be high. International trade tends to remove the special local advantage. Conversely, tariff protection tends to maintain the local advantage. In so far as factors of production move internationally in response to

[5] See, for example, Ronald W. Jones, "International Capital Movements and the Theory of Tariffs and Trade", *Quarterly Journal of Economics*, Harvard University Press, Cambridge, Mass., February, 1967, pp. 1–38. Other researchers in this field are Professor Murray C. Kemp, of the University of New South Wales, and Professor Ivor Pearce, of the University of Southampton.

differences in factor rewards, tariffs will tend to encourage the movement of relatively scarce factors across tariff barriers, such relative scarcity being looked at from the point of view of the country behind the tariff wall.

In general, the theory discloses that under a broad range of circumstances, though not all possible circumstances, the movement of goods between countries is a substitute, indeed a perfect substitute, for the movement of factors of production. It is a substitute in the sense that it allows an allocation of production between countries that will maximise the output of various mixes of goods such as could be achieved by the free movement of labour and capital between industries and countries. According to the theory of markets, these movements come about through producer and consumer responses to price under conditions of competition. Conversely, restrictions on the free movement of goods, such as tariffs, create market incentives for the movement of factors.

The answer to the question which factors will move where depends on particular circumstances. Applying this analysis to the USA and Britain in sufficient detail to answer the question runs into the problem of the complexity of the two economies, their respective tariff structures and, too, the consideration that both are advanced industrial countries. Analytical categories like labour and capital are increasingly felt by economists to be inadequate for the task. And the emphasis on equilibrium positions and perfect competition, ignoring the role of technology and other elements leading to monopoly, cast grave doubts. There certainly is no comfort in traditional analysis, however, for the view that freer trade would encourage direct investment.

If it were just a case of British tariffs coming down, there would be more presumption from simple theory that freer access to Britain for American goods would weaken the incentive for US direct investment. But the American tariff would, of course, be coming down as well. This increases the incentive to American firms to produce in the UK—rather than at home—for sale to the American market. Some American take-overs can correctly be viewed as international "vertical integration"; that is, the linking up under one ownership of successive stages in the production process. The British firm may have provided an intermediate input to the American firm. Just as firms sometimes acquire, through take-overs, their suppliers at home, they may do the same abroad. The growth of trade as a result of a multilateral free trade arrangement could well lead to more of this type of take-over.

Product Cycle View of Trade

Such an argument takes us away from the area of traditional theory. International trade economists are increasingly directing attention to explanations of trade and foreign investment which emphasise technology, behaviour over time, monopolistic advantages and economies of scale (particularly economies in research, marketing and management). Different writers emphasise different aspects, but in general this new approach can be referred to as the product cycle theory.[6]

The chain of causality in the product cycle view of trade begins with large firms and concentrated industries in the USA. These firms have sufficient volume of sales and established markets so that they can support extensive research programmes. New products are introduced first in the domestic market, where high income per capita and more knowledge of consumer preferences give the best chance of success. As output expands and unit costs fall, the product is exported. In countries where sales are substantial, this exporting success leads to some limited direct investment largely concerned with sales and servicing. When the foreign market is better established, direct investment expands to include light assembly and perhaps local purchase of components. If cost conditions are favourable, more direct investment and complete production abroad may follow. The cycle may be completed with the exporting of the product back to the USA. Meanwhile, the passing of time has led to new discoveries, which will generate new cycles.

The three most important contrasts between the new and the traditional approaches are: (1) the monopoly aspects, (2) the investment in technological change, with resulting proprietary rights over new discoveries, and (3) the importance of uncertainty. This last element is particularly important. At every stage the American firm is feeling its way along and learning from experience. In traditional analysis all firms in all countries have access to the same knowledge; everything is known about production costs and consumer responses. Given that it is cheaper to produce a product in one country than another, no elaborate trial and error process is needed to arrive at the

[6]Raymond Vernon, "International Investment and International Trade in the Product Cycle", *Quarterly Journal of Economics*, May, 1966, pp. 190–207.

correct allocation. No research effort is involved and no natural or legal monopoly position (through patents) plays any part.

More recent analysis, while being under-developed from the point of view of rigorous theory, makes an intuitive case for greater realism. It suggests a trial and error path leading through exports to direct investment. Had the American firm known that for a particular product, or range of products, production abroad would be cheaper, it might never have exported. But given the uncertainty of all economic activity, especially that involving new products and techniques, beginning by exporting gives assurance that a market exists and one can then proceed to substantial direct investment through successive stages.

The product cycle view does suggest that the NAFTA proposals, by encouraging trade, will lead to a greater volume of direct investment because of the acceleration of the flow of trade. Not a great deal is known as to why firms invest abroad rather than export. If asked, a spokesman for a firm is likely to reply that the decision to invest abroad was taken because the area chosen is a rapidly growing one. This implies an expanding market, but there is no reason why that market should be satisfied from local production rather than exports. There is a kind of presumption in this type of reasoning that exports are a marginal activity and full of uncertainty. If the market will really absorb the product, local production is cheaper and hence more profitable. The suggestion is that growing exports remove some of the uncertainty, show that the market is there and then lead to foreign investment.

Reasons for Foreign Expansion

Uncertainty plays another role in foreign investment in oligopolistic situations. A firm feels inclined to invest abroad because another competitor has done so. "We can't afford to be left behind," is the kind of remark made. The economist is inclined to reply: "You need not be left behind. You can keep up with exports." But in an uncertain situation it is not known whether or not production on the spot will give certain decisive advantages. Considerations of safety suggest going in first and finding out later.

Apart from costs of production there are a number of ways in which producing in the country in which one is selling can give advantages. Transport costs is an obvious one. These cover not just the freight rate, but the time factor, in the form of interest on the capital tied up in keeping goods in transit.

Many goods contain an important service component. This can be thought of quite broadly. It involves technical advice to prospective and actual customers, installation services, maintenance and other after-sales services, modifications after sales and provision of spare parts. Again, none of this, on its own, is an argument for investing in creating production capability abroad. Investment in the provision of sales and service can be undertaken quite separately. There may, however, be economies of integration to be achieved by combining production and servicing operations. There would then be a sound argument for foreign production as against exports.

It is a mistake to think of the incentives for foreign investment entirely from the point of view of conditions in the host country. American firms may be inclined to expand abroad as a natural outcome of their own growth processes. A number of writers on the firm, and on managerial capitalism generally, detect a tendency towards growth of the producing capacity as a part of the drive towards greater viability of each firm as an institution or organisation. One might ask: "Why not expand at home?" Such expansion, though, eventually comes up against two restrictions: the saturation of domestic markets and, secondly, possible anti-trust action by the US Administration.

With the ever faster movement of people about the world, faster and more reliable information channels and the greater ability to absorb, retain and act on larger amounts of information, there is less and less reason to see the firm as geographically bound to a single country. Instead of asking why firms invest abroad, it might be more reasonable to ask why they stay at home. The natural state is probably for very large firms to engage in production, at least some stages of their production processes, in a great variety of places. The current period in history is seen by many observers as a transition towards this state of affairs.

Sooner Inflow of US Investment

A number of points have been raised. An effort should be made to relate them to the likely effects of a NAFTA arrangement on the amount of US investment in Britain. These points fall under three headings: (1) the tariff effects themselves, (2) the effects from freer movements of goods and the presumably greater volume of trade this implies and (3) broad factors influencing the organisation and practice of firms.

The last set of factors would suggest more American investment in Britain, with the growth of the UK economy (and with a healthier balance of payments position, more investment by British firms abroad). This is independent of NAFTA effects. And it probably is the over-riding consideration when one speculates on the future amount of international investment. If so, a proper appraisal of the NAFTA effect should clearly isolate it from other considerations, and put NAFTA proposals in proper perspective with respect to them. In this light, the long-term effect on international investment of the free trade area proposal is likely to be small compared to what will happen anyhow.

The tariff effects, as indicated above, cut both ways.[7] In static competitive economic terms, British reductions should reduce the incentive to invest in Britain; American reductions should increase that incentive.

The most intriguing points follow from the expected greater current account trade. While the proposal for a multilateral free trade association does not have the Common Market implications of free factor movements and a certain political unity. It will— simply through trade—lead to greater economic mutual involvement. More American firms will have the British market brought to their attention more forcibly. For reasons discussed earlier, more US exports may well be followed by more investment in Britain, much of it tending to replace exports. My own surmise is that these considerations could well influence the timing of the flow of American investment in the UK. It would come sooner. In the long term, there is less reason to believe that a free trade treaty would, on balance, result in a great deal more.

In looking for subtleties and trying to list all effects, it is important not to overlook the obvious. For Americans, a major incentive to foreign investment is low production costs abroad, particularly low labour costs. This combines with an American comparative advantage in entrepreneurial skill. The NAFTA proposal is one intended, among other things, to raise productivity and incomes in

[7]For an empirical study of the effects of the European Free Trade Association (EFTA) and the EEC on American direct investment see Ralph D'Arge, "Note on Customs Unions and Direct Foreign Investment", *Economic Journal*, Royal Economic Society, Cambridge, June, 1969, pp. 324–333.

Britain (and elsewhere), in a way that government exhortation, special taxes and planning have failed to do. If successful this in itself will remove part of the incentive to invest in Britain. As output expands in those sectors where it is best able, and declines in other sectors, as competition and economies of scale make their contributions, labour costs should rise. Through raising efficiency and labour income, a broad free trade association embracing the USA would reduce the incentive towards inward investment.

Roughly, and in outline, the points and arguments discussed above are the major consideration in appraising the NAFTA effect on inward US investment. Much of it is speculative. An effect on the timing, and some increase in the overall volume, seems plausible. But one certainly cannot rule out the possibility of the free trade association proposal leading to a substantial increase. So the next question relates to feelings about this prospect. What are the effects on the UK economy of American direct investment in Britain? And what would be the effects if the investment were to increase?

O

3 BALANCE OF PAYMENTS EFFECTS OF DIRECT INWARD INVESTMENT

The distinction between direct investment and portfolio investment turns on the question of control. When a sufficient equity interest is concentrated in foreign hands, then a firm operating in Britain may legitimately be classed as foreign-owned. In principle it may be very difficult to determine when control, in the sense of ultimate decision-taking authority, has passed into foreign hands. In practice it is generally perfectly clear. Ownership is in the hands of a foreign firm, the parent firm, when it holds a large percentage (often one hundred per cent) of the voting shares of its British subsidiary. The subsidiary may have become foreign through a take-over or it may have been set up as a new establishment. The capital needed to set up or acquire the subsidiary could be raised by foreigners in the host country. But under UK regulations, along with preferred practice, it works out that in fact the investment is carried out with foreign financial capital.

The foreign firm exchanges, say, dollars for pounds, as if it were making an import, and uses the pounds to buy British shares, in the case of a take-over, or to buy factors of production—land, construction industry inputs, machinery and so on—if they are setting up a new establishment. This initial impact is favourable to Britain's balance of payments. As in the case of an export, it results in either fewer pounds being held abroad or more dollars being held by the UK monetary authorities. Likewise, an extension of an existing foreign investment, provided the funds are not raised in Britain, has an initially favourable balance of payments effect.

The financial transfer, which is the initial step, may or may not lead to a real transfer. By a real transfer it is meant that actual goods or services, either producer or consumer goods or services, are absorbed by the British economy. Whether or not a real transfer occurs depends on the behavioural responses of various actors in the British economy and on the action taken by the British Government. Consider the case of a direct investment by take-over. British subjects sell their shares in a British firm for pounds. The pounds were acquired by the American parent from the Bank of England's

Exchange Equalisation Fund, which now has the dollars. If the former shareholders then hold the pounds and do nothing with them, the UK balance of payments has improved by the full amount of the investment and there is no real transfer. Normally the British disinvestors will not hold the pounds. The Government will have to take steps, such as selling bonds, to neutralise the potential change in the supply of money due to the foreign investment. Successful neutralisation results in a financial transfer only, an immediate balance of payments gain of equal size, and no real transfer.

At the other extreme, consider the case of direct investment through a new establishment. Suppose that the economy was fully employed at the time the investment was undertaken. The real resources used for the investment now must be imported; alternatively, British resources must be used, but the goods these resources previously used to make then have to be imported. A real transfer takes place equal to the investment and there is no effect on the balance of payments.

One could say that the balance of payments is better off, given the inward flow of real resources, than if the direct investment had not taken place. That would be silly, though, because part of the current account inflow, equal to the direct investment, would not have occurred but for the direct investment in the hypothetical case considered.

If the host economy is in a state of unemployment when a direct investment is undertaken, the investment may in principle be achieved in the sense of buildings constructed, machinery installed and the like, without a real transfer. Real investment is done without a real transfer. The balance of payments then improves by the amount of the direct investment. Greater realism would suggest that domestic income will rise by more than the investment as the newly employed factors in turn spend money, generating the familiar multiplier process. The higher income will entail additional imports, but less than the amount of the investment. The first result to note is that when a direct investment takes place, either the balance of payments goes up by the amount of the investment, or a real transfer occurs, or some combination of the two.

Foreign Investment and Other Policy Options

In considering the balance of payments effects of direct inward investment, it makes sense to assume that a full employment policy prevails whether or not the investment takes place. Some people naively over-rate the importance of foreign investment by pointing to a foreign-owned firm and arguing that if that factory was not there, those people, or an equivalent number, would be unemployed. This does not follow. British workers as a whole might be working with less capital, but full employment is still possible without foreign investment. It is true that a fortuitous amount of foreign investment might bring about full employment where an inappropriate macro-economic policy would have resulted in unemployment. And foreign investment under aggregate economic mis-management might lead to the difficulties of over-full employment. But there always are appropriate policy options with and without the investment. To isolate correctly the effects of the foreign investment, it should be assumed that these policies are undertaken.

Financial investment, in the sense of a foreign take-over, changes the composition of assets held by the former shareholders. They now hold more money. Most likely they will not either continue to hold the money or consume more. They will acquire another paper asset or acquire a real asset through an intermediary. For the purposes of analysis it does not matter how many steps the buying and selling of assets goes through. In the end, the private sector must be induced to hold more money by lowering the rate of interest; or the quantity of money must be reduced by providing Government securities. Given full employment, additional real investment, equal to the foreign inward investment, is possible with no change in the balance of payments. This extra investment would come from a real inward transfer. Recalled here might be the first principle that a foreign investment adds an equal amount either to the reserves or to real absorption or some combination of the two.

Whether there is a gain in reserves, or in imports for consumption or investment, or in increased investment abroad without loss of reserves, the initial effect of foreign investment is beneficial to the host country. It is up to the host country to strike the optimum balance between the options which the foreign investment creates. In some instances, when the reserves are inadequate, the host country will take out the initial benefit in the form of increased reserves. Thus it avoids the necessity of improving reserves in other ways, such as reducing its own outward investment or its imports. In other instances, when the reserves are adequate, the host country will use the foreign exchange accruing from foreign investment for greater domestic absorption of foreign goods and services or for lending abroad.

Even in principle it is difficult to determine the optimum balance of uses of initial inward investment receipts. Treating a country as a single interest is part of the problem, but beyond this there is the need to translate reserves and the alternative uses into a common unit. The problem need not be solved at this juncture. The basic point to appreciate is the nature of the initial gain.

Once a foreign investment has been undertaken in the UK it sets in train a series of consequences which affect the balance of payments over time. Concentrating first on a new establishment, when the firm undertakes production after the investment is effected, it may import inputs from the parent country or other countries, and it may export to the parent or third countries. These are obvious effects. It may also affect the exporting and importing behaviour of the British firms with which it deals. Looked at more generally, foreign investment can affect the balance of payments through its effects on income and price levels in the host country. So there are the direct effects of the firm's activities, the effects through the economy generally and dealings with the parent firm. Some of these last are payments of research services, royalties and other fees. They can be treated conceptually as imports by the subsidiary to be used as inputs into its production. And then there is the matter of repatriated profits.

"Initial Benefit" Approach: Seven-Year Model

One way of viewing the balance of payments effects of inward investment is in terms of an initial benefit, followed by a stream of inward and outward payments, which probably net out to an annual balance of payments cost, stretching endlessly into the future. Later on I am going to suggest an alternative way which I think is more enlightening. But for the moment consider the approach which dominates current literature.[8] In the USA there has been considerable worry over the effect of the outward flow of direct investment on the American balance of payments. Economists have defended this flow on the grounds that the initial adverse impact is followed by a

[8]A highly sophisticated analysis along these lines is that of G. C. Hufbauer and F. M. Adler, *Overseas Manufacturing Investment and the Balance of Payments* (*Tax Policy Research Study No. 1*, US Treasury, Washington D.C., 1968). It contains many useful references.

stream of positive receipts from the balance of payments point of view. The question then arises as to how long is it before the inflow recoups the loss of the initial outflow.

The model employed in these calculations assumes that the subsequent payments of all kinds are each different, but constant, proportions of the stock of capital Americans have invested abroad. The categories of payments usually considered are (a) purchases and sales between the parent firms and the subsidiaries, (b) fees and royalties and (c) repatriated profits. The ratios of each of these flows to the stock invested is estimated by averaging over a number of years. Retained earnings, of course, add to the stock of capital abroad without additional balance of payments cost to the USA. With the ratios estimated, it is then a matter of arithmetic to calculate how long it is before an initial outflow comes back. This turns out to be about seven years.[9]

In a two-country world, the UK balance of payments effect would simply be the mirror image of the US effect. This would suggest that for seven years British balance of payments gains from American investment and from then on it suffers. But even staying within the terms of the model, this conclusion cannot be drawn because of the effect of US investment on British exports to third countries. Taken rather naively this effect appears to dominate any calculation. The ratio of annual exports from the UK to third countries by American-owned subsidiaries to the stock of American investment in Britain is very high. It is so much so that Britain's balance of payments appears to gain in the initial impact, and in all subsequent years, due to the induced exports.

Criticism of Seven-Year Model

A reasonable analysis requires that the export performance of American-owned subsidiaries be considered carefully. In the case of take-overs, obviously some of the exports would have occurred in any case. And new establishments may compete away some exports that would have been undertaken by British firms had the American investment not taken place. It is true that American-owned subsidiaries have a much better exporting record, in the sense of

[9]The range of variation in this estimate is very high, depending on the assumption used and the geographic area used. Under plausible assumptions, including the effect of exports lost because of direct investment, the balance of payments may never recover in any number of years. *Ibid.*, Ch. 5.

proportion of output exported, than UK manufacturing firms generally.[10] Whether or not this is a feature of American enterprise and decision-taking is less clear. These firms are concentrated in industries where British firms export a larger than average proportion. They also are large and large domestic firms do more than their share of the exporting. Whether being part of an international complex typically helps the exports of a firm located in Britain, or restricts it compared to a domestically-owned firm, due to the global strategy of the parent company, is not known. What is clear is that all these considerations are in no way captured by a ratio of exports to the foreign-owned capital stock.

There are ample other grounds for doubting the usefulness of the "seven-year" model, even correctly adjusted for third country effects. It only takes account of transactions between the subsidiary and the parent company, leaving out transactions with other firms in the parent country. No account is taken of the second round effects which the subsidiary brings about through its impact on the economy of the host country. Perhaps quite important in this approach to estimating balance of payments effects is the omission of import substitution from consideration. If a firm decides to produce in the customer country a product which it has been exporting to that country, a reduction in exports might be a natural consequence. This will not happen in every case. Direct investment might lead to a very sizeable increase in sales of the product in the host country. The subsidiary may use imported components, and, though some of the value added is now domestically generated, this could be outweighed by the increased throughput and the imports generated by it. Granting this is a possibility, it is still more likely that direct investment could be a significant substitution for imports. These three objections to the model are serious. And there are others.

The effect of direct inward investment on the balance of payments of a country is likely to depend on the state of the economy at the time the investment arrives and on the policy steps taken by the government. The major weakness of an approach of the kind being considered here is that it is purely mechanical. There is no room in it for economic behaviour. It suggests a rather simple type of view. Britain's balance of payments may benefit now, but the

[10]*Board of Trade Journal*, HMSO, London, June 30, 1967, p. xxviii.

country will pay for it in the future. Obviously a country is better off, all things remaining equal, the more the investment in that country is domestically owned. The point is that foreign investment causes things not to remain equal. The total amount of investment is raised and so is the income generated by it. Some of the extra income returns to the investor in repatriated profits. Again, this either damages the balance of payments, with no real transfer, or leaves the balance of payments unchanged, with a real transfer.

One way of conceiving the central point is to consider a time span under two conditions, including and excluding a foreign investment. In both cases the country will have to maintain balance of payments equilibrium. The relevant question is whether in the one case or the other income is higher in the receiving country over the appropriate time span. It is rather misleading to assert at one period in time that repatriated profits are damaging a country by creating balance of payments strain. It is more reasonable to evaluate the entire package.

If satisfactory policies are pursued by a country, it can have balance of payments equilibrium with and without having foreign investment. By satisfactory policies I mean essentially the correct exchange rate and the correct domestic pressure of demand. In this context the balance of payments aspect recedes in importance compared to the real effects. A country can absorb domestic and foreign goods and services at a higher level, for a period, because of an inward flow of foreign direct investment. When the inward flow stops and repatriated profits begin, balance of payments equilibrium means that the level of absorption will be lower than it would have been if the flow had continued. The relevant question, however, is: under which circumstance will the economy enjoy a higher level of consumption, with or without the investment? The balance of payments cost in isolation, at one moment in time, will not answer this question.

What is being suggested now is that more fundamental thought ought to be given to the effect of foreign inward investment on the income over time of the host country. (This is the subject matter of the next chapter.) The balance of payments problems then can be seen as problems in the aggregate management of that income so as to bring about the desired level of reserves or achieve any other balance of payments criteria. In this sense there is nothing special about inward investment. Domestic investment also has balance of payments implications. It is true that payments have to be made abroad and the capital comes from abroad. But given the effects on domestic income, it is then a question of macro-management.

The balance of payments management problem can conveniently be thought of under three headings: (1) the steadiness and stability of the "in" and "out" flows, (2) the transfer problem and (3) the inter-temporal aspects of the international payments. None is unique to inward investment. Nor is there anything original that I have to say. But a great deal of confusion and irrelevant argument can be avoided by clarifying these three points.

1. *Stability of Flows*

A large and sudden balance of payments inflow or outflow can be disturbing because it is large and sudden. It takes time for the economy to adjust to change. A given transaction might be beneficial in the long run or with the economy in equilibrium. The same transaction may be large enough to set up a disequilibrium situation, involving disequilibrium costs. A capital inflow of a purely financial kind, for example a take-over, may call for appropriate off-setting monetary action by the authorities to prevent an undesired rise in the quantity of money. If the inflow involves a real transfer, it provides the foreign exchange to effect the transfer and is unlikely to set up strains. In addition, some real absorption of domestic resources is usually involved. If the economy is at full employment, some freeing of domestic factors of production from non-investment activities is required in order to avoid excess demand. In the transition there can be miscalculations by the authorities, pockets of excess demand and also market dislocation. And, of course, if it is a sudden and not sustained inflow, comparable adjustments are required when it stops. The immediate and overt balance of payments problems, apart from the economic handling of a sudden surplus, are not very great.

On the outflow side, the problems will be more obvious. Casual inspection of the figures suggests that profit repatriation is likely to go on in a fairly steady and predictable way. Foreign subsidiaries

189

as a whole will, typically, be repatriating substantially less than they might. A sudden bunching of payments is conceivable, but very unlikely, given the law of large numbers. An exception to this could occur in response to a general policy move, or an economic crisis, here or abroad. Britain could, through her own policies, cause a disturbing bunching of payments. But the actual flow is subject to regulation, which is discussed in the final chapter, and need not be accepted passively. Foreign disinvestment could also be awkwardly bunched, creating serious transitional strain. The decision to disinvest is a big one. It will not occur frequently, and not in the case of profitable enterprises. If the assets are sold to another foreign interest, nothing follows. If they are sold to British interests, it is likely to be at a low price, but the balance of payments could suffer transitional strain. (It is inconsistent to argue, except in the transition, that foreign investment is both bad when it comes in and bad when it goes out.)

The above few paragraphs have indicated possibilities. Post-war British experience suggests that foreign investment, and the repatriation flows generated, are characterised by considerable stability. A careful statistical analysis could be undertaken to quantify and place in perspective the degree of fluctuation and its importance. Short of this, one can report that the numbers appear consistent with the general view that inward investment has not been a source of instability. Great concern over the issue of possible sharp fluctuations does not seem to be warranted.

2. Transfer Problem

The second balance of payments consideration is identified above as the transfer problem. Suppose in some future period new inward investment ceases. This concerns the relation between financial transfers and real transfers between countries. Let us say that the economy is in balance internally and with respect to foreign transactions. A group of American subsidiaries are operating in Britain and are making profits. The profits are in pounds. These are taken to the Exchange Equalisation Fund and are converted into dollar balances in the USA. That, after all, is the ultimate object of the parent companies' operations in Britain. The fund must be in a position to effect this conversion. That means that the UK must acquire dollar claims or other foreign claims convertible into dollars. Apart from capital transactions, ruled out by assumption to elucidate the principle, a current account surplus must be achieved. Two steps are involved here. Starting from a position of full employment, there must be a reduction in the domestic absorption of goods and services. This reduction is the cost in terms of host country income of the imported capital. The second step is that foreigners must be induced to buy the extra potential exports made available. Principally this means that there must be some movement in the terms of trade such that British goods are cheaper *vis-à-vis* foreign goods. The money transfer to the USA should create some extra demand for British goods, but relative price changes will be required to do the rest. This would be easier to achieve in a world of freer trade.

About all this there is nothing different in principle from a rise in domestic investment leading to greater imports and hence to a need for more exports. The goods must be made available and the demand for the goods has to be induced. Whether the reduction in real income necessitated by profit repatriation makes the foreign investment uneconomic for Britain is another matter. From the balance of payments point of view a real reduction must be brought about and a real transfer achieved. The fact that profits are repatriated will itself help the transfer. In a fully employed world, if the profits are consumed or invested this will cause the transfer. Both income and price effects will be working in favour of the UK current account. More realistic and less mechanistic is to regard the repatriation and the conditions to effect a real transfer as ongoing processes. That foreign investment is involved in all of this is of no special significance.

3. *Need for Adjustment*

The third balance of payments point is the question of inward investment and its effect over time on the need for balance of payments adjustment. Discussion in this paper has frequently been about comparing levels of income, with and without inward investment. This comparison involves two time profiles, not just two absolute numbers. It involves evaluating income today as against income tomorrow. Inward investment increases the degree of choice a country has in the timing of its consumption. By somewhat relaxing the balance of payments constraint, the option is opened of greater consumption sooner. The necessity of consumption reductions to achieve balance of payments may be postponed.

The impression which some writers give is that inward investment affords an illusory current benefit in return for a perpetual cost. From the balance of payments point of view it makes the situation easier today in return for making it harder tomorrow. Again, it obviously is harder tomorrow than it would be if, *ceteris paribus*, repatriated profits were not occurring. Sometimes it is noted that for some countries the annual outflow of profits exceeds the annual inflow of new investments, and it is incorrectly concluded from those statistics alone that inward investment is bad for the balance of payments. The income side of this fallacy will be reached shortly. If one can borrow at 3 per cent in perpetuity, and lend at 6 per cent, there is profit. The number of years required for interest *payments* to equal the principal is of no interest. The relevant point here is that freedom to spread adjustment in the balance of payments over time is itself a benefit, as all countries recognise by holding reserves or by trying to do so.

Strictly speaking, it is not necessary for a country to gain initially in balance of payments terms and lose thereafter. Professor E. D. Domar, of the Massachusetts Institute of Technology, has pointed out that it is possible for a country to enjoy continuous balance of payments benefit from inward investment and never have to incur an outward flow on that account.[11] He was thinking of the case where the new inflow rises each year and always exceeds the repatriated profits. To stay ahead in this way the inflow will have to rise, as the foreign capital stock is rising, from new investment and retained profits and hence the rising repatriation of profits accruing to that stock. In such a situation the share of foreign investment in total investment within a country is likely to rise. But it need not. New investment can exceed repatriated profits for each and every year. The foreign proportion of total investment need not rise if the rate of increase of domestic investment exceeds the rate of increase of the foreign capital stock. Nothing in logic rules this out.

As a practical matter, the combination of a net inflow, new investment exceeding repatriated profits and a total foreign-owned sector which is not growing faster than the domestically-owned sector, is unlikely to occur. As roughly half the foreign-owned profits are in fact repatriated, this happy combination of events means that the

[11] E. D. Domar, "The Effect of Foreign Investment on the Balance of Payments", *American Economic Review*, American Economic Association, Evanston, Illinois, December, 1950.

domestic rate of growth must be about 8 per cent, assuming typical rates of return on foreign capital of about 16 per cent. The appeal of the Domar case is not its realism, but is the hope, within the terms of the model, of unequivocal benefit from inward investment. It is not very relevant. More to the point is an appraisal of the economics of foreign direct investment outside the terms of the model, including periods of net outflow.

Consideration of the balance of payments effects of inward investment has directed attention to two topics, the balance of payments adjustments which this investment calls for, and the effects on the domestic level of income. The conclusions which emerge are that the adjustment problem cannot be ruled out *a priori*, but no very strong theoretical case can be made for it. Britain has considerable control in this area if she wishes to use it. The second conclusion is that the effect on income is the fundamental one.

4 EFFECTS OF INWARD INVESTMENT ON DOMESTIC INCOME

In this chapter consideration will be given to a most important question, the effect of foreign investment on the level of income in the host country. Here it will be necessary to abstract from certain factors which will be taken up in other chapters. Primary among these factors, which also affect income but are left out for the moment, are special entrepreneurial skill, technology and the effect of the foreign firm on the competitive structure of industry. The concern now is with quantity rather than quality. What is being asked is how more inward American investment, as such, changes domestic income. There are several issues: how foreign investment affects (a) the total volume of investment within the country, (b) the volume of domestically-owned investment, (c) the relative income of labour and capital and finally (d) total domestic income.

It is always possible, in principle, for the authorities to respond to a foreign capital inflow in such a way as to reduce domestic capital formation. The foreign inflow has the effect of raising reserves in this perverse case. More normally a real transfer takes place and total investment rises. Under almost any plausible theory of domestic capital formation it is likely that total investment will rise. In the case of a new establishment the extra capital formation is most clear. In the case of a take-over, the foreigner has the plant, which is still in the country, and a national has its value, which will probably still be in the country and a proportion of which will find its way into new domestic capital formation. Assuming full employment throughout, in either case the increased capital stock means that each employee now has more capital with which to work. Output per man rises and so total national income rises.

Factors Determining Division of Income

The next question that might be asked is what general factors determine the division of the income between domestic labour, domestic capital and foreign capital. The usual assumptions made in answering this question are that the two sources of capital are rewarded at the same rate and this rate declines as the amount of capital rises. (The inward flow comes to a halt when the rate of return in the country equals the rate abroad.) Wages, it can be assumed, are the same whether earned by working with foreign or domestic capital. They rise as the total capital stock rises. In this simple model the loss of income on domestic capital is exactly offset by the gain to domestic labour. In addition, there is some extra wage earned on the foreign capital beyond what would have been earned without that capital. This is the net gain in income to the host country. The profit income on the foreign capital accrues to the foreigners.

This is a basic point in examining the economic implications of a capital inflow. Apart from the special considerations (market imperfections, managerial skill, technical knowledge) and complicated interactions set off by the inward flow, the more capital in a country the higher the real income. And part of the extra income is captured by labour in the host country. Taxes also capture part of the income of foreign capital. Intuition may be helped by considering an extra amount of domestic capital. This raises income by more than the profit income of the domestic capital owners. In this respect foreign investment is exactly the same.

Professor Ivor Pearce, of the University of Southampton, has argued that the rate of return on capital need not fall as the capital stock rises.[12] His argument rests on a more complicated model in which there are several sectors and the output of some sectors is an input of other sectors. The argument is formally correct and makes an even stronger case for the benefits of inward investment to the host country. Domestic capital also gains from the arrival of the foreign capital. I am doubtful about the empirical relevance of this argument. For one thing there appears to be no end to the process. With the yield on capital rising one would expect to attract more capital with all the world's capital eventually collected in one place. Conversely, if the yield on capital falls very slowly as the capital stock grows, which means that the extra income going to labour is very little, then the gain to the host country is small.

Consider next the case where the presence of foreign capital, by raising income, raises the volume of domestic capital. This would not be the case in a strict Kaldorian world where saving is done by

[12]Ivor F. Pearce and David C. Rowan, "A Framework for Research into the Real Effects of International Capital Movements", in Tullio Bagiotti (ed.), *Essays in Honour of Marco Fanno* (Padua, 1966).

recipients of capital income and all wage income is consumed. But in a looser and probably more realistic setting—with income transfers, taxes and public investment—higher income probably yields more domestic investment. Some writers emphasise the concept of a relatively fixed stock of profitable investment projects within an economy. Canadian researchers, for example, have been attracted by this line, which is a more plausible one, especially in the short run in a host country which is heavily based on extractive industry. If there is such a stock, foreign investors may capture opportunities which domestic capital would have taken; and with a lack of alternative projects, domestic investment could be reduced. For the UK one is very much inclined to reject this hypothesis and reason instead that the level of income is the main determinant of investment. In this case more foreign investment adds to total and to domestic investment.

Within the framework of a simple competitive model, one way that foreign investment can hurt the host country is by turning the terms of trade against it. Increases in investment may increase the supply of exports. If foreign demand for exports is very inelastic, in principle the terms of trade can deteriorate sufficiently so that income actually declines. Domestic investment can also bring about this result for a country whose welfare is very dependent on foreign trade. Such evidence as exists suggests that this perverse result is very unlikely for the UK. It also seems improbable that under these conditions an inward flow of investment would persist.

All of the discussion of the effects on income of capital imports treats capital as a homogeneous quantity. For these purposes foreign capital is the same as domestic capital, except that profits on it do not accrue to Britain's nationals. The rate of profit is the same regardless of source. In a competitive setting of this kind a country either exports capital, or imports it, but not both. Clearly if actual capital flows are to be understood other factors must be brought to bear. But there are important points to be made, even at this level of abstraction. The most important is the strong general presumption that a capital import raises income in the host country. The total volume of capital rises and thus raises wages. The volume of domestic capital may well rise. The return on capital goes down, but this loss is captured by domestic labour. These are the most likely general effects on income.

5 ENTREPRENEURIAL SKILL AND EFFICIENCY

Economic analysts do not usually pay a lot of attention to ownership. If it is assumed that all firms are profit maximisers and their behaviour is the same whether they are domestically or foreign-owned. But along with American capital is acquired American decision-taking. There is reason to believe that this alters behaviour. Some people see in this the greatest advantage of capital imports. (Others see the greatest danger here. But discussion of this question will be postponed until the concluding chapter.)

Professor John Dunning, of the University of Reading, found that American-owned firms operating in the UK were more productive and more profitable than their British counterparts.[13] It is often alleged that American management is superior. Much *ad hoc* evidence supports this contention. Better training, a more scientific and professional approach along with greater energy and application are widely believed to characterise the management in a US firm *and* its subsidiary abroad.[14] It is not intended to explore this contention here or quantify its importance. Assuming that it is true, what economic implications might one try to draw?

Very little is known as to whether more efficient and energetic management on the part of foreign subsidiaries has a tendency to spread to domestic firms. Competition and simple emulation would suggest that it does. A proper appraisal of this factor would involve determining the efficiency of the competitive system itself. Obviously this is not possible. Economic analysis can bring to light, however, the inherent complexity of the task of evaluating the effects of alleged superior American efficiency.

It is worth pointing out, as some people believe otherwise, that this efficiency is not necessarily of any benefit to Britain. For the sake of illustration, suppose that a UK firm is taken over and that a similar output as previously produced is now achieved by using

[13]John H. Dunning, *American Investment in British Manufacturing Industry* (Allen and Unwin, London, 1958), pp. 180-183.
[14]James E. Kenney, "American Enterprise in Western Europe: The Case of Great Britain", *Review of Social Economy*, Catholic Economic Association, Chicago, September, 1968, pp. 145-155.

fewer inputs and less labour and material. To take the worst case, let it be further assumed that these factors are now unemployed. The output, unchanged, is disposed of at the same price. And to complete this unfortunate picture, instead of generating higher profits, the saving in costs is disposed of in the form of higher executive salaries, these executives being Americans. In this case it is hard to see any benefit for Britain. The value of the illustration is only trivially to suggest that subsidiary efficiency is not automatically beneficial. More important, it indicates where to look for the benefits.

Benefits of Efficiency Accompanying Investment

If the efficiency results only in higher profit, some gain is secured for the host country through taxation. The factors released, however, must be employed elsewhere in order for there to be real gain. There is no reason why indeed this should not occur. A rise in productivity in one firm, with full employment, raises total output. As long as the rise is not entirely captured by the foreign parent, and apart from hypothetical cases it is difficult to see how it can be, there is gain to the host country. The gain occurs through extra output (either in the firm or by factors released), higher payment to factors, increased government revenue via profits tax or through lower product prices.

This welfare analysis is particularly complicated because normally when large profits are made, and there is free entry, the excess profits are expected to be competed away. In the case at hand it is assumed that the higher profits are achieved by special managerial know-how which cannot be emulated by other firms. Under these circumstances it is still the case that some, though not all, of the extra income will accrue to the host country. Where the more productive foreign subsidiary expands its output, and this is a likely event, less efficient domestic firms may well be put out of business or at least be reduced in scale. Apart from transitional costs, this is not a bad thing. The factors released may then be more productively employed in the more efficient firms, whether domestic or foreign owned.

While this is open to debate, it is not necessarily the case, or in my view even likely, that the inward investment, and the accompanying import of managerial skill, will flow in to those sectors particularly in need of improvement. One could make a kind of infant-industry argument that superior foreign techniques could inhibit the development of these skills in domestic firms who would eventually acquire them on a learning-by-doing basis. Such a case is not likely to be persuasive when set against the view that the competition itself is a spur to improve. It would, however, be overly optimistic to expect US inward investment to go into areas particularly needing productivity improvement through better management. So many factors are operating on the decision to invest abroad that it is more realistic to expect that high-powered foreign management will in some cases be expanding at the expense of Britain's poorest management and in some cases at the expense of her best.

So far this chapter has been considering the economic effects of better American management on the British economy, assuming no improvement in domestic management. Not all of the extra output achieved, it can be concluded, will be lost to the UK through higher foreign profits. But if there *is* a spill-over effect, and subsidiary efficiency is passed on to domestic firms, the gains will be much greater. Broadly, there are two ways this can occur: through competition and through imitation. Better ways of doing things may be taken up by firms in an industry in which there is no US investment or competitive consequences. But how likely is this?

Expectations of Benefit Need to be Tempered

Certainly American advances influence other countries. These advances may conveniently be grouped under four headings. These are: (1) basic additions to knowledge of relevance to production, (2) the application of knowledge to production, (3) new products and (4) management techniques. (The first three will be discussed later.) No one would deny the important role of these developments for the American economy and their contribution to other economies. But is it really true that direct investment is an especially important way of spreading the use of modern management methods? Clearly there are other channels of information. Observation of the techniques of US firms is almost as easy in the home country as through the subsidiaries operating in Britain. Recent British advances in management education, such as establishing the London Graduate School of Business Studies, and a similar school in Manchester, are patterned directly on American methods. Given the ease of travel today and the rapid spread of information, there is less special advantage to physical proximity. A London firm is as likely to learn from a firm in New York as from a subsidiary of the New York firm in Dundee.

A possible counter point is the movement of British personnel into American subsidiaries and then back to British industry. Casual discussion, however, suggests that this, too, is not very important. The numbers involved are small; they tend not to be at a high enough level, and they are not sufficiently concentrated in a receiving British firm. The managerial improvements of the kind being discussed require a will to act at the highest levels. If the will is there, the lack of a handy subsidiary to learn from is not a serious block; and if it is not there, the presence of a subsidiary seems unlikely to bring it about.

The one exception is competition. This can come as much through current account trade as through direct investment. In appraising the likely effects of an Atlantic or wider free trade association, improved firm-efficiency through competition is clearly one of them. The extra gain due to competition through more direct investment, if any occurs, is not likely to be important.

The American firm abroad appears to be more profitable than its UK counterpart, although determining an appropriate counterpart is not easy. There is also independent evidence that American management is in general superior to British management. Some observers see this as both a major incentive for US firms to set up subsidiaries in Britain and as a major source of benefit to the country when they do come to the UK. The force of this chapter is to somewhat damp down expectations of benefit due to foreign managerial skill. The phrase, "America has a comparative advantage in management", is succinct but not enlightening. One way to think of the economics of the situation is to suppose that Americans were no more efficient but instead used more capital. That would also result in a higher output per man. There would in this case be less profits tax, but otherwise the effect would be the same as from the alleged superior efficiency. The foreign skill only helps in so far as product prices fall, factor prices rise and the efficient foreigners are imitated. The last argument seems doubtful and the other two not very different from just seeing the investment as bigger than otherwise. The major economic impact, it is concluded, comes from the quantity of capital, not from the skills of those who manage it.

6 AMERICAN DIRECT INVESTMENT AND BRITISH TECHNOLOGY

American investment in Britain is concentrated in such sectors as electronics, some parts of mechanical engineering and chemicals where research plays a critical role. Characteristically it flows into industries with advanced and rapidly evolving technology. (Aircraft is the outstanding exception.) Many writers take the position that it is "the transference of knowledge which is the crux of the direct investment process".[15] The technology aspect of direct investment is not restricted to the complex and advanced sectors. In all economic activities it is possible to improve products and productivity through the discovery and application of scientific knowledge.

Before proceeding further the concept of technology should be clarified. Advances in the engineering sense, such as building a supersonic passenger aircraft, may or may not add to economic welfare. Inherently interesting developments in technology may turn out to be economic disasters. An important distinction is to be drawn between production of new knowledge and the increased application of superior techniques. Finally, when one speaks of the benefits of technology, it should be asked who is benefiting. Broadly there are four interests: (1) the technology producing sector itself, which is to say those engaged in research and development; (2) the owners of technology who are granted patent rights, can charge monopoly prices, or lease the right to use inventions; (3) factors of production whose productivity is increased through a technological advance; and (4) consumers who enjoy superior products. While all these interests can, in principle, gain simultaneously, there are obvious conflicts of interest as well.

When attention turns to economic autonomy, and the avoidance of too much foreign investment in key sectors, it frequently is the issue of technology and technological dependence which is paramount. Something will be said about these matters. On the general

---

[15]Johnson, "The Efficiency and Welfare Implications of the International Corporation", Paper prepared for a seminar on the International Corporation at the Sloan School of Management, Massachusetts Institute of Technology, Spring, 1969.

point there is ample evidence of concern in Britain over technology. Much of the case for increased investment in education, and the establishment of the new Ministry of Technology, spring from the view that backward technology in the UK is lowering economic welfare compared to what it might be. Poor technology is a major explanation of past setbacks. Improved technology is a major hope for future advances.

Of the many factors bearing on the state and development of British technology, American investment is one of the more important. Two themes dominate this topic: an optimistic and a pessimistic one. The older view is the optimistic one. It holds that American investment in Britain is beneficial to the country's technology. This benefit is held to come about in a number of ways. (1) The foreign subsidiary introduces new and improved products which improve welfare directly as they enter the consumption stream. At the same time, improved intermediate goods help the productive efficiency of many domestic firms. (2) New production processes are introduced into Britain through American subsidiaries who employ in Britain the advanced techniques of the parents. (3) Often the most important feature is held to be the ability of the subsidiary to draw on the research efforts of the parents, the research inputs of these companies in the USA being much larger than the total UK input into research and development. In these three ways American direct investment is held to be a stimulus to British technology.

A newer and less optimistic theme sees direct investment as a hindrance to British technological development. (1) In the case of take-over, a major incentive to foreign investors is often held to be a stock of unexploited research ideas. Through its newly founded subsidiary, the foreign parent acquires the property rights in these ideas causing the benefits of them to accrue abroad rather than to the domestic economy. (2) A desire on the part of multinational corporations to centralise activities may mean that the research division of taken-over firms are reduced or eliminated and in the case of new establishments little or no local research may be undertaken. (3) Part of the product cycle view mentioned earlier is the implication that subsidiaries will always be working with older and less developed techniques and products. So some *a priori* grounds exist for judging direct investment to be competitive rather than complementary from the point of view of its effect on British technology.

The purpose of this chapter is to examine the economics of these six points bearing on technology, three allegedly favourable and three allegedly unfavourable. One man's platitude is another's revelation. While there is a danger of attacking straw men, all of these arguments, pro and con, have been put forward with seriousness. Even among those who would say that not all the points deserve attention, there would not be complete agreement as to which are the unworthy arguments.

In any issue as complex as the present one it would be surprising if all the arguments went one way, if inward direct investment were unequivocally good or bad for British technology, and through its effects on technology, good or bad for economic welfare. It is hoped that some clarification of the issue will aid in forming reasonable policy judgements in this area.

Buying Unexploited Research?

The take-over arguments are the ones which arouse the most concern. For small, science-based firms, with histories of considerable research activity, stocks of patents may well constitute their most valuable assets. Two examples frequently quoted are Solotron and Cossor. Clearly it is possible for firms of this type to be undercapitalised and ripe for take-over. If that happens, the investment is undertaken by British interests, but the pay-off, in terms of the profitability of the products, accrues to foreign interests. The first point to recognise is that there must be some take-over price at which it is in the national interest to sell, or at least it is no loss, regardless of the size of the future profit stream which is forgone. This, then, suggests two possibilities. If there is a national loss through such take-overs, either there is a divergence between social and private evaluation of the future income, or the firm is being sold out below the private value.

To appraise the present value of a collection of patents is obviously a very speculative and uncertain matter. The most desirable collection is one with a high present expected value, and with a low degree of attendant uncertainty. Normally one would expect riskiness to be associated with a large departure from past practices. Such a departure might bring large gains or large losses. The expected value of each collection of patents is a weighted average of the various possible outcomes, weighted according to the likelihood of each outcome occurring. In the case of a relatively small departure from the past, it may be clearer what the innovation is worth, and the possibilities of going much above or below would be less. The expected value of innovations involving small changes is likely to be small. The expected value of a risky project, involving the possibilities of large losses as well as large gains, and being an average across these, may also be small. To determine the present expected value involves discounting future streams back to the present. Some projects may have much more distant pay-offs in time than others. But the main two items to focus on in determining the value to individuals, or to the economy, of research-oriented firms are the most likely value and how much the actual value is likely to vary above or below this value.

If individual British firms with property in research ideas sell out too low to other British firms, that is not a loss from the national point of view. The American take-over case with adverse consequences requires that British interests in general appraise the company at a lower value than its true value, and a a lower value than the American purchaser. The adverse nature of the sale can only come about if competition among potential American purchasers is not sufficient to drive the price to an equitable level. Setting this question aside for the moment, are there reasons for British interests to systematically undervalue firms rich in research induced innovations?

One possible answer to this question can be found in the self-insuring nature of large-scale operations. British and American interests might take an identical view of both the expected value and the riskiness of a particular firm, but the risk would be a rational deterrent to one from buying, but not to the other. If the American firm is larger and able to make many purchases, the element of riskiness fades in importance for that firm and expected value is what matters. The greater the size, and the more take-overs which are possible, the less does the variance about the expected value matter to a prospective purchaser. Considerations of size would then give a bias in favour of US buyers.

The key point here is a discrepancy between individual and national interests. For the UK as a whole the risk element in a large number of science-based firms tends to cancel out. A single British interest may not be large enough to acquire enough companies through take-over to achieve the necessary self-insuring. This is a delicate argument, but not impossible, in favour of the view that some American take-overs, largely oriented towards technology, may be uneconomic from the UK point of view.

More robust, but harder to reason about, are arguments such as the one about UK decision-takers being less apt at realising the value of research ideas. What seems implausible is that they should have less ability than the Americans at appraising the potential value of successful research, but be equally good in developing that potential. Another argument to account for possible underbidding on the part of British interests is a different attitude from Americans to trading-off risk as against expected return. The British might require a higher expected value to compensate for a given degree of risk. This trade-off may be a function of income levels. To the wealthier, risks may be less threatening. Again one gets a departure between social and private value. To the country as a whole a large number of research achievement firms are not a risky asset when viewed as a group. Thus the fact that individual investors evaluate risk differently in Britain than in the USA, or may do so, is relatively unimportant for socially optimum judgements.

Returning to the question of competition between American firms, even if for various reasons—appraisal ability, scale and differing risk and expected value trade-offs—there is a British tendency to undervalue science-based potential growth firms, would not competition between American interests insure that take-over prices were roughly at economic levels? This depends on the ideas being potentially valuable to a number of competing American firms. The theory is often advanced, particularly with reference to aircraft, but many consumer oriented products as well, that many British developments are worth more to the USA than they are to Britain. A sizeable sales programme, a complementary product line, and similar selling advantages, could put an American firm in a position to profitably exploit an idea which would be unprofitable, or much less profitable, if developed by British interests. The question then arises if there are likely to be many, or any, competing American firms of this scale.

While examples can be found, or concocted, of innovations which are valuable to many firms, and of innovations which are of real value only to one, generalisation on this topic is not possible. To be clear, however, there is an important distinction between take-overs at prices less than the value to the buyer, on the one hand, and take-overs at prices that do not reflect the value to the UK of retaining the firm. The latter is the result of misperceived private advantage or is a result of a discrepancy between private and social advantage. The former, buying at less than the firm is worth to them, is still a gain to Britain. There is little point in retaining a claim on innovations in Britain that cannot be profitably exploited in the country. If they can be sold for more than their present discounted expected value, should they be retained, so much the better. In that sense, the fact that they are worth more to others is irrelevant. The only point it might raise is whether there is some tendency for British research to be directed to activities which cannot be very profitably exploited in Britain. This could come about through a mistaken imitation of American research programmes.

Centralising Research Away from Britain?

After the loss of technology-rich firms through take-over, the next problem is the disbanding of the research department or, in the case of new establishments, a failure to undertake research efforts of a size comparable to domestic firms. The new establishment and the take-over cases are similar, although not exactly the same. It can take considerable time and expense to develop a good research organisation. And an ongoing research operation is not an asset of the firm which can be sold. Why, then, might the parent firm reduce or eliminate the research capability of a taken-over firm? Assuming informed rationality, either the research programme did not make sense, as such, or it could be done more cheaply by the parent firm. In both cases the benefit of the research team was illusory.

In point of fact, it is usually held that new American subsidiaries do engage in research in Britain, at least to the extent of their domestic counterparts. This is generally taken to be a point on their side. I regard that as not very sensible. If a British scientist goes to work for Ford in the USA that is regarded as a loss from the national point of view. (The benefit to the individual is usually not weighted very heavily in these calculations.) But if the same man goes to work for the Ford subsidiary in this country that is evaluated differently. From the point of view of his research output it should not be. For in either case the ideas he produces become the property of the multinational Ford corporation wherever the man is located. Of course there are economic differences between a man working for a foreign-owned subsidiary and working abroad. His expenditure has different implications, as do his taxes, and there are many other sources of difference. These factors may be classified under the general heading economics of emigration. But from the sole point of view of the implications for technology, working for a foreign subsidiary is like working for its parent. Either way foreign interests are buying domestic ability to produce ideas. If it is bad for British technology when a scientist emigrates, it is bad when foreign subsidiaries hire, or retain, British scientists.

A recent study of the British economy by the Brookings Institution, in Washington, D.C., characterises UK industry as being seriously undermanned from the point of view of technically-trained people.[16] The proportion of science-based, or research-dependent, economic activity is higher in Britain than in any other country, including the USA. At the same time, the proportion of the workforce receiving scientific, or more broadly technological, training is among the lowest in industrial countries. Several different measurements all come to the same conclusion: too few scientists in British industry. A much greater use is made, of necessity, of technicians. But the general conclusion of shortage of scientific labour is well supported. Obviously there is difficulty in determining comparable industrial categories and comparable people from the point of view of training and ability. The evidence is so strong, however, that even allowing for a very wide range of error it would still lead to the same conclusion.

The Brookings Institution's study concludes that in the long run the answer to the shortage of scientific personnel is much greater inputs into education. Only in this way will people be trained in sufficient numbers, not only for research and development purposes, but for management, sales and other areas where increasingly more technical knowledge is required. In the relatively short run they urge concentration—letting go in some areas so that necessary scientific buildups can be achieved in other areas. If this analysis is broadly correct, it has definite implications for the domestic view of foreign-owned firms and domestic technology. Any building up or maintaining of research organisations in Britain, either in new establishments or in taken-over firms, will be done almost entirely with British scientists and technicians. Every man employed by a US subsidiary is a man taken away from domestic industry, at least in the short run. So the view that there is danger to British

[16]Merton J. Peck, "Science and Technology", in Richard Caves (ed.), *Britain's Economic Prospects* (Allen and Unwin, London, 1968).

207

technology when foreign subsidiaries fail to initiate or maintain research efforts appears to be misconceived. The direct opposite view appears to make more sense. The more British scientists that are put on, or left on, the labour market by American subsidiaries the better it is.

As a slight digression from the six points on technology, it is worth examining an implicit assumption of much popular thinking in this area: namely, the implication that from the social point of view research effort is grossly underpaid. The feeling that these activities are so beneficial for the economy as a whole suggests that the financial inputs, in particular scientific wages, are well below what the outputs are worth. As a corollary, it is much better to hire *scientists*, and undertake the other necessary inputs, than it is to pay for *ideas*. Once stated it is clear that there is nothing *a priori* in favour of this view. It seems a rather romantic one. Very special market factors would be required for the return to investment in this one activity, research, to be so far above all others. And how to establish a very sharp divergence between social and private return, the other plausible avenue, in this area is not easy to see. Considerations of this kind may somewhat dampen the uncritical enthusiasm for research which can be encountered in Britain.

Subsidiaries Employ Outdated Techniques?

On the third allegedly adverse effect of American direct investment on British technology, the view that the subsidiary is continually employing an outdated technique compared to that of the parent, it is argued that new products are marketed first in the parent company's country and enter the subsidiary company's country some time later as imports into that country where eventually they are produced, by which time the parent company has undertaken a new round of innovation. There are two very doubtful points about this argument; it runs counter to the view of the international firm as an integrated operation, and one must consider the effect of technological competition without investment to isolate the investment effect.

It seems most implausible that if the investment link is removed in this product cycle chain, this would have a favourable effect on technology in Britain. While it is true that some theory and some evidence support the view that innovation is an important explanation of certain trade flows, it is much less clear that this type of flow

208

lowers the rate of adoption here of newer techniques. If the goods are produced in Britain, rather than imported, there is nothing to suggest that domestic factors will be used less productively compared to their alternative employment. In short, comparison with their counterparts in the USA is not relevant.

In a world where the subsidiary is a relatively self-contained operation, and the parent company relation is that of a holding company, it may make some sense to think in terms of an independent state of technology in the subsidiary operation and the parent operation. But as the multinational firm becomes one large and integrated production unit with international division of labour and capital, factor costs may influence factor combinations. Yet the best technique known and available to the firm will be employed in each operation in each country.

Technological Benefits of US Investment

Turning from the allegedly harmful effect to technology of American investment in Britain to the benefits, it should be remembered that the concern is not with all the benefits, but only with those involving technology. (In the previous chapter there was some discussion under a separate heading of the question of management technology.) A frequently quoted effect is the introduction of new products which, apart from being beneficial in themselves, stimulate product innovation in domestic firms. There is probably a tendency to exaggerate this effect. Direct investment may speed product diffusion through better servicing, adapting the product for local markets and perhaps reduced cost. But it is an alternative to American exports. For the products can come to Britain in any case.

The issue of intermediate and capital goods is a more potent one. First, these are more likely to call for modification to local specifications. In addition, servicing and technical advice will typically play a considerable role both in the decision to adopt the advanced product and in its successful use. These are spheres where on-the-spot knowledge, and continuing direct contact with actual and potential customers, give an advantage to the direct investor over the exporter. And so the rate of adoption of new production techniques may be considerably speeded by direct investment.

Apart from its effect on domestic firms, the incoming firm itself will, on average, employ more advanced techniques. The extent to which this is a benefit to the British economy depends on how much of the extra productivity remains private to, and is captured by, the subsidiary. Spill-over benefits to the host economy occur through taxes on profits, lower product prices, higher payments to domestic inputs and effects through imitation. All but the last of these have been considered in Chapter 3, dealing with income effects of direct investment, and to some extent under the management question. That the American subsidiary uses better techniques does not help Britain in and of itself, but only in the ways mentioned. Capital which is more productive is, from the British point of view, rather like a larger quantity of capital, without any special technological advance.

Discussion of the technological effects of American direct investment may be completed by considering the third potential source of benefit to the British economy, which is the advantage to Britain that arises from the access which subsidiaries of US firms operating in Britain have to the research efforts of the parent companies. It is perfectly reasonable to point out that an appraisal of the research activities of a subsidiary in Britain means little if considered in isolation from the parent company. The possibilities for technical advance on the part of a subsidiary are clearly not dependent on its own research efforts conducted in Britain. Only scattered and impressionistic evidence is available, but this suggests that subsidiaries of American firms operating in the UK, and in other countries, do not in general carry their share of research costs. The question is complicated and involves not only direct charges by the parent firm, but tactics of product-pricing as well. A less contentious generalisation would be that subsidiaries draw on the research of parent companies, typically freely and without direct charge.

Problematical Nature of Technological Arguments

It is often pointed out that American parent-company research exceeds total UK research. Some caution should be exercised in interpreting this phenomenon. For one thing, if there were to be an expansion of US direct investment as a result of a multilateral free trade association being formed, embracing the USA and the UK, it is unlikely that the newer arrivals would be as heavily committed in research activity as the firms already in Britain. But more important, there are two great sources of slippage when considering UK benefit from parent research. Not all of the parent research will be relevant to the subsidiary. Much of it, for example, is geared to the US military programme. It is rarely the case either that the subsidiary is engaged in as wide a range of activities as the parent. The second source of slippage from the host country point of view is the advantage to the subsidiary which is captured by it and not transmitted to the host.

Drawing together the six technology arguments, for and against, one is left with certain impressions. In all cases the initial appeal of the arguments, on both sides, rapidly fades and becomes much more problematical. Considered in concert, there is an important conclusion to be found. It is that Britain should resist any temptation to set other economic arguments aside on account of appeal to the overwhelming importance of factors to do with technology. Without much stronger evidence in favour of a particular influence, neither great harm nor great benefit appears to be forthcoming on grounds of technology.

An interesting question is the possibility of discriminating between potential investors in Britain on the grounds of being good or bad for British technology. An aspect of the question is the notion of autonomy, and the desirability of insuring sizeable British interests, in a proportionate sense, in certain allegedly key or critical areas. Often this line of enquiry has military overtones, which are not being considered in this paper. But it also has more strictly economic aspects. A possible ground for discrimination is that an industry has reached a level which threatens British autonomy. The issue is taken up in Chapter 8 on foreign investment and economic autonomy.

The second ground for discriminating from a technology point of view is in terms of the behaviour of potential incoming firms, irrespective of the key industry question. The force of this chapter has been to suggest that rational discrimination on these grounds is hard to undertake. One reason is that the most often raised question, will the new establishment undertake research in Britain, is not a sound economic ground for discrimination. Similarly, discrimination in the take-over case involves judgements which are unlikely to have a rational basis. Some further attention to discrimination will be given when Chapter 7 takes up issues of competition in industrial structure and American investment.

7 REGIONAL IMPACT OF AMERICAN DIRECT INVESTMENT

Apart from official regulation of the location of investment, there are several reasons why incoming American firms tend to locate outside the usual industrial conurbations. The newcomer, who approaches the country with a fresh eye, is less bound by habit and example to expand into traditional areas. If one incentive for coming is the prospect of a less expensive supply of labour, the new establishment is likely to determine to locate where that supply is greater, in parts of Wales and Scotland for example. The first choice, then, would be towards areas of traditionally higher unemployment, and not to the industrial south. An additional economy in locating away from the main concentrations is the reduced cost of land and buildings.

It might also be speculated that the American investor, by contrast to his British counterpart, is less put off by physical distance from sources of supply, from markets and from communication with the nation's capital. Once in operation he may discover that problems with road, rail and telephone services add to the difficulties of communication beyond what the same geographic distance would entail in the USA. But taking all the points together, there is a tendency for the American to be more imaginative and adventurous in his location choice than the British investor with traditional ties. A firm which is in a mood to strike out in a foreign country is not likely to huddle up next to existing establishments when it arrives there.

In addition to the economic and other incentives towards outlying location, there is the question of regulation. Every incoming firm has to obtain permission, which may be subject to any conditions. Location of new establishments is typically an important aspect of the conditions for entry. Naturally the American firm is directed towards high unemployment areas in accord with national policy on the location of industry. The combination of the existing tendency in any case to locate away from the centre, and the regulation policy, means that a disproportionate number of new US establishments have located in atypical industrial areas for such firms, in high unemployment areas and especially in Scotland. And if American investment in Britain were to expand as a result of a world-wide free trade association initiative, regional policy could be implemented to a considerable extent by intensive location control of this investment.

The existing economic and regulatory forces, and the possible extension of them, mean that a special property of inward direct investment in the UK is its location. The social impact of foreign firms is likely to be less if mixed among domestic firms. And the economic impact of investment is influenced by location. The purpose of the present chapter is to consider these special aspects.

In earlier chapters it was argued that the effect of foreign investment on domestic income was the important effect, and balance of payments considerations, for example, had little meaning when taken on their own. The discussion of income effects was carried on under the assumption that full employment is maintained, whether the foreign investment occurs or not. In that case the extra output which results from foreign investment comes from an increase in the capital per worker, not from employing extra workers. But what of investment in high unemployment areas? If labour is fairly immobile, the whole of the wage bill of the new establishment may be regarded as an addition to domestic output, not just the change in wage rates due to a change in the ratio of capital to labour. So in this sense the contribution of foreign American investment to domestic welfare could be very great indeed.

Measures to Protect Local Firm's Labour Interests

While granting the special benefits to Britain of American direct investment in development areas, some research suggests that the hiring and training policies pursued may limit the benefit to the host community.[17] The incoming Americans are interested in higher quality labour. Typically they pay something above the going rates, at least in the early period of establishment, and they hire their labour from other domestic firms rather than from the unemployed. Surprisingly little emphasis is placed on training. A stylised description of American employers in the outlying regions would be that the physical plant is relatively new and up to date

[17]R. M. Jones, "The Direction of Industrial Movement and its Impact on Recipient Regions", *Manchester School*, Manchester Statistical Society, June, 1968, pp. 149–172.

and management is prepared and able to use labour efficiently. The broad policy is to hire the more able and better motivated workers. This means hiring from other firms, for the higher quality workers will not normally be among the unemployed, and certainly will be harder to locate if they are. Prolonged unemployment, and in these regions that is often the case, has tragically damaging effects. Rehabilitation to successful employment can be a lengthy process. So both supply and demand considerations lead the Americans to turn to other domestic firms for their labour.

The natural expectation would be that this would still aid employment in the area as the domestic firms replaced their lost employees by hiring from the unemployed. No doubt such a desirable outcome does occur. But there are special problems. In order to make good use of unskilled labour, skilled labour must also be available. If the American firms are creaming off the best workers, it may not be possible to return to full strength rapidly due to time taken for retraining. If there is the likelihood of further expansion on the part of the subsidiaries, domestic firms may be reluctant to undertake the necessary training.

As the depressed region is often anxious to attract American investment, public support—especially for executive housing—may be forthcoming for the new firm, thus placing the existing domestic employer at a disadvantage. Even in a transitional sense it is not equitable or economic to attract foreign capital and thereby seriously weaken local domestic industry. The policy conclusions which suggest themselves are that the incoming firms should be required to make substantial efforts at training and rehabilitation and not merely reduce unemployment at one remove through the good offices of the domestic firms. They may often not be able to undertake this extra expense. Concessions given for the purpose of attracting outside capital should be designed so as not to weaken the position of the traditional employers in the area. With these safeguards, the contribution of American capital to the economic life of depressed areas could be very great.

Fear of Local Domination

Such limited knowledge as is available indicates that the American firm is a relatively isolated region has little desire to exert a social or political influence on the area. Instead, it wants to fit in, to lead a quiet life, to be inconspicuous. Its record as far as supporting local activities is probably as good, or bad, as the existing local domestic firms. Fears that special problems arise when an American is a dominant employer in a region do not appear to be justified. For one thing, it is unlikely to be the case that a single American employer, or even all American employers taken together, will hire more than a small proportion of the workforce in the employment area. This is a likely outcome if one keeps in mind several considerations. It is difficult to attract labour to areas of high unemployment even if a job is assured. So the firms will be using local labour. With reluctance to train, and a skill requirement which is likely to differ in many cases from the local skill mix, a relatively small proportion of the workforce will be of interest to the incoming firm. To be a truly dominant employer, then, in the sense of hiring a large proportion of the labour in an area is unlikely. It would imply that the area skills exactly matched the requirements of the firm.

Isolation is, after all, a relative concept. With improved transportation, there are few areas which are feasible locations for a new establishment and where the area workforce will be much under one hundred thousand people. This alone makes a single, dominant employer unlikely. There is nevertheless some fear of foreign ownership which is stronger among workers located away from the main centres. The feeling is that the foreign subsidiary will not care deeply about the interests of the local community. In addition it will be hard to influence policy by trade union or other means when the ultimate owners are in a distant land. And the outsider may not be sensitive to the local traditions of employment.

It is true that all three factors appear, at one time or another, to have led to costly industrial disputes. In appraising the foreignness itself as an explanation one must try to separate out the factors of size, being a subsidiary of a big parent firm, and the consideration that the type of activity is strange to the area. On the plus side one may note that the multinational corporation is less likely to suffer a falling off in demand because of regional, or even national, factors. But it is in a position to close down locally and continue to produce elsewhere, perhaps even in a different country. This is bound to change the power relations in the region. It is not easy to show exactly how this intangible consideration causes concrete harm. The topic leads naturally into questions of competitiveness and autonomy. It is these that will now be discussed.

8 FOREIGN INVESTMENT AND COMPETITIVE NATURE OF INDUSTRY

The changed nature of the multinational corporation is relatively easy to understand. Improvements in managerial techniques, the ability to handle larger volumes of information, more rapid and reliable means of transport and communication: all these have tended to integrate the operation. The "holding company" relationship between parents and subsidiaries is ending and in many cases has ended. The world-wide organisation for production and distribution is emerging or has already arrived. This greater unity of operation is becoming more and more clear and is relatively understandable. More difficult to explain than the changed nature of the multinational firm is its increasing growth. International investment is growing at roughly twice the rate of world trade. Why?

The economist's natural tendency is to explain this success in terms of returns to scale. The larger organisation is more efficient and so entails lower costs of output. Few people today would see these advantages of size in the traditional static terms. The exigencies of the relation between factor inputs and product output on a technical, establishment, level do not call for an international scale of operation. I believe this to be generally the case. At the same time, it may be recognised that in special cases a product may be produced more efficiently through an international division of labour. Relative wages for different types of labour may differ across countries, as may the distribution of different skills. If transport costs are not too high relative to the value of the product, different phases of production may efficiently take place in a variety of countries. This international division of labour does not depend on a single corporate entity managing the various activities. Staying within the realm of technical considerations, it is difficult to see how these managerial returns to scale arise at the international level.[18]

[18]See Charles P. Kindleberger, *American Business Abroad* (Yale University Press, New Haven, 1969). The first of these six lectures on direct investment explores fully the issues raised in this paragraph. The third lecture on Europe is of particular interest in the present context.

Coming down to earth a little, it should be recognised that multi-national corporations are, on the whole, giants and that they operate in an oligopolistic competitive structure. This suggests the possibilities of returns to scale in marketing and particularly in research. The first, and no doubt less important, phenomenon comes about through international demonstration effects, the development of product image and, too, the applicability of marketing techniques, once developed, in more than one country. The more important part is the dual relation between size, as a support to research, and research yielding a competitive advantage which adds to size. These arguments do not really settle in a satisfactory way the choice between exporting and producing abroad. But they do locate the returns to scale, such as they are, in research and development.

Multinational Corporations and Competition

The inappropriateness of a purely competitive model of direct investment is highlighted by the phenomenon of "cross-freighting". Most developed countries are considerable senders *and* receivers of direct investment capital. Obviously the capital does not migrate to take advantage of a higher rate of return on capital *generally* in the receiving country. Rather, the parent firm in the USA has some special advantage if it engages in production in Britain; at the same time, a UK firm has some special advantage if it engages in production in the USA. The simple export of capital in order to take advantage of higher rates of return abroad, without the export of management decisions and the products they represent, will not account for the cross flow.

Three inter-related factors, in addition to returns to scale in research, offer potential explanation of the growth of international direct investment and the dramatic success of the multinational corporation. They are imperfections in the capital market, comparative advantage of managerial skills in certain activities and, thirdly, monopolistic positions which are primarily protected through patent rights. This last leaves unexplained the choice of direct investment as against a licensing agreement. The other two considerations also have weaknesses when taken on their own. Taken in concert, this type of explanation suggests that international investment can have serious consequences for competitive structure in the host country.

Everything that has been considered about the nature of, and the success of, the multinational corporation points to departures from perfect competition. Size alone would indicate this. Fewer than 10 per cent of the foreign-owned firms operating in Britain account for about 85 per cent of the sales of all foreign subsidiaries. Many of the smaller subsidiaries may still be dominant in their fields. The multinational corporation tends to be oligopolistic, both in the parent and in the host country. This should be taken into account when forming a judgement as to the effect of American direct investment on the UK.

Few would picture the private sector of Britain as being perfectly competitive and characterise inward investment as the entry of giant producers into an essentially atomistic structure. In many cases the only real competition British giants can have at home is from foreign giants operating in the country. These foreign contenders may come from America, or from third countries, which brings the discussion to a short but important digression.

Oligopoly, Technology and Welfare

The primary purpose in this paper is to consider whether the formation of an Atlantic-based free trade association would affect US direct investment in Britain and, if so, what would be the economic consequences. There has not yet been raised the question of changes in the flow of direct investment to Britain from third countries as a result of the free trade association being initiated. At present this source accounts for about 20 per cent of the inward flow. But while the effects on American investment will tend to cancel each other, the proposed multilateral free trade association should have a favourable effect on inward investment from third countries, although the broader the membership the lesser would be the effect. The formation of the European Free Trade Association, for example, has stimulated a substantial flow of direct investment to the member countries from outside. Being present in one member country allows tariff-free sales to all members. By the same token, producing in Britain would afford entry to the US market. It is difficult to see any counter influences which would tend either to reduce total direct investment to Britain and America combined, or to shift direct investment from Britain to the USA. It would follow that some increase in direct investment in Britain from third countries should be expected.

Returning to the issue of domestic competition, there are two factors to consider. One is a possible reduction in the number of rival firms in an industry as a result of expanded foreign investment in the UK. The foreign contenders are predominantly oligopolistic giants in the parent country and they strive for a similar position in Britain. Often expansion in the UK is by acquisition. On this count alone one would expect a reduction in competition. But the other factor turns on the similarity of concentration profiles as one looks across countries. So the foreign subsidiaries will often add to the number of oligopolistic competitors in the host country.

Economists know relatively little about oligopolistic competition. It remains one of the most intractable problems. Some studies have indicated for the USA that the cost in terms of misallocation of resources of monopoly are small in that country. The extent and costs of collusive behaviour in Britain may be small and are difficult to appraise. European advocates of a strong economic counter-offensive to *le défi Américain* plead for greater concentration and seem little worried about any possible loss through reduced competition in European industry. These writers emphasise competitiveness rather than competition and see competition at home as a hindrance to competitiveness abroad. Respectable opinion can thus be found deploring concentration and also advocating it. Reviewing the arguments in this area would carry discussion beyond the present topic. But what is pertinent is to note that increased inward direct investment is likely to be accompanied by an oligopolistic competitive structure. If oligopoly is based on, and fosters, superior technology, it is not necessarily true that the net results are a worsening of welfare.

9 DIRECT INVESTMENT AND NATIONAL AUTONOMY

The various threads of the discussion need to be pulled together and an attempt at an overall judgement made as to the validity of the direct investment arguments against the formation of a multi-lateral free trade association. These last have their roots in the possibility of American domination of the UK through an increased capital inflow. The discussion has run in two parts: the likely effects on the volume of American direct investment in Britain as a result of the free trade association; and the economic significance of direct investment when it does occur.

Summary

On the question of the quantity of investment, contrary to some popular conceptions, there is no obvious reason why the free trade association should result in it being increased. Indeed, one incentive for the flow, jumping over tariff walls, is removed and direct investment from the USA might well decline. Turning from the static to the dynamic arguments, there was some reason to expect an increase and, on balance, this is what might be anticipated, although not a very great change. The case for increased investment from third countries is stronger and so a rise in volume from them might be expected. Should this be viewed as an additional factor reducing British independence, or as an off-setting factor to the American inroad? To those opposed to private enterprise in general, or to the large firm, the answer is relatively clear. They reject both. For the rest, the best answer is a closer look at the economic nature of direct investment.

Beginning with the balance of payments question, it was argued that it was a mistake to focus here rather than on national income. It is quite feasible to achieve external balance with any particular level of direct investment. The problems of managing the economy from this point of view do not appear to become especially difficult as a result of direct investment. The relevant question, therefore, is the level of domestic income which obtains with more rather than less direct investment. The examination of the interrelations of the effects on domestic income is not easy, but it does point to favourable effects. Those cases where income falls are largely the very special cases where growth itself has adverse effects on income.

A theme running through several chapters is how much of the efficiency and extra output of the subsidiary is retained by it and how much is transmitted to the host country. An important factor in the answer is the degree of competitiveness. On this score there is reason to entertain important doubts. The typical oligopolistic nature of the direct investor has been emphasised. A label, however, is not an appraisal and it is here that the paper must confess to the most uncertainty. Some implications of that uncertainty will be drawn shortly.

On the issue of direct investment and technology, including management technology, the thesis is that this aspect has been over-dramatised by most writers. Both the beneficial and the harmful effects turn out to be less persuasive on closer examination. And in the area of technology, the pursuit of national autonomy appears to be an especially inappropriate and costly goal. Nationalistic research, with an emphasis on large, distinct and prestidgeous projects is to be contrasted, in my view unfavourably, with work which mingles freely with foreign efforts, pursues special advantages rather than "completeness" and is oriented toward economic gain.

The question of regional effects raises, among other matters, the topic of the multinational corporation as a transmitter of a way of life, of a life style. A brief pause in summarising could be made to comment on one aspect of social transmission, the field of industrial relations. Managers of American subsidiaries often explain their superior performance in labour productivity in purely management of labour terms. They tend to play down the role of more or better capital. They argue instead along the lines of motivating the worker better and deploying this factor more carefully than is done by the typical domestic counterpart firm.

This thesis of superior use of labour, while being flattering to the management of the foreign subsidiary, may nevertheless have an important element of truth. Where labour is used more effectively this is likely to entail a different rhythm of work and a different pattern of industrial relations. The American firm is more inclined toward plant bargaining than industry-wide bargaining and in some cases is not keen on the presence of unions at all. One should certainly consider the implications for UK autonomy of American subsidiaries operating in Britain in ways that depart from traditional British work practices and industrial relations.

Raising this question indicates some of the difficulties inherent in the concept of national autonomy. Is the British heritage to be thought of in terms of a particular mode of industrial relations, or in terms of a wider range of practices, hopefully with the individual having some choice among them? For reasons indicated in the chapter on regional consequences of inward investment, it is unlikely that a British worker will be, for all practical purposes, forced to work for an American subsidiary. Nor is it implied that all American subsidiaries depart from domestic labour and industrial relations practices. So expanded choice here need not imply any loss of autonomy or national character. The bounds on acceptable practices should be set by legislation which should afford adequate protection.

Uncertainty: Nature of the Exercise

It must be clear to the reader that both parts of this paper suffer from a large degree of uncertainty. This uncertainty, I would argue, is inherent in the material. While dramatic expansion of American investment in Britain as a result of a free trade arrangement between the two countries does not seem likely, it is possible. (On the other hand, substantial expansion may occur even without such an association.) Although the effects of inward investment appear to be favourable on balance, to raise domestic income without serious loss of autonomy or other adverse consequence, this judgement may also be in error. It must be admitted that a multilateral free trade association may have a tendency to encourage inward investment beyond some level which might be taken to be a desirable upper bound, in spite of the arguments as to why this is unlikely. If this essay is wrong on both counts, then the most important consideration to bear in mind is that the inward flow can be restricted without in any way contravening the free trade treaty proposal. The free trade area idea does not in any way imply free capital movements. To exercise this option would not even require a change in existing regulations. Foreign firms must obtain administrative permission to operate in Britain, and this permission may be withheld at the UK's discretion. This fact is the single most important answer to the question, will the NAFTA concept lead to American domination through direct investment?

The adverse effects, if they exist, of inward direct investment might not become clearly apparent until the level of investment was excessive. Regulation would thus have to be used to reduce the level rather than to prevent an additional inflow. This is more difficult. The difficulty does not arise at the formal level. It arises because of the strained relations engendered with American firms and with the US Administration. A strong implication of this line of thinking is the advisability of maintaining a close statistical and substantive review of the foreign investment position. Early warning is inexpensive in this area and could have a high pay-off. At the same time, one should not exaggerate the cost to foreigners of a forced reduction. Required domestic participation has precedent in other countries. And a pace of reduction no faster than depreciation should be sufficient from Britain's point of view. While it is unlikely that the UK would have to use outright prohibition, this is nevertheless an important potential line of defence against outside domination.

Finally, an emphasis on the positive aspect of direct investment is in order. If the multinational corporation represents an increasingly important part of economic organisation in the future, British policy should be directed to participation in this development rather than towards insulation from it. Participation can take two forms: the purchase of the shares of foreign-based multinational firms and, secondly, the encouragement of British-based international contenders. Post-war legislation in Britain has been extremely restrictive on both developments. The reason is the familiar one of balance of payments requirement. A major argument in favour of the free trade area option is the favourable effect it will have from the balance of payments point of view. An improvement on the scale anticipated would allow a greatly expanded participation in multinational operations by domestic interests. There is good reason to believe that this participation could be very significant.

INDEX

INDEX

227

NAFTA, 8, 27, 37, 71–94, 97, 99, 102, 104, 105–6, 107, 109, 115, 121–2, 123, 125–6, 128, 138, 142–3, 144, 145–6, 148–9, 151–2, 154, 155–6, 166–8, 174, 178, 179–81, 218, 222–3
national income, 194–6, 220–1, 223
nationalised industries, 118, 120, 122–6
Netherlands, 99, 130, 165
Neumark Report (1963), 134, 141
New Zealand, 57, 70, 71, 100
Nigeria, 29
non-discrimination, 13, 15, 18, 23, 38, 41–4, 46, 49, 73, 74–5, 76, 77, 87, 93–4, 121–2
non-tariff barriers, 7, 18–19, 23, 32–7 *passim*, 38, 47, 54–5, 78, 79, 103, 116–29
"North Atlantic free trade association": *see* NAFTA
Norway, 33

OECD, 15, 18, 54, 69, 72, 81, 115, 119n, 161
OEEC, 34
Ohlin, B., 140n, 153n
oil, 33, 57
oligopolies, 216–19, 221; *see also* competition
olive oil, 62
Organisation for Economic Co-operation and Development: *see* OECD
Organisation for European Economic Co-operation: *see* OEEC
overseas aid: *see* development aid
overseas investment, 70, 89, 93, 171–223
ownership of industry, American: *see* Americanisation

"Pacific free trade association", 8
Pakistan, 29, 76, 85, 89
Panama, 89
Partners in Development: *see* Commission on International Development (1968)
Pearce, I., 175n, 195
Pearson Commission: *see* Commission on International Development (1968)
Peck, M. J., 207n
payments: *see* balance of payments

per capita income, 76, 81
Peru, 89
Petersen Report: *see* Task Force of International Development (1970)
petroleum, 31n, 54, 55
Philippines, 35, 59, 89
Pincus, J., 31n, 58, 64, 68n, 71n
poor countries: *see* developing countries
population, 29, 30, 76–7, 81
Portugal, 34, 83
Prebisch, R., 13, 16, 17n, 50, 52
preference agreements, 13, 14–15, 17, 18–19, 23, 34–5, 43, 46, 50–1, 53, 64–9, 71–94 *passim*
Presidents of America meeting (1967), 69
prices, 13, 52, 56, 59, 60–1, 64, 83, 109, 110–11, 112, 129, 140, 149, 158
Prices and Incomes Board (UK), 90
prices and incomes policies, 159, 162–3
primary products, 6–7, 8, 13, 32–4, 47, 50, 52, 53, 54–9, 60, 62–3, 64, 66, 88–9
private overseas investment, 70, 89, 93
processing industry: *see* manufacturing industry
product cycle theory, 177–8, 202, 208–9
production, 175–9
Programme of Action (1963), 44, 46–8; *see also* GATT
protectionism, 4–7, 14–15, 19, 22–3, 32–7, 42–3, 46, 49, 53–4, 62–3, 79, 82, 92, 116–56 *passim*; *see also* competition; tariffs
Puerto Rico, 35, 59

quotas, 7, 14, 35–6, 40, 42, 46, 54, 55, 57, 62, 66, 73, 79, 80, 87, 90, 117, 158

railways, 149, 150, 151; *see also* transport
raw materials, 32, 36, 52, 56, 66, 84–6
reciprocity principle, 41–2, 49, 77, 93
Reddaway, W. B., 173
regional policies, 152–5, 212–15, 221
research: *see* technology
restrictive practices, 146–9
Restrictive Practices Board (UK), 90